Adolf Hitler
1889-1945

Contents

Introduction

It has been over half a century since the death of Adolf Hitler, yet even now he has the power to fascinate and horrify us. New books about Hitler regularly make the bestseller lists.

Photographs of him with his neatly trimmed moustache, and his ice-cold eyes turned to the camera, still send a chill down the spine. How can one man continue to create so much interest and so much fear?

History has had its fair share of evil characters, but Adolf Hitler is still considered by many to have been the most inhumane and dangerous of all. It was his hatred of communists, Jews and other minority groups that brought about the deaths of over six million people in Nazi concentration camps. And it was his lust for power that caused the Second World War. The nature of his evil is hard to comprehend, as is the blind devotion of the followers who acted on his orders.

As we search for answers we find contradictions in his character. Hitler was a man of culture who enjoyed paintings and the company of women and children. For a few years he brought prosperity and stability to Germany too. He was also the visionary behind Germany's great motorways and backed the development of the "people's car" (or VW Beetle, as we now know it). At the end of the war, when all hope had deserted him, this same man ordered that the very country he had tried to make so great should be destroyed. Can we ever understand such a man? As long as we keep trying, then there is always hope that history will not repeat itself, and that never again will the world be torn apart by the dreams and blind hatred of a single person.

What's in a name?

Adolf (male) German: composed of the Germanic elements: adal, which means noble, and wolf, which, of course, means wolf. This form of the name was first introduced into Britain by the Normans, but it did not become at all common in Europe until the eighteenth century. The name's association with Adolf Hitler has meant that the name has hardly been used since the Second World War.

The early years

Throughout his life Hitler was secretive about his childhood. If people delved into his background he feared that they would uncover the madness that was in his family.

They might even have found that he had Jewish blood; a fact that he could never disprove because his father had been illegitimate. Now, historians know that he didn't have a Jewish connection, but it's interesting that possibly one of the most anti-Semitic characters in history lived with that uncertainty. When Hitler wrote about his early life he claimed it had been poor and unhappy. In truth, Hitler's family were comfortably off, and, although his father was strict, his mother spoiled him.

Mother love

Adolf Hitler was born on 20 April 1889 in Braunau-am-Inn, Austria. His father Alois was an arrogant, hard-drinking customs official with an eye for women. Hitler's mother, Klara, had been the household maid and became Alois's third wife in 1885. She was quiet and obedient, and looked after Alois's two other children from his previous marriages, Alois and Angela. She bore her husband five more children but of these only Hitler and his younger sister Paula survived. Hitler was probably a normal healthy baby, but Klara feared she might lose another child so treated him as if he was sickly. She constantly fussed over him. Hitler's father was rarely at home so the bond with his mother grew stronger.

Life changed when Hitler was six. His father retired from the customs service. The family moved to a house with nine acres of farmland at Hafeld, near the town of Lambach. Suddenly, Hitler's drunken, domineering father was at home more often. He bullied and beat Klara and his eldest son, Alois. Despite the family traumas, Hitler looked back fondly on those years. Perhaps this was because he spent long hours in the fields surrounding the farm, playing his

▶ *Adolf Hitler as a baby and the notice of his birth in a local paper. His mother Klara fed him lots of cakes and biscuits to fatten him up.*

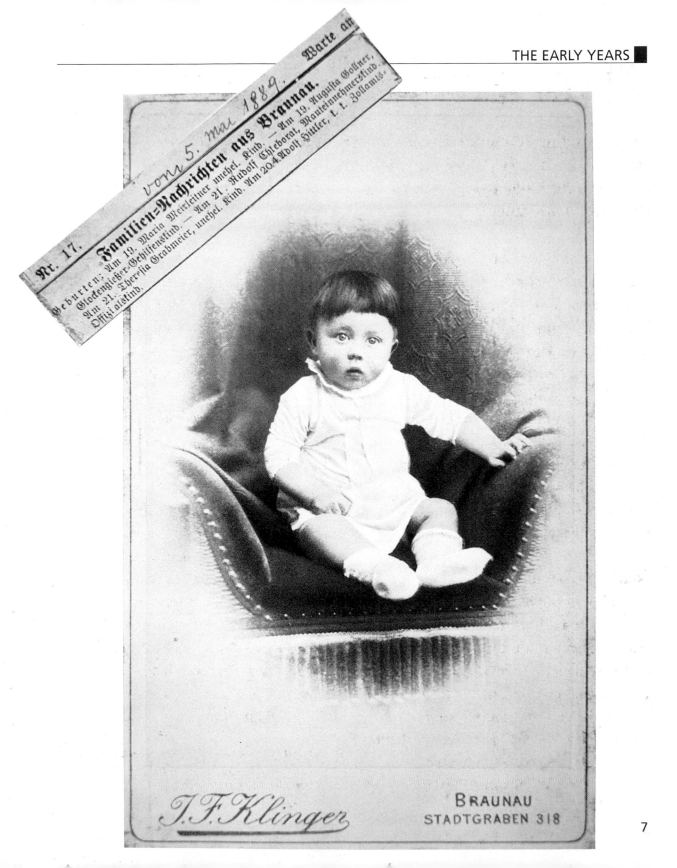

J. F. Klinger

BRAUNAU
STADTGRABEN 318

7

The ten-year-old Hitler (centre, top row) looks cocky and self-assured in this class photograph taken at the village school near Linz.

favourite game of cowboys and Indians. He did quite well at school.

When Hitler was seven his brother Alois left home. From now on Hitler was forced to do more chores, which he hated. His father kept a critical eye on him. Months later, the family moved into the town of Lambach. Hitler missed the countryside, but he didn't miss working on the farm. He continued to do well at school, but his father now beat him. On one occasion, Alois hit Hitler so hard he thought that he had killed him. Early on, Hitler decided not to cry when his father attacked him. Gradually, he became more rebellious and rude to his father.

War games

In 1899, the same year that the Hitler family moved to another new home near Linz, the Boer War broke out in South Africa. Hitler and his friends would recreate great battles between the Boers and the British. Hitler particularly enjoyed playing the part of the leader of the Boers – killing British soldiers. At other times, Hitler played more sadistic games. He'd sneak off to the local church-yard armed with his father's airgun, and take great pleasure in shooting rats.

Paula Wolff (née Hitler)

In 1959, Paula Hitler confided to a British journalist: "The autobahn and the VW are probably the best things my brother left behind." At this time, Hitler's younger sister was living by herself under the assumed name of Frau Wolff in shabby attic rooms in Vienna. She worked as an assistant for an insurance company and kept herself to herself. As Hitler's only surviving full sibling she had become the object of much curiosity and was interrogated by the Allies after the war. During those interviews she showed genuine emotion towards her brother: "His end brought unspeakable sorrow to me," she admitted before breaking down in tears.

In truth, Hitler had not been a brilliant brother. He had turned his back on his mentally retarded sister when their mother Klara had died, and had only given over his portion of their father's pension to help with her upbringing when pressed upon by his relatives to do so. In between the years 1908 and 1921 she never saw her brother; at times she believed he was dead. When he eventually came back into her life it was on his terms. They would meet very rarely – not even as often as once a year. He never spoke or wrote about her, but it's said that he granted her a small allowance to keep her out of the limelight. She died in June 1960. The whereabouts of her grave, like so many other details of her life, remain a mystery.

Teenage years

By the time Hitler was in his early teens, his school work had began to suffer. At secondary school in Linz he failed mathematics and natural history. His real talent was for drawing and he hoped to become an artist. He also became more interested in politics. In the early nineteenth century Austria had formed part of the German Confederation. Following the Franco-Prussian War of 1871, Austria had become part of the Habsburg Austro-Hungarian Empire. Meanwhile, other German-speaking territories had been united by Bismarck to form a great German empire. Hitler's father was a supporter of the Habsburgs while Hitler became more interested in German nationalism.

In January 1903, Hitler's father was drinking at a tavern when he died suddenly from a pleural haemorrhage. The tension at home lifted immediately but Hitler, who was now 14, remained stubborn and uncooperative at school. He eventually left school at 16 without a school-leaving certificate. With no father to bully him and a mother who allowed him to do as he pleased, Hitler was free to indulge in drawing, reading and listening

▲ *A sketch of Hitler by a fellow pupil in secondary school. Hitler, who was 16 at the time, already has a small moustache.*

the Academy of Fine Arts in Vienna. He'd visited the Austrian capital in 1906 and had been inspired by its architecture and culture. By September 1907, Hitler was on a train heading for Vienna – his dream was coming true.

Disappointment and despair

Hitler's dreams soon fell flat when the Academy judged his test drawings to be unsatisfactory. They believed his talents lay in architecture. To become an architect, Hitler needed to attend a technical college. But he needed a school-leaving certificate for that. Hitler was still determined that he'd get into the Academy to study art.

For a few lonely weeks Hitler fretted about his future. At home, his mother was becoming seriously ill. At the end of October 1907, Hitler rushed back to Linz. By now Klara had been diagnosed with cancer and she only had months to live. Hitler spent the next two months at his mother's bedside. She died a few days before Christmas and Hitler sketched her body one last time. Overcome with grief, he spoke to nobody for days. It is said that Adolf Hitler never liked Christmas again.

to the operas of Richard Wagner. His mother, who had a widow's pension, didn't pressurize him to look for a job as was expected of most young men. When he was offered an apprenticeship as a baker Hitler turned his nose up – he had grander plans! He wanted to study art at

Vienna

By February 1908, Hitler was back in Vienna. He had a small inheritance and a pension, but to make his money last he had to live frugally. He shared a tiny flea-ridden room with his best friend from school, a musician called Gustl Kubizek. Hitler spent most of his time practising his drawing and painting or reading. Sometimes he managed to get cheap seats at the opera and theatre. At least he felt he was living the life of an artist – although this young bohemian didn't drink, smoke or have girlfriends. In 1909 when he was 20, Hitler was rejected by the Academy again. By now his funds were running very low. He was poor, lonely and filled with self-pity, but he still refused to look for a job – in his heart he believed he was destined for higher things.

Life on the streets

By October 1909 Hitler was living on the streets, sleeping in doorways and selling his few possessions to survive. When it got colder he slept where he could: on the floors of bars or cafes, in cramped and

▶ *This watercolour of an old courtyard in Munich was painted by Hitler in 1914. By this time he had accepted that his talent was for painting architecture.*

13

dirty labourers' barracks and cheap lodging-houses. He sold most of his clothes, including his overcoat, and finally took refuge at an asylum for the homeless in the suburb of Meidling. He was painfully thin and his blue eyes looked sad and empty. In 1910, he moved to a slightly more habitable hostel called the Männerheim. Its reading rooms and library provided Hitler with the intellectual stimulus he'd been missing.

Political awakening

After a few months Hitler's strength returned, and with it came feelings of self-importance and confidence. At the Männerheim he became known for heading debates in the reading room. He directed months of frustration and anger at his own condition at the Jews and Marxists. At that time, Vienna was severely overcrowded, there was high unemployment and poverty. Many people blamed the large influx of immigrants, particularly Jews, for the worsening conditions. By 1910, Jewish people made up ten per cent of Vienna's population

◀ This early Nazi propaganda poster portrays a Jewish business-man as "the wire-puller" who controls the workers by force.

but a disproportionately high percentage of those worked in finance, medicine, law, the media and performing arts. There was a growing tide of resentment against the Jews in the city. Hitler became obsessed with the "Jewish problem". He believed the Jews controlled the economy and the arts and it was their fault that he had been denied success. As a child, Hitler had dreamed of a new German empire with Austria reunited with her fellow German-speaking nations. Once more, he found himself looking towards the "fatherland" and all things German.

The boy becomes a man

In 1910, Hitler was rejected by the Academy again, and once more they suggested he try architecture. In the following years he continued to live at the Männerheim, spending his days painting and reading about politics, developing a profound understanding of the use of propaganda. By May 1913 he realized it was time to move on; he hoped to continue his studies in Munich. About to leave Vienna, he reflected upon his life so far: "I had set foot in this town while still half a boy and I left it a man, grown quiet and grave."

The passionate soldier

Munich was the capital of Bavaria, and in 1913 it was considered to be, after Paris, the cultural centre of continental Europe.

Hitler felt immediately at home in Munich. But he steered clear of the lively culture that was based around people meeting in cafes and discussing politics and art. He rented a small room and spent much of his time painting architectural scenes which he very rarely managed to sell. Once again he found himself visiting libraries, but now he was reading about Marxism and its relation to the Jewish question. He talked of becoming a student at the Munich Art Academy but there's no evidence that he even applied. He was living a lonely, hand-to-mouth existence, seemingly without direction. Yet Hitler later claimed that he'd never been happier.

A call to arms

On 18 January 1914, it seemed as if Hitler's plans to become an artist might be thwarted again. Late that afternoon the unexpected knock on his door from a German policeman was followed by a notice to sign up for military service at Linz in Austria. If he didn't leave to do so at once he might be arrested and thrown in prison. In February, Hitler reported for military duty at Salzburg in Austria, but a medical officer found him unfit for military service. Apparently years of poverty had left him weak and run-down. Hitler returned to Munich to continue his lonely existence. He couldn't have guessed how political events in Germany were about to explode and change the course of his life.

In June 1914 the Austrian heir to the throne, Archduke Franz Ferdinand, was assassinated by a Serbian terrorist in the city of Sarajevo. By August 1914, World War One had broken out with Austria and Germany at war with Russia, Britain and France.

◀ An excited Hitler (circled) near the front of a crowd in Munich on 2 August 1914, the day after Germany declared war on Russia. The next day France joined the war against Germany and Hitler volunteered to fight.

At the Western front

When war fever gripped Germany, Adolf Hitler was infected too. Years later in his book, *Mein Kampf (My Struggle)* he said: "Even today I am not ashamed to say that, overcome with rapturous enthusiasm, I fell to my knees and thanked Heaven from an overflowing heart for granting me the good fortune of being allowed to live at this time." Hitler volunteered for action and this time he was accepted. By October 1914 he was at the Western Front fighting for the 16th Bavarian Reserve Infantry Regiment.

Hitler served as a regimental runner, a dangerous job that involved carrying messages and orders for officers through battlefields under fire. Fellow soldiers had mixed feelings about the young Austrian who preferred his own company, or that of a small white dog he'd named Fuchsl, and who didn't drink, smoke or talk about women. Some soldiers respected his intellectual air and the way he talked about art, architecture or politics. Others admired his bravery and leadership

◀ *Hitler (right) in 1916 with fellow soldiers Ernst Schmidt and Sergeant Max Amann. The little white dog is Fuchsl (little fox) which Hitler had taught circus tricks such as climbing ladders*

qualities, while a few were unnerved by his excessive sense of duty. In every way he seemed different, and perhaps for this reason he was never promoted beyond the rank of corporal.

A charmed life

Something else set Hitler apart from the other soldiers. He believed he was special and led a charmed life. On one occasion in the trenches he claimed he had heard a voice telling him to move. He did as he was bid and a few minutes later a shell hit the very spot he'd occupied previously. At other times he made strange prophecies about himself: "You will hear much about me," he told the other soldiers, "just wait until my time comes."

Hitler's bravery won him military honours; by December 1914 he'd won the Iron Cross, Second Class, for saving the life of an officer; towards the end of the war he collected the Iron Cross, First Class, for exemplary behaviour. In 1916 he was involved in the Battle of the Somme, but in October he was injured during a shell attack. He begged to stay at the front but was sent to a field hospital. In the following months he recuperated in hospitals near Berlin and in Munich.

Within a short time of being back in Munich, his anti-Semitism began to reignite, filling him with bitterness. This bitterness was made worse by his anger towards those who weren't fighting in the war, and the pacifists who were trying to stop it. His sense of German nationalism grew stronger still.

A losing game

In March 1917, Hitler was relieved to be back at the front in Belgium with his fellow soldiers and his dog Fuchsl. In between action there were often quiet periods when he could get out his water-colours and paint battle scenes. There was also time to read up on politics, history and philosophy. He had difficult times too; in August, Fuchsl went missing and then his paintings were stolen. When food was short the regiment were forced to eat cats and dogs, but following Fuchsl's disappearance Hitler couldn't bring himself to eat dog meat.

In the mud and chaos of the trenches it was hard to determine who was winning the war. The casualties on both sides were enormous, but by August 1918 the Allies broke through the German lines at Amiens. In September Hitler's regiment was moved to Flanders and in October Hitler was involved in a mustard-gas attack. The effects of the gas could be deadly and sometimes even those who wore masks went blind. Hitler was one of the lucky ones; his blindness would only be temporary.

A future in politics

In November 1918 Hitler was recovering in hospital when he heard that the German armistice had been signed. A German defeat was terrible but the effects of the war – the loss of two million German lives and a shattered German economy – made the blow even harder to bear. Hitler was devastated but made a pact with himself – if he recovered his sight then he would enter politics and forget about architecture. He later claimed he had a strange kind of vision, when he heard voices telling him to save Germany. He said that it seemed like a miracle when he suddenly found he could see again. Hitler wanted to feel that fate was pushing him towards a career in politics.

When Hitler was discharged from hospital in November 1918, Germany was in revolutionary turmoil. The war had caused terrible food shortages and Germans were angry with their leaders, especially their Kaiser, Wilhelm II, who had ruled as German emperor and King of Prussia since 1888. Wilhelm had dominated German politics until 1908 but in the following years illness had lessened his influence. By November 1918 mutinies in the army and navy and strikes by the workers had forced Wilhelm II to abdicate and flee to the Netherlands.

The Weimar Republic

On 9 November a republic had been declared, and a coalition government of the Social Democrat Party, the Catholic Centre Party and the Democratic Party was formed by Friedrich Ebert, the leader of the Social Democrat Party. This would be Germany's first encounter with a democratic government but it would be beset with many problems. In early 1919 the new government met in Weimar to draw up its constitution. Ebert was appointed president of the new Weimar Republic but he would have a difficult time holding together a government composed of so many political factions The Republic also had many enemies.

It was hated by the German nationalists, the socialists and the communists. These were unstable times, and the threat of revolution was never far way. The communist uprising by the Bolsheviks in Russia in 1917 was a chill reminder of how bloody and cruel revolution could be, and in December 1918 the Germans were about to get their first taste of a "Red" uprising.

In Berlin, a communist group called the Spartacists had attempted, and nearly succeeded, in calling a revolution. Ebert was keen to crush such rebellion and employed a group of right-wing ex-soldiers called the Freikorps (free corps) to crush the revolt. The Freikorps succeeding in stamping out the Sparticists, and Ebert eventually gave them the responsibility of defending the Weimar Republic from further attempts at revolution. Although they were employed as peace-keepers, the Freikorps would prove to be a bloodthirsty mob. Their brutality only served to destabilize Germany even further. Opposition street armies, mainly composed of communists, soon gathered, and in a matter of months the country had become a dangerous place to live.

The experience of war

Hitler responded to these events with anger. He blamed the situation on the enemies from within – Jews, Bolsheviks and those who believed in democracy. War had brought millions of ordinary Germans nothing but poverty. The Treaty of Versailles, which would officially end the war, took land away from Germany and was a terrible humiliation. But years later Hitler said: "If I weren't myself hardened by this experience, I would have been incapable of undertaking this Cyclopean task which the building of an empire means for a single man." After World War One most Germans craved peace, but Hitler wanted revenge.

▼ *During the communist Spartacist uprising in Berlin in 1919, members of the Freikorps crushed the opposition using armoured cars and flamethrowers.*

GERMANY IN 1919

Germany 1919

Frontier of German Empire 1914

Terms of the Treaty of Versailles

- Germany and its allies to take responsibility for causing World War One
- Germany to lose an equivalent of 13 per cent of its pre-war area: Alsace-Lorraine in the west to be given to France; part of Posen and West Prussia in the east to be handed to Poland

- Allied troops to occupy the Rhineland for at least five years
- A reduction of the German army to 100,000 men
- Germany to pay reparations for war damage; fixed at 132 billion gold marks (about £6,600,000,000 today)

Hitler and the start of the Nazi Party

When Hitler returned to Munich in December 1918, soldiers and workers had taken control in a rebellion and a Bavarian Republic had been proclaimed by the communists.

To add insult to injury – from Hitler's point of view – the rebellion had been led by a Jewish left-wing socialist called Kurt Eisner. Unsure of his future, Hitler volunteered as a guard at a prisoner-of-war camp 96 kilometres away at Traunstein. While Hitler was away from Munich, Eisner was killed and a communist group proclaimed the German state of Bavaria a part of the Soviet Union. Hitler returned to the city in March and witnessed the bloody street battles in which the Freikorps crushed this communist uprising. Soon after, Hitler was employed by the army as a propaganda officer, to assess and monitor the revolutionary atmosphere prevalent in Munich.

Effects of Versailles

In June 1919, the new German government was forced to sign the Treaty of Versailles. People had hoped that the Allies would look favourably upon Germany's new democratic government and that the terms of the treaty would be lenient but they were not (see box on p. 23). There was no room for negotiation: the Allies said that they would continue to wage war against Germany if the government didn't agree to the terms of the treaty. One of the greatest blows was the reparation payment. It was to cripple Germany's already shaky economy. Very soon, Germany was suffering from high unemployment and inflation. Millions of unemployed and disillusioned soldiers added to the general climate of misery and resentment. The crime rates soared as people struggled to survive.

An opening in politics

In September 1919, Hitler was ordered by the army to spy on a small right-wing group called the German Workers' Party

▼ After 1918, thousands of injured soldiers were forced to beg on the streets of Germany. Scenes like this made most Germans fear another war.

(DAP). The group seemed badly organized yet it was fiercely nationalistic and blamed the Jews and communists for Germany's problems. At first, Hitler wasn't impressed, but he had been looking for a way into politics and perhaps this was a good opportunity. After his second visit to the party, he was offered a position organizing recruitment and propaganda. He accepted, and in October gathered an audience of over a hundred people for a meeting at which he spoke for 30 minutes. For the first time, he realized he had talent as a speaker. Within months the gatherings got larger, as students, shopkeepers and army officers crammed into the meetings held in beer halls. Most of those crowds had heard about a new and brilliant speaker – Adolf Hitler.

The lone wolf

On 24 February 1920, 2,000 people were drawn to a meeting of the DAP. Hitler was going to read out the main points of the new party programme (see the box on p 27) which he had helped to compile. His speech lasted for nearly two and half hours, but the crowd was transfixed throughout. They cheered when he ranted and shouted about bringing down the Jewish threat. They listened carefully as he altered his pitch and quietly talked about the union of all Germans. They believed he was honest and, still more importantly, capable of liberating Germany. As he went through each point the audience cheered. Anyone who jeered was forcibly removed by a band of ex-army officers. From now on Hitler called himself "the wolf" – it would become his nickname amongst close friends, but he personally liked the name.

A new image

Inspired by Adolf Hitler, the membership of the DAP increased steadily throughout 1920. The party changed its name to the Nationalsozialistische Deutsche Arbeiterpartei (National Socialist German Worker's Party) (NSDAP) or the Nazi Party, for short. With his flair for propaganda, Hitler set about making other changes. He chose red as the new party colour, a deliberate move to provoke the communists, as this was their party colour. He picked the swastika as the party's symbol. The swastika was already used by some of the Freikorps, and against a black, white and red background it made a simple and effective banner. Publicity material advertised all Nazi meetings. Flags and posters adorned the meeting halls. Party members wore swastikas on their armbands. At demonstrations, Hitler's army band marched and sang songs with rousing choruses of "Sieg Heil, Sieg Heil!" Nazism was on a roll and making its mark upon the political fabric of Bavaria.

A campaign of terror

The party had other influential members such as the writer Dietrich Eckart. He helped Hitler with his poor grammar and improved his public-speaking techniques. He also introduced him to rich, influential people. Another important member was Captain Ernst Röhm, who brought with him loyal soldiers ready to create terror among the communists on the streets of Munich. This same fearsome army eventually evolved into the Sturm Abteilung (SA) or storm troopers.

Hitler's reign of terror and intimidation was set to begin and it was calculated and cruel. "Cruelty impresses," he claimed. "People need a good scare. They want to be afraid of something. They want somebody to make them afraid, someone

Hitler's DAP manifesto

- We demand the union of all Germans in a Greater Germany
- We demand... the revocation of the peace treaties of Versailles and Saint-Germain
- We demand land and territory to feed our people and to settle our surplus population
- Only members of the nation may be citizens of the state. Only those of German blood, whatever their creed, may be members of the nation. Accordingly no Jew may be a member of the nation

to whom they can submit with a shudder. Haven't you noticed, after a brawl at a meeting, that the ones who get beaten up are the first to apply for membership of the party?"

The leader

By July 1921, Hitler's extraordinary ability to rouse a crowd had made him one of the leaders of the Nazi Party. The Nazis were fast becoming one of the largest nationalist parties in Bavaria. Party membership had increased to 6,000 by early 1922 and at a rally in Munich in

November 1922 there were 50,000 people in the crowd. In January 1923, at the time of the First Reich party rally, there were 20,000 members: a figure which rose to 55,000 by the end of the year. Although the party represented all classes, most of its membership was made up of social groups such as skilled craftsmen, civil servants and students. Hitler also realized the importance of friends in high places. He was now a guest in respected households such as the Wagners, the esteemed relatives of Hitler's favourite composer.

Germany in crisis

For Germany, 1923 had been a terrible year. In January, following late reparation payments, French troops had occupied the Ruhr, Germany's most important industrial region. As a result the mark had plummeted, there had been enormous inflation, and unemployment had risen. Suddenly, the middle-classes saw the value of their savings slump and the working man couldn't feed his family.

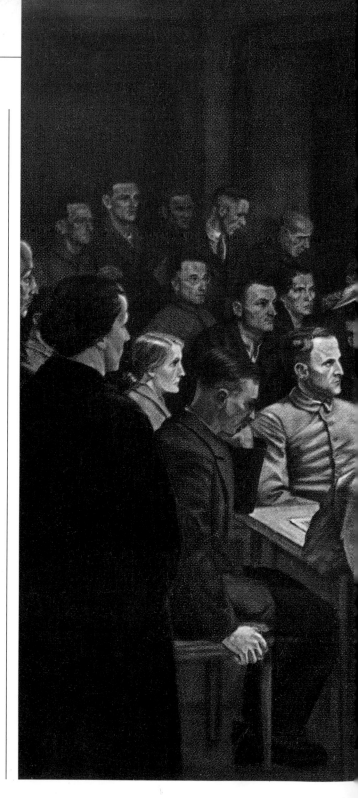

▶ The artist H.G. Boyer captures the intensity of Adolf Hitler at a Nazi meeting, circa 1922. In his neat suits, Hitler looked the picture of respectability but he was quite prepared to use force.

► Hitler takes to the snowy streets of Munich in 1923. He rarely missed the opportunity to promote the Nazi Party.

Communist revolts in Saxony, Thuringia and Hamburg made people believe there could be a communist revolution throughout Germany. Hitler believed the time was right for a national revolution or Putsch (purge). The plan was to overthrow the Bavarian government, then force them to join the Nazis in a march on Berlin and impose a Nazi regime throughout the whole of Germany. In Italy the Fascist leader Benito Mussolini had staged a similar coup in 1922 and Hitler had very much admired his style.

The Beer Hall Putsch

The plan was put into action on 8 November 1923. Hitler ordered the meeting of the Bavarian government at a beer hall called the Bürgerbräukeller to be surrounded by 600 storm troopers. With a gun in his hand, Hitler took the stage and proclaimed that the national revolution had begun. Members of the Bavarian government were seized and persuaded to support the plan.

In many ways the Putsch was badly organized – after seizing the government leaders, Hitler then allowed them to go free. This was a foolish decision that gave the leaders time to gather the army and police and put a stop to the coup. The next day, when 2,000 storm troopers attempted to enter Munich, there were street battles in which 16 Nazis were killed. Hitler was also injured but he managed to run away and hide at the home of his friends, the Hanfstaengls. At first Hitler believed he'd been shot but his injury turned out to be a dislocated arm. That evening, Hitler suffered pain and humiliation and even considered suicide. Helene Hanfstaengl, his friend and supporter, hid his revolver. She told him to continue with his struggle.

Hitler's views, in his own words

"What we must fight for is to safeguard the existence and reproduction of our race and our people, the sustenance of our children and the purity of our blood, the freedom and independence of the fatherland, so that our people may mature for the fulfilment of the mission allotted by the creator of the universe."

"The cleanliness of this people [the Jews], moral and otherwise, I must say, is a point in itself. By their very exterior you could tell that these were no lovers of water, and, to your distress, you often knew it with your eyes closed. Later I often grew sick to my stomach from the smell of the kaftan-wearers. Added to this, there was their unclean dress and their generally unheroic appearance."

"If, with the help of his Marxist creed, the Jew is victorious over the other peoples of the world, his crown will be the funeral wreath of humanity and this planet will, as it did thousands of years ago, move through the ether devoid of men ... Hence today I believe that I am acting in accordance with the will of the Almighty Creator: *by defending myself against the Jew, I am fighting for the work of the Lord."*

Behind bars

Hitler was arrested the next morning and taken to Landsberg Prison. He would be charged with high treason and sentenced to five years in prison. Humiliated and dejected by the defeat, Hitler went on hunger strike for two weeks. Eventually he was persuaded that the failure of the Putsch had been a good thing as people's enthusiasm had been stirred. When the revolution came it would require a leader, he was told, and that leader would be Adolf Hitler.

Life at Landsberg was comfortable and Hitler was treated well. He was exempt from manual work and allowed visitors. He mixed freely with other Nazis. He was also allowed books so he spent hours reading Nietzsche and Marx. However, the greatest luxury was having the time to write about his life. These memoirs, later published as *Mein Kampf*, revealed how passionately he hated the Jews and the communists, and how he would strive to make Germany great again.

▶ *Hitler looking defiant as he stands trial for his part in the Beer Hall Putsch. He stands between Ernst Röhm (front right) and General Ludendorff.*

Building the Nazi Party: 1925–1929

Hitler was released early from prison in December 1924. He had served little over a year of his sentence, but it had been time to gather his thoughts and assess the future of the Nazi Party.

He realized he had work to do as many people had turned their backs on the party and membership was now less than 28,000. Realistic about the problems ahead, Hitler told his secretary Rudolf Hess: "I shall need five years before the movement is on top again." In many ways the political situation in Germany didn't favour Hitler's return to power. With the help of foreign loans, primarily from the USA, the dark days of 1923 seemed to have lifted. Money had been poured back into industry, there were more jobs and the German economy was looking healthier. To gain a foothold in politics, Hitler decided to change his tactics. The Jewish issue would be downplayed; instead he would concentrate on organization and policy. Rather than overthrowing the government, he would have to work within the government framework and win seats in the Reichstag (the German parliament).

A new beginning

Hitler made his re-entry into public life on 27 February 1925. For dramatic effect he chose the Bürgerbräukeller – the scene of the disastrous Putsch – for his first public speech. Over 4,000 people jammed into the beer hall and a further thousand were turned away. As he walked towards the stage, the crowd cheered, women started to cry and men pushed forward to congratulate him. For two hours Hitler held the audience's attention. He demanded solidarity within the party but he told them that he could only do this if he was the undisputed leader of the Nazis.

▶ *Hitler poses for a photograph as he is released from Landsberg prison in 1924.*

If he was in charge, he reasoned, then he would take responsibility for leading the party to greatness.

Winning back control

In fact it would take Hitler until 1926 officially to win back control of the party: after that time he was called *Führer* (leader) at all times. In the meantime, his comeback had not gone unnoticed by the Bavarian government. They quickly banned him from speaking in public, a boycott that was later extended to the states of Prussia, Saxony, Baden and Hamburg. Undeterred, Hitler spoke at closed meetings in front of wealthier supporters, while concentrating upon measures to build the Nazi Party. In 1925 the party was the smallest in Germany, but Hitler could appeal to all kinds of supporters. He could turn to the working man, and tell him that he too had worked as a labourer on building sites. At the same time, his artistic background meant that he could appeal to bohemians. In his speeches he would almost hypnotize the audience, using powerful rhetoric,

◀ *A portrait of Hitler signed by him on 28 April 1924 while he was still a prisoner. He's also written, " Erst recht!" ("Now I'll show you!").*

repeating his simple ideas over and over again. He told people the things they wanted to hear and he restored their confidence by telling them that Germany's problems were not their fault but those of Jews and communists. He appealed to people's sense of patriotism and told them the way forward for the German people was to restore one race – the Aryans – to Germany.

When *Mein Kampf* was published in July 1925 its high sales were a sign of Hitler's growing popularity.

A vision for the future

In the following years Hitler set about reorganizing the party and creating departments for industry, agriculture, economy, foreign policy and publicity. The SS (Schutzstaffen) guard detachment were recruited to act as personal bodyguards to Hitler and the other Nazi leaders. The SA was reformed. Hitler Youth, the Women's League, and the Leagues of Nazi Lawyers, Nazi Doctors and Nazi Teachers were all launched. When the party held its first rally in Thuringia, the crowd used the raised-arm Nazi salute for the first time. By the end of 1926, membership was back up to 50,000.

Behind the public face

Much has been written about Hitler since his death, as authors attempt to make sense of possibly the most evil man in history. In many ways Hitler was a straightforward man with simple tastes. He continued to live in cheap rented accommodation until 1927, when he rented a villa in Obersalzberg on the German-Austrian border as a place to relax at weekends. He enjoyed outdoor living and was never happier than when walking in the hills wearing lederhosen, a part of the traditional German dress. One of his early extravagances was a brand-new red Mercedes which he enjoyed driving to picnics in the woods and lakes outside Munich. Some of the picnickers enjoyed a swim, but Hitler refused to undress in front of the others and would usually read a book.

"Uncle Alf"

Hitler genuinely enjoyed the company of women and children. He also loved dogs, but his sadistic streak was never far from the surface as he regularly threatened his animals with whips. Hitler was particularly secretive about his love life – probably because he seemed to prefer

the company of younger women. The relationship with his niece Geli Raubal was perhaps his most passionate but historians cannot agree how intimate the relationship actually was. Hitler was in his late thirties when his fun-loving nineteen-year-old niece caught his eye.

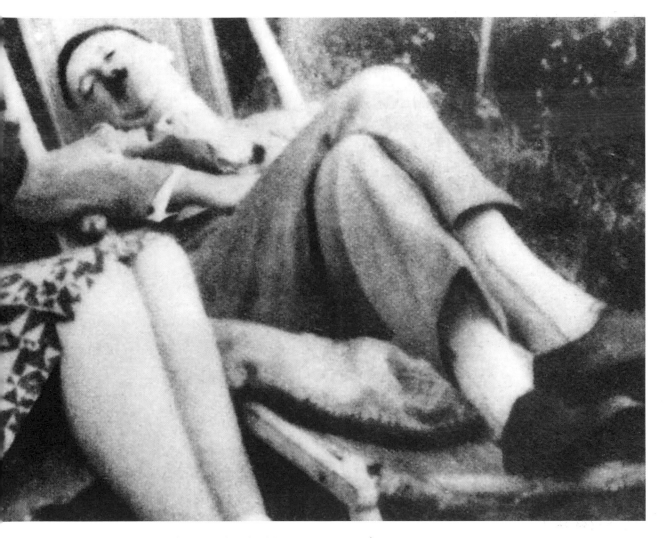

Geli was the daughter of his half-sister Angela. The relationship between Hitler and Geli began when Geli's mother became housekeeper of his villa in Obersalzberg. In 1927, Geli moved to Munich to be near Hitler. For the next few years she accompanied him to the

"Uncle Alf" and his niece Geli share a quiet moment. Not much is known about Hitler's taste in women, but Ernst Röhm once suggested that Hitler was partial to peasant girls with large round bottoms.

▲ Following the Wall Street Crash scenes of poverty and hardship became common in Germany. This photograph shows people queueing for soup outside the Salvation Army in Berlin in 1931.

theatre and opera and even to a few Nazi Party events. She loved it when "Uncle Alf" mimicked people, something he was good at, and he found her company relaxing.

Throughout this period the German economy had been growing. By 1928 the national income was 12 per cent higher than it had been in 1913. In his speeches Hitler claimed that he alone could save Germany, but what was he actually saving Germany from? Hitler was beginning to sound out of touch, something that was reflected in the poor results for the Nazi Party in the 1928 elections for the Reichstag. So Hitler continued to work at restructuring the party; in January 1929 he recruited Heinrich Himmler as the leader of the SS, and put him in charge of building an army of elite soldiers.

From October 1928 to September 1929 the membership of the party rose from 100,000 to 150,000, and in August 1929 the Nazis held their biggest rally yet at Nuremberg. Special trains transported party members to take part in the event and during one of the many spectacular parades, 60,000 storm troopers waving Nazi banners marched past Hitler. It took three hours for the parade to finish.

The Depression hits

In September 1929, Hitler and Geli moved into a luxurious flat in Munich. "Uncle Alf" would prove to be a jealous and possessive lover who wanted to know how Geli spent each day. Meanwhile he was romancing another young woman called Eva Braun. Eva was a fresh-faced eighteen-year-old who worked in a photography shop. Hitler would take her on dates during the day in order to keep the liaison secret from Geli. For a while, Hitler's private life infuriated Nazi Party members as it seemed to take over from his political responsibilities. However, in October 1929, events in the USA were about to change the lives of everyone in Germany – including Hitler's. The Wall Street Crash on "Black Thursday" heralded an end to the new prosperity and when the USA called in loans they had made to Germany in the early 1920s, businesses began to fail. Unemployment rocketed and Germany was plunged into depression. This climate of desperation would make the perfect setting for the rise of Adolf Hitler and his Nazi Party.

Creating the Third Reich

Between 1928 and 1930 Germany's unemployment rose from about one million to over 3 million.

The Weimar Republic eventually broke up in 1930 and Heinrich Brüning of the Centre party was made Chancellor (the equivalent to Prime Minister). The situation did not improve and people still looked for a new political figure, one who could steer the country back to prosperity. Hitler sensed imminent success. That August he told his colleagues that he expected a breakthrough within a year. In his speeches Hitler gave Germans the hope of a brighter future. He called for an end to democracy and offered a unified and stable government in its place. He spoke out against the Treaty of Versailles and denounced the reparation payments. He railed against the Jews and the communists and blamed them for Germany's problems.

▼ Hitler appears calm and relaxed as an adoring crowd of SA and other onlookers surround him in Munich, circa 1930.

He made promises he couldn't hope to keep, but in doing so he appealed to a wider spectrum of voters including farmers, workers, middle-class intellectuals and industrialists. By September 1930, the Nazis had gained 107 seats in the Reichstag and had become the second largest party in parliament.

Personal tragedy

Behind the scenes, Hitler's life wasn't quite so triumphant. His work took him away from home a great deal and his relationship with Geli became strained. The affair ended in tragedy in 1931 when Geli was found, shot dead, in the flat. The verdict was recorded as suicide, but some people suggest that Hitler had killed her because she had taken another lover. We will never know the truth, but Hitler never forgot her and her photograph remained by his bed for the rest of his life.

In 1932 unemployment in Germany hit six million and industrial production was half that of 1928. In the presidential elections in May that year Hitler stood against the respected war hero, General von Hindenburg. Hitler was defeated but still gained 30 per cent of the votes.

Hitler's popularity was undeniable and certain politicians invited Hitler to join the coalition. But years earlier Hitler had promised himself that the Nazis would never be part of a coalition, and only he would be leader of the government. His steadfast belief in himself paid off. In the September elections of 1932 the Nazis took 230 seats and became the largest party in the Reichstag. Despite losing 34 of those seats in a second bout of elections in November, Hitler still refused to join the coalition. By now Hitler spent little time in Munich as his work was on the road, touring the country and preaching Nazism to an adoring public. Hindenburg had always distrusted Hitler. But in January 1933, in the face of Hitler's growing popularity, he appointed Hitler as Chancellor. He believed that if Hitler led a Nazi-Nationalist coalition government, with a cabinet which had a majority of Nationalists in it, then Hitler could be kept under control. It was a massive underestimation of Hitler's power and determination. Now that Hitler was Chancellor he aimed to secure complete control of the country.

▶ *An election poster from 1932 featuring von Hindenburg and Hitler.*

„Nimmer wird das Reich zerstöret — wenn ihr einig seid und treu"

1 Nationalsozialisten

Determination and fire

One of Hitler's first moves as Chancellor was to apply for another election in March 1933. He hoped for a Nazi Party majority. That way he'd be even closer to his dream of creating a dictatorship. Within weeks he also gave the SA and the SS more power to deal with those considered enemies of the Nazis. Jews, communists and rival politicians were arrested, tortured and sometimes murdered. Hitler was hell-bent on success. When the Reichstag building caught fire on 27 February 1933 he blamed a Dutch communist, and in turn all communists. In truth, the fire was probably started by the Nazis to gain support in the upcoming election and also to enable them to pass emergency laws that would help them to crush the communists.

These new laws effectively legalized the reign of terror the Nazis were about to unleash. Now the police could arrest and hold people indefinitely, as well as censor post and make searches of people's houses. In the next few months it is

Women seemed to adore Hitler. On a few occasions teenage girls threw themselves under his car, hoping that he might comfort them afterwards.

estimated that about 25,000 people were arrested by Hitler's henchmen, the SA and SS. With the rights of the press withheld, and the right to hold public meetings curtailed, the Nazis were removing any opposition. Only the Nazis and Nationalists could campaign freely for election. But in March 1933 the Nazis still only managed to win 288 seats – which was 44 per cent of the votes. Hitler had anticipated a bigger majority but his plans for imposing total Nazi rule on Germany were still on track.

Complete control

That same month the Reichstag passed the Enabling Law. It would give Hitler full dictatorial powers for four years. Now Hitler could establish a one-party system, with the Nazis in Berlin in complete control. With hindsight it's easy to ask why Hitler was given such free passage to the top, but the Nazis' reign of terror cannot be underestimated. On the day the Reichstag voted for the Enabling Law the building was surrounded by the SA, and Hitler had crushed much of the opposition. We must also remember Hitler's uncanny ability to sway people with his false promises, something that he continued to do throughout his leadership. Within months of taking power, Hitler had banned trade unions and replaced them by the German Labour Front. It was just one example of how Hitler would court a group to win their support, then completely betray them at the last minute.

Hitler moved quickly to establish Nazi rule across Germany. He placed his most loyal supporters in top-ranking positions. He chose Joseph Goebbels as his Minister of Propaganda and Hermann Goering as Prussian Minister of the Interior – both men would be key players throughout the existence of the Nazi regime. By a process called Gleichschaltung (co-ordination) all public groups were brought under Nazi control. Now teachers had to join the National Socialist Teachers' Organization, while all German employers had to join the Estate of German Industry. By July 1933, the last of the rival political parties, including the Nationalists, had been shut down. With effective manipulation of the media, Goebbels ensured that the only way forward for millions of Germans was Nazism. Towards the end of 1933 only the ageing President, Hindenburg, the army and the Catholic Church were not controlled by Hitler and the Nazis.

The "Night of the Long Knives"

The only real threat to Hitler came from the SA. It now had over a million members. The fear and intimidation meted out by the SA, under the leadership of Hitler's old friend Ernst Röhm, had been instrumental in Hitler's rise to power. Now Hitler needed more support from Germany's middle classes, its leading industrialists and the army. To gain a larger foothold in these camps he needed to clean up his image and distance himself from the SA. On 30 June 1934, in an act of ruthless treachery, Hitler had 150 SA leaders, including Röhm, murdered by the SS. Perhaps as many as a thousand others were killed during a bloody night of terror known as the "Night of the Long Knives". The army leaders were pleased with Hitler's treatment of the unruly SA. When Hindenburg died on 2 August 1934 Hitler was declared Chancellor and President. From now on Hitler demanded that he be called Führer at all times.

▶ *Hitler addresses a Nazi rally in the 1930s. Such events were well rehearsed so they appeared perfect. Behind the scenes the SA were not so orderly.*

Domestic policy – propaganda and the dictator

If you had been alive in Nazi Germany during the 1930s you would have been bombarded by Nazi propaganda and expected to follow the party religiously.

Posters and pictures showed Hitler as an all-powerful dictator, often making him look bigger and more handsome than he actually was. Everybody was expected to obey their Führer. To show their support people had to hang swastikas in their windows and greet each other with "Heil Hitler". Wardens were employed on each neighbourhood block to keep an eye on people and report those who didn't obviously show their allegiance to the Nazis. Everybody was being watched. There was a real fear that if you didn't support the party fully, then neighbours, or even your children, would inform the authorities. Once more fear was used as a key tool, and it became extremely difficult to rebel against the Nazis.

The 1936 Olympic Games

The Nazis couldn't have maintained their control through terror alone. After defeat in war, depression, and years of political upheaval the Nazis offered German people a sense of pride and even a chance to have fun. Parades and celebrations of key dates in the Nazi calendar (see the table on p.53) were opportunities for people to gather together, sing and dance and generally forget about the bad times. They were, of course, carefully organized events designed to show off the new regime and allow Hitler to speak to his people. Most occasions were filmed or recorded for the radio. Perhaps the greatest of these Nazi extravaganzas was the 1936 Olympic Games in Berlin.

▲ The black athlete Jesse Owens wins one of his four gold medals at the Berlin Olympic Games in 1936.

Hitler was proud to show off his dynamic new country to an international audience. Germany scooped most of the medals, but when the black American sprinter Jesse James Owens won four gold medals, Hitler was said to be so angry he left the stadium rather than congratulate him. It was an early indication of how Germany's leader was really thinking.

The Nazis gave the impression of organization and efficiency, but in truth the administration was in a mess. All decisions were made by Hitler, but in running his government, he adopted a divide and rule strategy. He'd assign the same task to different people or offices and in doing so he would deliberately play people off against each other in order to safeguard his own position as master of the party. In that way, he could claim that without him it would all fall apart.

The visionary

Despite their lack of organization, the Nazis were successful. Between 1933 and 1939 the German economy was recovering and unemployment fell to

Hitler launches the beetle-shaped Volkswagen in 1939. The car would become popular throughout the world after World War Two.

Calendar of Nazi celebrations

- **30 January** Hitler's appointment as Chancellor
- **24 February** Refounding of the party in 1925
- **24 March** Heroes' Remembrance Day for war heroes
- **20 April** Hitler's Birthday
- **1 May** National Day of Labour
- **2nd Sunday in May** Mothering Sunday
- **June** Summer Solstice
- **September** Nuremberg Party Rally
- **1 October** Harvest Thanksgiving
- **9 November** Anniversary of the 1923 Putsch in Munich

below one million. This recovery was partly because the world economy had improved, but it was also because Hitler had invested heavily in industry and rearmament. Naturally, in his speeches Hitler highlighted his own part in the new prosperity, but in some ways Hitler was a visionary. He masterminded the construction of canals, motorways and mass housing. It was his dream that one day every German would have a reliable car to drive on the new fast motorways.

Within a short time Hitler had brought a sense of stability to many Germans.

People could support their families and self-worth was restored. But behind all this success was a long-term goal. In 1936 Hitler hatched his Four Year Plan in which he stated his aims: to make Germany self-sufficient in food and raw materials, and prepare its armed forces in anticipation of war within four years.

Persecution of the Jews

In 1933 there were about 500,000 Jews living in Germany. They made up less than one per cent of the population yet the Nazis blamed them for all of Germany's misfortunes. For years Hitler had raged against the Jews. He had likened them to germs that poisoned pure German blood. He looked forward to the day when Germans would become a racially pure race – the Aryans.

Now, as Führer, Hitler was in a position to pass many of his long planned anti-Jewish policies. Within months of becoming Chancellor, the SA were ransacking Jewish properties, arresting Jews, and sending them to concentration

◀ *A Jewish synagogue is destroyed on Kristallnacht. Such images provoked outrage abroad, and people finally began to question what was happening in Nazi Germany.*

camps. Then, on 30 March 1933, Hitler ordered a one-day boycott of Jewish shops and businesses. When foreign powers threatened to boycott Germany, Hitler realized he would need to tread carefully. However, he soon managed to introduce new laws to whittle away at Jewish liberties. To start with, Jews were expelled from the civil service and media, then they were banned from higher education. In 1935 the Nuremberg Laws stripped them of German citizenship, and marriages between Jews and people of German blood were forbidden.

Kristallnacht

In 1938 life got even harder for the Jews. On 9–10 November 1938, the Nazis staged Kristallnacht (Night of the Broken Glass). The Nazis burned down about 200 synagogues and smashed and looted Jewish businesses and homes. Over 20,000 Jews were arrested and taken to concentration camps, and about 90 Jews were killed. By September 1939, nearly half of Germany's Jews had emigrated to other parts of Europe or the US. Many believed they were escaping to a better life; but they were actually running for their lives.

Brainwashing the children

At Nuremberg in 1935 Hitler told the crowd of Hitler Youth that they were to be, "Fast as a greyhound, tough as leather, and hard as Krupp Steel." In these words he had encapsulated the Nazi philosophy of strength and racial superiority. He'd also struck at the hearts of those he believed to be the future of Germany – its children. Hitler always maintained that education was the only means of creating good Nazis. So schools and colleges were brought under Nazi control and the school curriculum carefully tailored. Subjects like biology could be used to promote racial superiority, while history could teach of Germany's great past. Foreign languages were dropped and replaced by character training in loyalty, obedience, courage and sacrifice. Physical training played its part too, in creating a stronger and healthier nation. Even though Hitler did not play any sport himself he placed great emphasis on games and physical fitness.

In 1926 Hitler started the Hitler Youth movement. By 1933 all other youth

▶ *When young boys became members of Hitler Youth they were given a dagger engraved with the words: "Blood and Honour".*

movements had been merged under its banner and by 1934 there were over 3.5 million members. Towards the end of the 1930s all children aged between ten and

eighteen were expected to join; membership had risen to about 7 million. There were penalties for those who refused to join, but most children were happy to participate in a group that played sports and games and sang rousing anthems and brought them closer to their beloved Führer.

Hitler the man – his private life

As he became more powerful, Hitler distanced himself from other leading Nazis, but he still liked to surround himself with beautiful women.

In early 1932 Hitler took Eva Braun as his mistress. It was an unusual affair, as Eva never appeared with him in public, while in private he was domineering and cold, banning her from dancing and smoking. Perhaps his enduring love for Geli meant he didn't have much more to give. It must have infuriated Eva that Hitler had kept Geli's room as it was when she was alive, and that he had fresh flowers placed there each week. In a desperate attempt to attract Hitler's attention, Eva attempted suicide, both in 1932 and in 1935 – but he continued to neglect her. In 1932 Hitler met Magda Quandt. He thought he'd found a woman he could marry. The fact that she was Goebbels' mistress didn't deter him, but when she did eventually marry Goebbels, he didn't seem too troubled by her loss. There were rumours of many other mistresses as well. But in truth Hitler probably just liked the attention and company of beautiful actresses and singers, rather than wanting a close relationship with any of them.

The summer home

By the end of 1936 Hitler was spending a lot of time in the Austrian Alps, at his new summer retreat in the Berchtesgaden, the Berghof. The house had been developed on the site of his old villa, and though Hitler liked to portray himself as a man of simple tastes his new home revealed a more extravagant side to his nature. He collected Persian carpets, rare tapestries and fine art, and dinner was served on beautiful Dresden china with silver cutlery. There were fourteen bedrooms for guests, each supplied with a

▶ *Hitler poses for a photograph with Eva Braun and her niece in about 1937. Not many people knew that Hitler had a mistress until the end of the war.*

portrait of Hitler and a copy of *Mein Kampf*. Hitler held conferences there, but he also enjoyed entertaining. It was an honour to be invited to the Berghof, but all guests were aware of the strict rules (see the table below).

The bohemian

In his youth Hitler had fancied himself as an artist, and a touch of the bohemian remained with him throughout his life. In his Vienna days he had devoured books about politics, but as he got older he

turned to literature. He rarely read German books, his tastes were more international, and included *Robinson Crusoe*, *Uncle Tom's Cabin* and *Don Quixote*. Another favourite was the Bible in which he hoped to find justification for his anti-Semitism. He enjoyed the music of Beethoven and Weber, but his greatest love remained opera, particularly the works of Richard Wagner. In Vienna, Hitler had enjoyed the theatre. Now he was a fan of the movies too, including American movies and the Hollywood star, Greta Garbo. He continued to be interested in art and in 1933 laid the foundation stone for the Munich House of German Art. However, when he saw the first selection of paintings he was so furious with the modern art he saw there that he threatened to shut the exhibition down. Hitler believed that modern art was evidence of a decadent Western world. In 1938 he passed a law that banned modern art from being exhibited.

Culture and Nazi Germany

Behind his back some of his Nazi colleagues joked about Hitler's interest in culture and the arts, but Hitler recognized that art and politics went hand in hand.

Some of Hitler's instructions to guests at the Berghof, 1938

- Smoking is forbidden, except in this bedroom
- At all times the Führer must be addressed and spoken of as such and never as "Herr Hitler" or other title
- Women guests are forbidden to use excessive cosmetics and must on no account use colouring materials on their fingernails
- Guests must present themselves for meals within two minutes of the announcing bell. No one may sit at table or leave the table until the Führer has sat or left
- Guests must retire to their rooms at 11 p.m. unless expressly asked to remain by the Führer

---

He realized that the arts could influence people so it was important that access to the arts was strictly controlled. For example, in 1933, he ordered the mass burning of Jewish, communist and gay-authored books. Later in the same year, the Nazis set up the Reich Cultural Chamber, a building with separate chambers for literature, theatre, music, fine art and films. The Nazis also tried to

▲ Paintings of the perfect Aryan family were acceptable in Nazi Germany. This oil painting by Wilhelm Haller shows a blond German couple with their five children. Rolling hills in the background complete the idealized vision.

bring high culture to the people. In factories, workers would have to take breaks from the production line in order to listen to orchestras playing rousing German classical music.

Body matters

When most people think of Adolf Hitler they often picture his hard expression and his stiff demeanour, and they think of his lust for power and propensity for evil. In many ways it's easy to forget that he was a real person who felt pain and suffered from illness. In fact, from the middle of the 1930s Hitler was seeing more and more of doctors and

▼ *Almost human: Hitler relaxes at his Berghof mountain retreat. This photograph was probably taken by Eva Braun.*

psychiatrists, and relying upon greater and greater doses of powerful drugs to keep himself going.

Some of Hitler's ailments, such as high blood pressure, eczema and stomach problems, could be clearly put down to stress, made worse by his bad temper. Other problems could be blamed on his diet. Since Geli's death he had become a vegetarian, but this made his stomach problems and flatulence worse. Hitler also had a sweet tooth and as he got older he was inclined to put on weight. Hitler feared death, but it only worried him because he believed he had so much to achieve and that he might run out of time. In 1935, when his voice became hoarse, he was afraid that he might have cancer of the throat. It turned out that the small growth on his larynx wasn't malignant. The operation to remove it was a success – but like so much of his private life, it was kept secret.

▲ *Almost mad: Hitler rehearsed for his speeches as if he were an actor. It's easy to believe there was insanity in Hitler's family when you see pictures like this.*

In the hands of fate

As extraordinary as it might seem, Hitler, the all-powerful dictator, also believed in fate, and dabbled in astrology. In 1933, he sought help from one of Europe's leading astrologers, Erik Jan Hanussen. Hitler wanted to find out if the famous astrologer could advise him about his future. Hanussen more or less told him that he would rise to power. We don't know if Hitler believed the astrologer's predictions, but it's interesting that he was prepared to listen to them.

Foreign policy: 1933–1940

Hitler's greatest ambition was to make all German-speaking people part of the Reich.

Many years before, Hitler had also written about Germany's lack of living space (*Lebensraum*) in *Mein Kampf*. He believed that the country could only be secure if it had more land and space. "The greater the quantity of space at the disposal of a people, the greater its natural protection," he wrote. So we know that expansion into foreign territories was always in his mind.

The aims of Hitler's foreign policy are still disputed by the historians and experts on Nazi Germany. Hitler's first goal was to dismantle the Treaty of Versailles, but what did he intend to do next? Did he aim to take over Europe and create a German empire, or was he looking towards Russia and its collapse? Some people assume he was an opportunist who was just aiming to make Germany great and implemented his aims one step at a time, as and when suitable chances arose.

► German troops march into Vienna in spring 1938. Nazi Germany was on the road to war.

Preparation for war

In the 1930s, ordinary people in Germany craved peace. But as early as 1933, Hitler was preparing for war. Under the rearmament programme, Germany had been building its military machine, and in 1935, in direct contravention of the Treaty of Versailles, conscription had been reintroduced. In 1934 Hitler had signed a ten-year non-aggression pact with Poland, but he had no intention of keeping the peace. It was probably a diversionary tactic that helped him to persuade France and Britain that rearmament and conscription weren't acts of aggression: that he was merely restoring Germany's military honour. He must have convinced them, as Britain signed a naval pact with Germany allowing them to rebuild their navy – up to one-third of the size of the Royal Navy. This would prove to be just one of the many occasions when Hitler managed to

Lebensraum

"The aim of German policy is to make sure to preserve the racial Community and to enlarge it. It is therefore a question of (living) space…"
Hitler on 5 November 1937 speaking in the Chancellery.

blind his enemies with a diplomatic smokescreen.

Occupation of the Rhineland

By the middle of the 1930s, new wars threatened to disturb the peace in Europe. Hitler waited for the right moment for Germany to enter the arena. In 1935–6 when the Italian Fascist dictator Benito Mussolini invaded Ethiopia, Hitler noted that France and Britain failed to rein Italy in with economic sanctions. He decided the time was right to strike a blow of his own. In March 1936, Hitler ordered his German troops to occupy the demilitarized Rhineland. It was another challenge to the Treaty of Versailles but Hitler predicted, correctly, that France and Britain wouldn't do anything about it.

Invasion of Austria

Later in 1936, when the Spanish Civil War broke out, Hitler forged an alliance with Mussolini. In the same year, Hitler signed a pact with Japan to fight the spread of communism. Within a short time, Hitler had made new allies. In 1938 when he took control of Germany's armed forces he was prepared for his next

▲ *Fascist leaders unite. Hitler pays a state visit to Italy in May 1938. The pact between the two dictators Mussolini (left) and Hitler lasted until 1943.*

move – to unite the German-speaking people of his native Austria with Germany. In March 1938, after months of threats, Hitler ordered German troops to enter Vienna, in Austria. Within days, Hitler was able to lead a triumphant celebration – a motorcade – from Munich to Vienna. It would be an emotional homecoming at which Hitler proclaimed an *Anschluss*, or union, between Germany and Austria. He later told his valet, "It is fate, Linge. I am destined to be the

Führer who will bring all Germans into the Greater German Reich."

Claiming the Sudetenland

Hitler planned his next campaign carefully. This time he aimed to reclaim a German-speaking region of Czechoslovakia called the Sudetenland. In September 1938, he met with the British and French Prime Ministers, Neville Chamberlain and Edouard Daladier, and the Czechoslovak President, Eduard Benes. France and Britain were eager to avoid war. Eventually an agreement was signed whereby 18,400 sq km of Czechoslovak territory were given to Hitler. Hitler promised that this would be his last demand. But on 14 March 1939, Germany invaded the rest of Czechoslovakia. The era of appeasement was finally at an end.

Final steps to war

In January 1939, Hitler turned his attention to Poland. He began by demanding that the Poles hand over the corridor of land that separated East Prussia from the rest of Germany. The land was important to Poland as it was

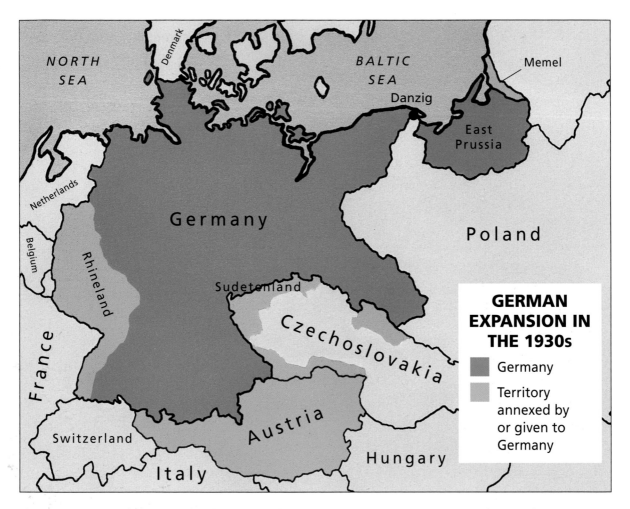

GERMAN EXPANSION IN THE 1930s

Germany

Territory annexed by or given to Germany

the country's only access to the sea and it contained the valuable seaport of Danzig. Fearing that Hitler would use force, Britain and France guaranteed Poland military protection. Meanwhile, Hitler was making alliances of his own. In May 1939 he signed a pact with Mussolini (the "Pact of Steel"), in which they agreed to support each other in any future war.

Then, in August 1939, he made a non-aggression pact with the communist Soviet leader, Joseph Stalin. Hitler's hatred of communists was well known so the pact came as a shock to France and Britain, but Hitler believed that with the Soviets on his side, France and Britain wouldn't help the Poles. It was to prove a terrible miscalculation.

Poland is blitzed

Hitler planned surprise attacks on Poland using concentrated firepower over short bursts of time. This was a tactic known as Blitzkrieg (lightning war). On 1 September 1939, the blitzkrieg on Poland began. Two days later, when Britain and France declared war on Germany, war between the European superpowers had begun. Hitler had a genuine admiration for the British. He had hoped that they could be talked out of war. But when he realized that he would have go to war with them, he was resolute. In a speech on 1 September, he told the Reichstag, "I will carry on this fight, no matter against whom, until the safety of the Reich and its rights are secured! From this moment,

▶ *This cartoon from 1939 makes fun of the alliance between Hitler and Stalin.*

my whole life shall belong more than ever to my people. I now want to be nothing but the first soldier of the German Reich. Therefore, I have once again put on that uniform which was always so sacred to and dear to me. I shall not take it off until after the victory – or I shall not live to see the end!"

On 17 September the Soviets entered Poland from the east. The attack on Poland happened too quickly for the Allies to help, and defeat for the Poles came about within six weeks. Believing he should lead by example, Hitler stayed near the action and arrived at the front line each day, armed with his pistol and whip, to inspect proceedings. In Germany the news of another war hit people hard. But they were living in a dictatorship and criticism was forbidden. Nobody was allowed to listen to foreign radio transmissions and, within Germany, Nazi propaganda presented the war as a necessary evil.

Days of victory

Hitler then turned his attentions to the West. With massive numbers of aircraft, tanks and lorries the German war machine would prove to be too powerful for other European countries to be able to put up much resistance. In April 1940, Germany conquered Denmark and Norway. Hitler's sights were now set on France. The French had built a line of defence called the "Maginot Line" along their border with Germany. Meanwhile the British had dug trenches at Lille, near the Belgian border. On 10 May 1940, the Germans found an easy way around the Allies' defences. First, they began attacking northern Belgium and the Netherlands by air. So the Allies responded by advancing north, leaving the south of the Maginot Line, near Sedan, open to the German tanks. The German war machine advanced rapidly. By 23 May 1940, the Germans were a few miles from Dunkirk on the English Channel, and the British forces were retreating. It was at this point (against the wishes of his generals), that Hitler ordered his tanks to stop. Invasion of Britain had seemed inevitable, yet Hitler's orders enabled 338,000 British servicemen to escape from Dunkirk. It seems that Hitler had hoped that he could still make peace with Britain. But Britain was in no mood to make peace with Nazi Germany, and its new prime minister Winston Churchill had promised his country victory at any cost.

▶ *Hitler enjoys a moment of triumph in front of the Eiffel Tower in Paris, soon after the German invasion of France in June 1940. Hitler was "fascinated" by Paris.*

War on all fronts: 1940–1942

On 22 June 1940, the French armistice was signed at Compiègne. This was poignant, because Germany had surrendered here at the end of World War One. The French were now under Nazi rule.

Hitler was in a triumphant mood and spoke of destroying everything that reminded the world of the shame of 1918. He later travelled to Paris, a city that had always fascinated him, and visited the Eiffel Tower and Napoleon's Tomb. With its fine architecture and art, Paris was everything he had always imagined and he talked about making Berlin more beautiful than the French capital one day.

Blitzing Britain

Hitler's confidence in his own judgement and military planning was on a new high. He became less likely to listen to the advice of his generals and more likely to issue counteractive orders. In July 1940, Hitler spoke to the Reichstag of his hope for peace with Britain: "Mr Churchill ought perhaps, for once, to believe me when I prophesy that a great empire will be destroyed – an empire which it was never my intention to destroy or even to harm…" Hitler's threats did nothing to dent Churchill's iron will and Hitler was forced to continue to wage war against Britain.

So, in August 1940, Hitler planned to wipe out the Royal Air Force and make a naval invasion of Britain. On 13 August 1940, German bombers attacked British airbases; in September they blitzed London. Hitler was convinced that the British would surrender, but despite high civilian casualties and heavy losses to the RAF, Britain soldiered on. Hitler felt compelled to change tactics, and, once more, he halted an offensive which might have won him the war. Instead he looked towards the defeat of the USSR in a campaign named "Operation Barbarossa". A year earlier, Hitler and Stalin had

▲ Hitler and Mussolini discuss tactics for the Eastern Front with Field Marshal Wilhelm Keitel (background) and General Alfred Jödl (right).

signed a non-aggression pact, but Hitler had never really trusted Stalin. He believed the threat of Soviet intervention against Germany kept Britain in the war. If Germany defeated the USSR then Britain would be forced to surrender.

The desert war

In Britain, Churchill was doing his best to get the United States to join forces with the Allies against the Nazis, and by September a deal had been struck whereby the USA provided Britain with warships. Ever mindful of possible American intervention against Germany in the war, Hitler had strengthened his alliance with Italy and Japan, with the

Tripartite Pact. But this brought him new problems. Italy had been fighting against the British in North Africa, so in January 1941 Hitler was forced to send one of his finest generals – Field Marshal Erwin Rommel – to Africa to help the Italians. By April 1941, Rommel had driven the British back towards Egypt. Germany appeared victorious, yet in undertaking a war in the desert Hitler had been forced to take men and military machinery away from the war in Europe.

Operation Barbarossa

In June 1941, as the war in Africa progressed, Hitler launched Operation Barbarossa against the USSR. Stalin was unprepared and by early July Germany had advanced deep into the USSR. However, Hitler was about to make another decision that would cost him dearly. In the past, the success of blitzkrieg had been based on speed and concentration of military power. Now Hitler planned to divide the German forces into three, and make a three-pronged attack upon Leningrad, Moscow and the Ukraine. Spread so thinly, the German army was not easily able to tackle the large numbers of Soviet troops,

nor was it equipped for the bitterly cold Russian winter. As the rains came down, the roads were turned to mud so thick that the German tanks couldn't move. By November, snow and freezing conditions meant that German troops were trapped 100 kilometres outside Moscow. Dressed in light summer uniforms, many German soldiers perished in the snow. Hitler insisted that all his men fight on: "There must be no withdrawal ... The enemy will gradually bleed themselves to death with their attack."

War with the USA

By December 1941 it was clear that the war in the USSR wasn't going to plan. Nor were the British any nearer to surrender. That same month, Hitler appointed himself Commander-in-Chief of the army – the generals who secretly called him the "bohemian corporal" would now have even less influence over his decisions. The Japanese attacked Pearl Harbor on 7 December 1941, and Hitler declared war on the USA on 11 December. By acting against the wishes of many of his army generals he was taking his country to war with the largest industrial nation in the world.

The "New Order"

By 1942 victory in Europe was by no means certain, yet Hitler's vision of a German empire was taking shape. He'd envisioned a great state, a "New Order", with all Jews removed. After taking over Austria, Czechoslovakia and Poland there were an estimated four million Jews living under Nazi rule. Within the Soviet Union, which Hitler still believed he would conquer, there were millions more. How did Hitler plan to deal with the "Jewish problem" there?

The "Jewish Problem"

As in Germany and Nazi-occupied countries, what happened in Poland revealed the brutal treatment that the Nazis were capable of inflicting. In 1939, at the start of occupation, Jews there were forced to wear a yellow Star of David to identify them. They suffered humiliation and terror, and, in many instances, had their homes and businesses confiscated. Eventually, they were herded into ghettos or concentration camps to live in appalling conditions with no heat or food, while being forced to work for the Nazis. Many people died from malnutrition or disease, while others were killed by firing squads. It soon became obvious to Hitler that this wasn't an efficient method for getting rid of the large number of Jews throughout Europe. At one point Hitler showed an interest in setting up a "devil's island" for the Jews on the island of Madagascar. Then, in July 1941, he had handed responsibility for the Jewish problem to Heinrich Himmler and Reinhard Heydrich.

The "Final Solution"

In 1939, Hitler had already demonstrated the lengths he'd go to "cleanse" Germany of those he considered to be imperfect or non-Aryan stock, when he had ordered a euthanasia programme. On this occasion over 80,000 disabled, mentally ill, criminal or long-term unemployed Germans had been killed by lethal injection or carbon monoxide gas. A public outcry had brought that programme to an end but now Heydrich and Himmler planned the "final solution", a term used by the Nazis to describe the mass genocide of Jews, communists and other "undesirables", such as gypsies and homosexuals. Although Hitler distanced himself from the final solution, there is little doubt that it was acted out under his orders. For years he had spoken out against the Jews and in 1942 he talked of "extermination" and "elimination" of the Jews (see page 78). The details of the final solution were finalized in a conference at Wannsee, near Berlin, in January 1942. Heydrich read out a report that detailed how Jews capable of work would be employed on behalf of the German war effort. While most of those were expected to work themselves to death, other Jews would be put to death by an "appropriate treatment".

The death camps

The "treatment" that Heydrich proposed was death by poison gas. The Nazis quickly set up concentration camps throughout Nazi-occupied Europe, the first of which was at Chelmo in Poland. Jews and other victims were rounded up from occupied territories and taken by train to the camps. At the camps the fittest were selected to work, while young children, older people and those considered unfit, were taken away to be gassed. By 1942, some Nazi concentration camps had evolved into highly efficient death camps run by the SS. Prisoners

▲ In Germany and Nazi-occupied countries, Jews were forced to wear a yellow star so that they would stand out from their non-Jewish neighbours.

▼ Another Nazi measure to isolate Jews was to make them carry Jewish identity cards which bore their photograph and fingerprints.

▲ *The Warsaw Ghetto had been created by the Nazis in 1940 soon after the invasion of Poland. By 1943 most of the Jews in the Ghetto had been rounded up and taken to concentration camps.*

were herded into gas chambers disguised as shower blocks. Once the victims were inside the chamber, the doors were locked and lethal Zyklon-B or carbon monoxide was pumped in. Afterwards, the bodies were searched for jewellery and other valuables such as gold teeth. The corpses were later burned in furnaces that blazed day and night, destroying the evidence of such an evil crime. The concentration camps harboured other Nazi attrocities too. At Auschwitz, Dr. Josef Mengele, also known as "the Angel of Death", selected people he wanted to perform medical and surgical experiments upon. In other camps, starving people were forced to work until they were too weak to carry on and were exterminated. Today, historians argue about Hitler's role in the Holocaust. A few suggest that there is a lack of evidence against him. But most say that his speeches make his involvement apparent. They claim he was a manipulative politician who realized that the mass murder of millions would shock and appal too many people, and, to survive as leader, he had to distance himself from such events.

Hitler's plans for the Jews

"One must act radically. When one pulls out a tooth, one does it with a single tug, and the pain quickly goes away. The Jews must clear out of Europe. It's the Jews who prevent everything. When I think about it, I realize that I'm extraordinarily humane. At the time of the rules of the Popes the Jews were mistreated in Rome. Until 1830, eight Jews mounted on donkeys were led once a year through the streets of Rome. For my part, I restrict myself to telling them they must go away . . . if they refuse to go voluntarily I see no other solution than extermination."
Hitler, in the presence of Himmler, at lunch on 23 January 1942.
quoted in *Hitler* by John Tolland

"If the international Jewish financiers in and outside Europe should succeed in plunging the nations once more into a world war, then the result will not be the Bolshevizing of the earth, and thus a victory of Jewry, but the annihilation of the Jewish race in Europe."
Hitler, quoted in *New Perspectives: The Holocaust* by R.G. Grant

▶ *In the barracks at camps such as Buchenwald (shown here) disease was rampant. The seventh figure from left in the second row (with face partially hidden) is the Jewish writer Elie Wiesel.*

The misfortunes of war

The year 1942 would prove to be a turning point for the warlord Adolf Hitler. The German Reich was at its greatest extent, yet by declaring war on the USA Hitler had caused a world war – a war that would be long and costly.

United in their mission to crush the Nazis, the American, British and Soviet allies worked closely together on strategy, while the Germans, Italians and Japanese did not work together as effectively.

Germany is attacked

In May 1942 the Allies began bombing major German cities. For the next three years, bombs rained down on Essen, Düsseldorf and Cologne. In a series of day and night raids thousands of civilians were terrorized and killed. For the first time, ordinary Germans were experiencing the horror of war on their own doorsteps. They had not expected death on this scale and morale plummeted. As usual Hitler and his propaganda machine tried to convince them that waging war was the right thing to do. In speeches he claimed that the American President, Franklin D Roosevelt, was mentally ill and a "pawn" of the Jews. He said that Germany would save Europe from Bolshevism. He also favourably compared himself to another warlord, Napoleon: "We have mastered destiny which broke another man a hundred and thirty years ago," he told the Reichstag in early 1942.

The Soviet offensive

German soldiers had held out throughout the cold Soviet winter of 1941–1942, and by spring 1942 Hitler was considering his next move against the USSR. Against the advice of his generals, Hitler was planning a two-pronged attack on the industrial city of Stalingrad on the Volga,

EUROPE IN 1942

Germany and its allies

Nazi occupied countries

Under Vichy government (controlled by Nazis)

NORWEGIAN SEA

NORTH SEA

Norway

Sweden

Finland

USSR

Estonia

Latvia

Lithuania

BALTIC SEA

Great Britain

Germany

Poland

France

Switzer-land

Hungary

Spain

Italy

Yugoslavia

ADRIATIC SEA

Romania

Bulgaria

BLACK SEA

Turkey

Corsica

Sardinia

Albania

Greece

Algeria

Sicily

Crete

Cyprus

Syria

Iraq

Palestine

Transjordan

Saudi Arabia

MEDITERRANEAN SEA

Libya

Egypt

and the Soviet oilfields of the Caucasus. It was an overly ambitious plan that would mean dividing his forces between two fronts. It was the same mistake he had made during Operation Barbarossa, yet if anybody tried to reason with him, Hitler's temper flared and he lashed out unreasonably. Around this time, his health began to decline seriously and he suffered with pounding headaches and hours of sleeplessness. He now spent most of his time hidden away in the forests at Rastenburg in East Prussia at his headquarters, the *Wolfsschanze*, or Wolf's Lair, and people rarely saw him.

The Battle of Stalingrad started on 19 August 1942. Hitler was confident that seizing Stalingrad, and then the Caucasus, would be easy. His confidence had been boosted by German successes in the USSR and North Africa. In the past two months thousands of Soviet troops had been killed in battles at Kharkov and Voronezh. Meanwhile, in Africa, Rommel had driven the British back from their stronghold of Tobruk and was advancing towards El Alamein. Hitler had reason to feel triumphant – but the tide was about to turn against the Nazis and in favour of the Allies.

The turning tide

By concentrating on the war in Europe, Hitler had neglected the war in North Africa. Throughout this offensive Rommel had been outnumbered by enemy soldiers and military machinery, yet he'd still managed to break through the British defences. In early November 1942, Rommel's luck ran out and the Germans were defeated at El Alamein. Rommel contacted Hitler and requested a retreat, but Hitler was adamant that he should hold out: "The choice is victory or death," he told him. Rommel acted against his Führer's wishes and withdrew his men, although historians aren't sure whether he had actually received Hitler's orders or not.

Defeat in Africa was followed by setbacks at Stalingrad. By 18 November 1942, the Soviet army had managed to surround the German Sixth Army. General Friedrich Paulus had asked Hitler if his men could retreat but once again Hitler refused, and told his generals to "fight to the last man". Paulus's men managed to hold out for two more months, but during that time, 146,000

▶ *German troops surrender at Stalingrad on 31 January 1943 and are taken prisoner.*

soldiers were killed. On 2 February 1943, against Hitler's wishes, Paulus surrendered and 90,000 men were made prisoners of war. Hitler was furious; he believed Paulus should have shot himself rather than surrender.

Events at El Alamein and Stalingrad shook Hitler. He became depressed and unreasonable, mainly choosing to eat and sleep at the Wolf's Lair with only his dog, Blondi, for company. He no longer listened to music, and on the rare occasions he had visitors he talked long into the night about his early years in Vienna, or about history, rather than face the reality of the war he was losing. Throughout Germany people reacted to the war news with shock and dismay. Hitler had assured them of victory, yet Germany had been beaten. He'd promised them better lives, but the war was draining the economy. In Berlin there were three days of mourning for the missing soldiers. With theatres and bars closed, the mood was grim – and deteriorating fast. More than ever the

◀ *A Nazi propaganda poster urges German civilians to do their bit for the war effort. The poster reads: "Just as we fight so will you work for victory!"*

Nazi propaganda machine was needed to cast its spell over ordinary Germans.

"Total War"

By 1943 Goebbels had become the pubic mouthpiece for Hitler. In fact, the Führer only delivered two more speeches in public. On 18 February 1943, Goebbels launched the "Total War" campaign. The aim was to raise the same "Dunkirk spirit" in the Germans that had been observed in the British public. The message was that Germany could still win the war if everybody pulled together for the war effort. In the past Hitler had believed that a woman's place was in the home; now women were needed in the factories. By 1944 Germany's 14.9 million women workers made up over half of Germany's native workforce. The Hitler Youth had been set up to educate the children. Now those children aged between 10 and 15 were expected to volunteer for war work such as farm work or collecting rags. From all over Nazi-occupied territories more and more people were drafted in to man the munitions factories. Many of these non-German speaking people came unwillingly, and were treated little better than slaves. During the years 1941–1944 war production increased by 230 per cent, but the Total War campaign had come too late to save Germany.

Operation Gomorrah

The German people were told that production was increasing, yet everywhere they looked they saw destruction. The saturation bombing of German cities and industrial areas had been devised by the Allies to halt industrial production, and cause such panic in the population that they would plead for peace. From March to July 1943, the RAF targeted the Ruhr's industrial towns, but in July and August of that year the Allies turned on Hamburg. Operation Gomorrah, as it was aptly called, began with intensive air raids; for over a week bombs rained down on the city, with the RAF bombing it by night and the American Air Force (USAAF) bombing it during the day. The blazing inferno destroyed nearly three-quarters of Hamburg. Over 44,600 people were killed and approximately 1.2 million people fled or were evacuated. At last, the Allies had found a way to defeat Germany. That autumn they targeted Berlin in the hope that this might crush Germany

completely. Again the attack was relentless and over half the city's homes were flattened, but the war was far from over.

At the Wolf's Lair

By 1943, Hitler divided his time between the Berghof and the Wolf's Lair. By now his tempers were so bad that his staff were frightened to tell him any bad news. Instead there was an atmosphere of enforced pleasantness, with Hitler following a daily schedule that included a mid-morning briefing before entertaining his waiting guests. Hitler refused to visit the bombed-out cities; he left that job to Goebbels. When he talked of the air raids he became angry and accused certain British commanders of being part-Jewish. Most evenings he refused to sleep until he knew that all enemy planes had left Germany's airspace. As the great cities of Germany burned, Hitler was enjoying himself making new town plans and models of cities such as Munich and Linz. From now on his detachment from reality seemed to grow more and more evident.

▼ *The Allies bring death and destruction to the streets of Hamburg during Operation Gomorrah in July 1943.*

Final collapse of the Nazis

By 1943 many of Hitler's generals doubted that Germany could win the war. But Hitler believed that Germany could not be seen to falter, and talked of renewed efforts against the Soviets.

This time Hitler planned an attack on the Eastern front at Kursk. The offensive was a gamble, but Hitler promised his forces up-to-date equipment and more men to fight this difficult campaign. By July the new tanks hadn't arrived, but a million back-up soldiers had poured into the region. Hitler felt uneasy about the attack and postponed it three times. Unwittingly, he had given the Soviets enough time to regroup and build up their defences. On 4 July 1943, more than 6,000 tanks clashed in what would be the biggest tank battle of the entire war. Over 70,000 Germans were killed and 1,500 tanks were lost. Previously Hitler had always told his soldiers to stand up and fight to the death, but on 13 July 1943, he ordered his men to stop fighting. Germany had lost the Battle of Kursk and it had been Hitler's own fault. From now on, all Germany's efforts in the East would amount to one long retreat.

A fight to the end

By the end of July 1943, against all odds, Hitler still believed he could win the war. But the Battle of Kursk had been a disaster. Then, on 10 July 1943, news reached him that the Allies had landed in Sicily. By 25 July, Hitler's closest ally, Mussolini, had been arrested and the new Italian government looked set for peace talks with the Allies. To add to the humiliation, American and British bombers had almost destroyed Hamburg. Yet still Hitler wasn't ready to admit defeat and he ordered the evacuation of 60,000 German troops from Sicily. In a

▼ *A wrecked German tank and dead soldier after the Battle of Kursk in 1943.*

speech broadcast on 10 September 1943, he told his country: "My right to believe unconditionally in success is founded not only on my own life but also on the destiny of our people." Within days the Germans had seized Rome, and Hitler had arranged a daring mission to rescue Mussolini.

In October 1943, the new Italian government declared war on Germany; however, the German occupation of Rome and northern Italy meant it would take the Allies nearly two years to fight their way through Italy. Hitler remained out of sight, hidden away at the Wolf's Lair. Christmas of 1943 was a bleak time. Hitler wanted no Christmas tree or decorations. Meanwhile, far away on the Eastern front in Russia, his troops faced another cold winter. By January 1944, the Germans had been pushed back from Leningrad and the Soviets had claimed back much of the Ukraine. The picture was gloomy but Hitler still believed Germany should fight to the last man. His health was growing steadily worse, but his spirits were lifted by the successful development of the V-1 rocket. He believed that these flying bombs targeted at mainland Britain could win the war for

Germany. It was a glimmer of hope, as all his other plans for a victorious Germany crumbled about him.

The D-Day Landings

On 6 June 1944 Hitler awoke late to the news that the Allies had landed on the north coast of France at Normandy. It was the beginning of the D-Day landings. Hitler's generals had heard about the invasion a few hours earlier but had been too scared to rouse the Führer. Hitler's reaction was strange; one moment he was angry, the next he was chuckling with excitement at the thought of being face to face with his enemies. In truth, he didn't believe this was the real invasion; he had expected the Allies to land at Calais. Once again, he had misjudged the situation and given his military commanders no clear indication as to how they should proceed. Within weeks, over one million Allied troops and huge amounts of ammunition had been landed on the beaches of northern France. The Germans were outnumbered on land, at sea and by air; the situation looked

▶ *Hitler was still asleep when American troops came ashore at Omaha Beach in Normandy on 6 June 1944.*

hopeless. Rommel wrote to Hitler suggesting it was time to stop fighting, but Hitler still believed that with the V-1 rocket the British would surrender. Later that month, Germany launched its deadly V-2 rockets at London and other major cities in Britain. Within a few weeks 6,139 British civilians had been killed, but in France, the Allies fought on.

The July bomb plot

Hitler was no stranger to attempts on his life. Since 1938 there had been at least five plots to kill him, but in July 1944 one man got close to ending the Führer's life. For months, senior members of the German army had realized that a German victory looked very unlikely, and that Hitler would never consider peace talks. A group of conspirators headed by a respected war hero called Colonel Claus von Stauffenberg, believed that the only way to save Germany was to assassinate Hitler and stage a coup. On the morning of 20 July 1944, Stauffenberg had managed to smuggle two briefcases containing bombs into the Wolf's Lair

▶ *Hitler shows Mussolini the damage caused by the bomb at the Wolf's Lair. Both men were deeply shocked but Hitler said he felt "new courage".*

and had hidden them under a map table. When Stauffenberg left the room, the fuse had been set and Hitler was just metres away from the activated bomb.

As Stauffenberg reached his getaway car, he heard the explosion. Convinced that he had killed Hitler, Stauffenberg escaped to Berlin. In fact, Hitler managed to walk away from the blast with only a few cuts and bruises, perforated eardrums and a slight limp.

He later told his doctor: "I am invulnerable, I am immortal." More than ever, he believed that he'd been specially chosen to continue the fight for Germany.

Those that had conspired against the Führer paid the highest price. Stauffenberg and the other senior army officers in the conspiracy were arrested and shot. A further 5,000 suspects were executed. Not even the outstanding commander Rommel was spared. Although there was no evidence he was involved in the plot, he'd been a close friend of many of the conspirators. Hitler gave him a choice of facing trial or taking poison. On 14 October 1944, Rommel committed suicide.

Hitler's health

Anyone who saw Hitler at this time was shocked to notice that he had aged dramatically and his health had deteriorated terribly. His right hand now shook so much that he could no longer shave himself, and he'd even started to forget people's names. Historians now believe that he might have had the first symptoms of Parkinson's Disease, a neurological disorder which can cause dementia. He was also taking a cocktail of drugs to help him sleep and, in turn, other drugs to keep him awake. Perhaps these facts can explain Hitler's steadfast but, by this time, utterly deluded belief that Germany could still defeat the Allies and win the war.

End of the dream

On 25 August 1944, after four years of Nazi occupation, the Allies liberated Paris. From there they advanced through France, while Soviet troops swooped through Romania and into Poland. As his enemies drew closer, Hitler's thoughts turned to the death camps. By August 1944, it is estimated that six million people, mainly Jews, had been murdered in the Nazis' death camps. It was now time for a massive cover-up. Hitler told Himmler to begin shutting down all the camps – except Auschwitz as he believed there was still work to do there – and ordered that all the buildings and documents relating to the camps should be destroyed.

The last stand begins

On 16 December 1944, Germany made a last stand, with a surprise attack against the Allies via the Ardennes in Belgium. "No one can last forever. We can't, the other side can't," Hitler said. "It's merely a question of who can stand it longer. The one who must hold out longer is the one who's got everything at stake." Despite early success, the Germans withdrew in January 1945. An earlier retreat might have saved some of the 100,000 German casualties, or the 600 tanks and 1,600 aircraft that were lost, but Hitler insisted that his men fight on. Later in January, when the Soviets took Warsaw and part of East Prussia, Hitler had already returned to Berlin. While his soldiers fell, he hid away in a concrete bunker underneath the Chancellery taking comfort only in the company of his dogs.

The last months

Hitler claimed he moved to the bunker at the Chancellery to get some sleep during the air raids.

In fact his final days, lived out in a few darkened rooms, probably passed like a nightmare, as his existence now hung between life and death. He made few appearances above ground again, and on 30 January 1945, exactly twelve years to the day since he became Chancellor, he made his last radio broadcast. He had nothing new to say; Germany had heard it all before. He urged his people to do their duty to the last and rid the world of Jews and communists. "However grave the crisis may be at the moment," he told them, "it will, despite everything, finally be mastered by our unalterable will, by our readiness for sacrifice and by our abilities." In truth, Germany had already given everything it could.

▶ *In April 1945 the Allies began liberating the Nazi concentration camps. The experience was often likened to a living nightmare. These ravaged and starving inmates from Dachau would be some of the lucky ones.*

The final word

By the end of January 1945, the Soviets had crossed the Oder River, the last natural barrier before Berlin. As American bombers rained bombs down on the German capital, leading Nazis believed that time was running out. During one raid the Chancellery itself was hit so badly that the lines of communication, the power and water supply were all destroyed. Yet Hitler remained defiant and began dictating his final interpretation of the war to his secretary Martin Bormann. He wanted to record how close he had come to winning, and he wanted to apportion blame for the mistakes that had brought about his downfall. He pointed the finger at the British, who he claimed could have ended the war in 1941 if they had surrendered. He ranted about Jews and communists, and found a way to blame everybody except himself. His companions in the bunker were startled by his detachment from reality. Even as the bombs roared overhead, Hitler still dreamed of victory.

▶ *Dresden, the seventh largest city in Germany, was virtually destroyed by Allied air raids. On 13 February 1945 the blazing city was visible from 320 km away.*

Desperation and destruction

Between 13 and 15 February 1945, the Allies bombed Dresden. A massive firestorm destroyed much of the city and reports suggested that as many as 25,000 civilians had been killed, while 35,000 were missing. Hitler was angry, but ruled out executing prisoners of war in retaliation. By 3 March 1945, when American and British troops crossed the Rhine, his mood was less forgiving. But this time, he turned against his own people: "If the war is lost, the German nation will also perish," Hitler told his armaments minister, Albert Speer. "There is no need to take into consideration the basic requirements of the people … Those who will remain after the battle are those who are inferior; for the good will have fallen." In the following days he ordered the destruction of anything of use to the Allies, including industrial sites, bridges, waterways and energy sources. Hitler had always demanded loyalty from his people but ultimately he never returned it to them. Although retreating German troops did do some damage, Speer managed to prevent any large-scale destruction.

The enemy at the door

In February 1945, Eva Braun had joined Hitler in the bunker. Her devotion touched him, but his moods continued to swing from high to low. On 12 April, his spirits were raised considerably at the news of President Roosevelt's death. Perhaps this was a turning point? A few days later, when he heard that Soviet troops were in the suburbs of Berlin, his anger returned. The German army battled against the enemy, but the Soviets moved ever closer to the centre of Berlin. By 20 April 1945, all hope had gone, but there was a forced sense of celebration in the bunker. The occasion was Hitler's fifty-sixth birthday, and among those present were the leading Nazis: Goebbels, Goering, Himmler, Bormann and Speer. Earlier that day, Hitler had met a group of Hitler Youth volunteers. They were preparing to fight against the Soviets in a last bid to save Berlin. Meanwhile, their Führer was deciding whether he should quit Berlin for the safety of the Bavarian Alps, or die alongside them in the city they were defending.

◀ *The final humiliation: surrendered German troops march through a captured Berlin on 2 May 1945. The capital city is already in ruins and their Führer is dead.*

101

The bitter end

Hitler's decision to remain in Berlin was not an act of bravery. As an ex-soldier Hitler believed there was honour in death and by 22 April 1945 he was talking about suicide. The Soviets had now surrounded the city and Hitler finally admitted that it was all over. For a while he seemed calm and emotionless, but when Goering wrote to him asking if he should assume leadership of the Reich Hitler was furious. A few days later his anger erupted again when he heard that Himmler had tried to negotiate peace.

On 29 April 1945, the news that Mussolini had been killed and strung up in Milan for all to see must have haunted Hitler. Having lost the support of his closest Nazi colleagues and with Berlin crumbling, Hitler decided to kill himself.

The atmosphere in the bunker had become gloomy and stifling, and even those who remained loyal to Hitler found his behaviour bordering on the insane. In the early hours of 29 April, Goebbels, Bormann and the other remaining occupants of the bunker gathered for the wedding ceremony of Hitler and Eva.

The human cost of World War Two

	Peak size of wartime population	Total armed forces	Total forces killed/missing	Total civilians wounded	Total civilians killed/missing
Germany	79.4 mill	10 mill	3.5 mill	2 mill	2 mill
Britain	47.8 mill	4.7 mill	420,000	377,000	70,000
USSR	193 mill	20 mill	13.6 mill	5 mill	7.7 mill
USA	132 mill	16.4 mill	292,000	675,000	Under 10
Italy	45.4 mill	4.5 mill	80,000	25,000	180,000
Japan	73.1 mill	6 mill	2.6 mill	26,000	953,000
France	41.9 mill	5 mill	245,000	90,000	173,000

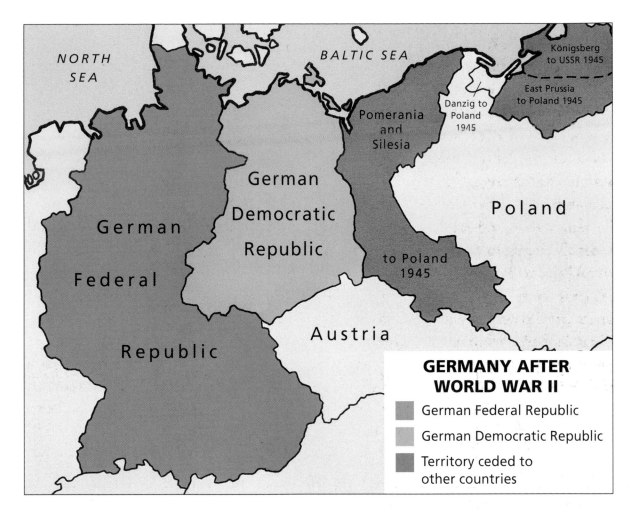

NORTH SEA

BALTIC SEA

Königsberg to USSR 1945

East Prussia to Poland 1945

Pomerania and Silesia

Danzig to Poland 1945

German Democratic Republic

German Federal Republic

Poland

to Poland 1945

Austria

GERMANY AFTER WORLD WAR II
- German Federal Republic
- German Democratic Republic
- Territory ceded to other countries

Everyone drank champagne and Hitler reminisced about his life. The following morning he said his goodbyes to his staff and his dog Blondi who was taken away to be put down. Everybody knew what Hitler was about to do. He had even given orders about how he would like his body to be disposed of. At 3.30 p.m. that afternoon a single shot was heard. Hitler had put a bullet through his head, and Eva had taken poison. Their bodies were later taken upstairs, doused with petrol and burned – the Führer's directions had been followed to the bitter end.

On that same day Red Army soldiers waved a Soviet flag from the top of the Reichstag building. The streets below were filled with rubble, while clouds of smoke and dust filled the air. In the final battle to save their capital, 100,000 German soldiers had been killed, and perhaps as many civilians. Hitler's dream of a thousand-year Reich had brought nothing but death and destruction.

Victory in Europe

On 7 May 1945, Germany signed an unconditional surrender, but there were many things worse than losing the war. German cities had been flattened, millions of soldiers and civilians had been killed, and Germany would lose territory and ultimately be divided into two countries – the Federal Republic in the west and the communist Democratic Republic in the east. But the greatest humiliation came when the world heard about the Nazi concentration camps. When the Allies liberated the camps, they found the people who had been lucky enough to escape death. They also found piles of corpses and other evidence. Germans were made to visit the camps to see what had happened. We'll never know how much ordinary Germans knew about the Holocaust, but the hatred and evil caused by Adolf Hitler had brought shame to all of them.

▶ *"Der Befreier Deutschlands" (The man who made Germany free) photographed at Obersalzberg in 1933.*

Glossary

abdicate To give up the throne.

allegiance Loyal support.

allies Countries that have made an agreement to work together towards a common goal.

anti-Semitism Hatred of and prejudice against Jews.

appeasement Giving in to a potential aggressor's demands to try to prevent war.

armistice An end to hostilities, reached through an agreement between all sides.

Aryans The highest racial group of people, as defined by the Nazis.

bohemian An unconventional person – often used to describe artists and writers.

Bolshevism Russian communism – the Bolsheviks were a group of communists who seized power in Russia in 1917.

boycott A ban imposed on people to stop them doing certain things.

coalition A government made up of many different political parties.

communism A way of organizing a country so that the land, its housing and its industries belong to the state, and the profits are shared among everybody.

concentration camp A place where political prisoners were usually murdered.

coup A successful move – often used to describe the seizure of power in politics.

curriculum A programme of study.

demilitarize To remove armed forces from an area.

democratic Describes a system where the government is voted for, and is accountable to its people.

dictator A leader who has complete control of a country.

elimination To get rid of somebody or something by taking it away or killing it.

exemplary To be outstandingly good at something – an example to all.

extermination The total destruction of something or someone.

high treason A crime against the government or ruler of a country.

inflation The rate at which the cost of living goes up.

inheritance The property or situation, passed from one generation to the next.

inhumane To lack all consideration for another living thing.

intimidation Frightening tactics used to overpower someone.

left-wing The radical and socialist side of a political party and their followers.

mark The German unit of currency.

munitions factory A place where weapons and ammunition are made.

mutiny A rebellion against authority.

natlonalism Extreme patriotic feelings.

pacifist A person who believes in peace.

patriotism Devotion and loyalty to one's country.

pleural hemorrhage A ruptured blood vessel in the lining of the lungs.

plummet To fall rapidly.

Reich A German word meaning realm.

reparation payments The money paid by a country to make up for the damage they caused in a war.

rearmament The process whereby a country builds up its army, its weapons and military machinery.

right-wing The conservative section of a political party and their followers.

solidarity Agreement to stick together between those with a common interest.

synagogue A Jewish place of worship.

treaty An official agreement between different countries.

USSR (Union of Soviet Socialist Republics) The Russian state which existed from 1917 to 1991.

Further reading

Hitler and Stalin by Alan Bullock (HarperCollins Publishers, 1991)

Hitler: A Study in Tyranny by Alan Bullock (Penguin, 1980)

Hitler and Geli by Ronald Hayman (Bloomsbury Publishing, 1997)

Mein Kampf (My Struggle) by Adolf Hitler (Hutchinson, 1969)

The Mammoth Book of How it Happened edited by Jon E. Lewis (Robinson Publishing Ltd, 1998)

Hitler: Diagnosis of a Destructive Prophet by Fritz Redlich, M.D. (Oxford University Press, 1998)

Explaining Hitler: The Search for the Origins of His Evil by Ron Rosenbaum (Random House Group Ltd, 1998)

Adolf Hitler, in the Profiles series, by Richard Tames (William Heinemann, 1998)

Hitler by John Tolland (Wordsworth Editions Ltd, 1976)

The World at War: The Reader's Digest Illustrated History of World War Two (The Reader's Digest Association Ltd, 1989)

The Third Reich, in the Witness History Series, by David Williamson (Wayland Publishers, 1988)

Bloomsbury Thematic Dictionary of Quotations (Bloomsbury, 1997)

Oxford Dictionary of Quotations (Oxford University Press, 1999)

Timeline

1889 20 April: Adolf Hitler is born at Braunau-am-Inn, Austria.

1903 Hitler's father dies.

1905 Hitler leaves school.

1907 Hitler moves to Vienna; mother dies.

1914 Hitler lives in Munich; at the outbreak of World War One he volunteers for the German army.

1916 Hitler is wounded and recuperates in Munich.

1918 Hitler is awarded the Iron Cross, First Class, and is temporarily blinded in a gas attack; World War One ends; an armistice is signed in France.

1919 A constitution for Germany is drawn up at Weimar.

28 June: The Treaty of Versailles is signed

September: Hitler joins the National Socialist German Worker's Party (DAP).

1921 The DAP is renamed the Nazi Party; Hitler becomes President of the Nazi Party.

1922 Mussolini's "March on Rome"; he becomes prime minister of Italy.

1923 French and Belgian troops occupy the Ruhr. The German mark collapses. Germany is hit by huge inflation.

8–9 November: the Putsch in Munich fails; Hitler is imprisoned at Landsberg near Munich, where he writes *Mein Kampf*.

1924 23 December: Hitler is released from prison.

1925 The Nazi Party is refounded; the SS is formed; *Mein Kampf* is published; Hindenberg is elected as President of Germany.

1927 The first Nazi mass meeting is held at Nuremberg.

1928 The Nazi Party wins 12 seats in the German parliament (Reichstag).

1929 29 October: The Wall Street Crash in the USA is followed by massive unemployment in Germany.

1930 The Nazis win 107 seats in the Reichstag.

1931 German banks collapse; Geli Raubal dies in Hitler's apartment; Hitler stands as a candidate in the presidential elections, but is defeated by Hindenburg.

1932 31 July: the Nazis win 230 seats.

November: the Nazis win 196 seats.

1933 30 January: Hitler is appointed the Chancellor of Germany.

27 February: the Reichstag is set on fire.

23 March: The Enabling Law is passed, giving Hitler the powers of a dictator for four years.

March: The Nazis win 288 seats in the Reichstag.

1934 30 June: 150 SA leaders are murdered in the Night of the Long Knives.

2 August: President Hindenburg dies. Hitler is pronounced Chancellor and President and takes the title of Führer.

1935 September: The Nuremberg Laws concerning German Jews are announced.

1936 7 March: Hitler orders the army to occupy the Rhineland.

September: Four Year Plan introduced. Hitler becomes an ally of Mussolini's. The Olympic Games are held in Berlin.

1938 Hitler becomes Commander-in-Chief of Germany's armed forces.

12 March: Germany takes over Austria.

20 May: Hitler plans an attack on Czechoslovakia. Hitler claims the Sudetenland.

1939 March: Germany invades Czechoslovakia.

1939 23 May: Hitler plans an attack on Poland.

23 August: Hitler signs a non-aggression pact with Stalin.

1 September: Germany attacks Poland.

1940 April: Germany occupies Norway.

May–June: Germany attacks France.

June: Italy declares war on Britain and France. Hitler decides to invade USSR.

1941 Hitler declares war on the USA.

1942 20 January: The Wannsee Conference takes place.

August: The Battle of Stalingrad begins.

November: The Germans are defeated at El Alamein.

1943 February: The German army in Stalingrad surrenders.

July: British and American troops invade Sicily. Italy surrenders to the Allies.

1944 6 June: The D-Day landings occur.

20 July: The plot to murder Hitler fails.

1945 30 January: Hitler makes his last broadcast to his people.

30 April: Hitler commits suicide.

7 May: All German forces surrender.

8 May: VE (Victory in Europe) Day takes place. End of the war in Europe.

Index

The complete guide to referencing and avoiding plagiarism

Colin Neville

 Open University Press

Open University Press
McGraw-Hill Education
McGraw-Hill House
Shoppenhangers Road
Maidenhead
Berkshire
England
SL6 2QL

email: enquiries@openup.co.uk
world wide web: www.openup.co.uk

and Two Penn Plaza, New York, NY 10121-2289, USA

First published 2007

A catalogue record of this book is available from the British Library

ISBN-13: 978–0–33–522089–2 (pb) 978–0–33–522090–8 (hb)
ISBN-10: 0–33–522089–4 (pb) 0–33–522090–8 (hb)

Library of Congress Cataloguing-in-Publication Data
CIP data applied for

Typeset by RefineCatch Limited, Bungay, Suffolk
Printed in Poland EU by OZGraf S.A.,
www.polskabook.pl

The McGraw·Hill Companies

Contents

Preface

The title of this book is a somewhat impertinent one, for reasons that will become clearer later in this preface. The book is likely to be of interest to you if you are currently studying in higher education or on a pre-degree course in a school or college. It presents, discusses and gives you examples of the main referencing systems found in higher education in Britain. However, it also tries to explain the principles of referencing: a practice that often worries, exasperates or baffles many students.

It also describes and illustrates, what often seems to the casual observer, the often small differences between the main referencing styles applied in Britain. They may be small differences, but their academic guardians will often fiercely defend the referencing styles described in this book. Particular referencing styles are adopted by subject disciplines, for reasons linked to history, professional practice, or for reasons of personal whimsy by heads of department – and defended thereafter by them, often out of sheer cussedness, against administrators who try to introduce uniformity of referencing practice across an institution.

The guide, I hope, may prove particularly useful to those of you who encounter a range of referencing styles in your progression through pre-degree, undergraduate and postgraduate studies. Undergraduates, for example, on a combined studies degree, may find themselves having to reference sources in two or more styles as they encounter different disciplines, with each discipline wedded to its own referencing style preference. The graduate may then move on to a postgraduate programme and encounter a completely new referencing style – and with tutors insistent that they meticulously cite and reference their sources in line with departmental practice.

Although the author–date (Harvard) referencing style appears to be a significant one in higher education in Britain (see results of a survey, Chapter 5), the American Psychological Association (APA) and Modern Languages Association (MLA) styles still retain their firm holds respectively in psychology and language disciplines. In addition, numerical referencing styles, including those recommended by the Modern Humanities research Association (MHRA) and Institute of Electrical and Electronic Engineers (IEEE), still maintain a strong presence in a wide range of humanities, science and technology courses.

However, although the author–date (Harvard) referencing style, followed by the two numerical styles, appear to be most significant referencing styles in Britain, the benchmark guides for their application, British Standard recommendations, are less satisfactory, compared with others, particularly APA and MLA. The referencing style guides produced by the APA, MLA, MHRA and IEEE are all written by their respective associations in clear prose, with easy to follow referencing examples and with the rules of the referencing game spelt out unambiguously to their disciples.

British Standard (BS), however, presents the author–date (Harvard) and two numerical styles in a rather desiccated and unimaginative way, and one reads with no great surprise that a committee comprised of representatives from 19 bodies were responsible for drafting them. The examples presented in the BS recommendations also do not seem quite to connect with the sources the average student, outside Oxbridge, encounters and applies in Britain today. No wonder then, that the transformation of author–date (Harvard) and numerical style references, from 'British-Standard speak' into more accessible, student-friendly prose, has been undertaken over the years by countless librarians, editors, study skills advisers and publishers.

In the process, however, each interpretation has been distilled with the essence of the individual writer. Most adapters of BS recommendations have kept to BS recommendations for presenting the order of elements in references, but you will find subtle variations on BS wherever you look. British Standard, for example, illustrates full source references showing:

- Name (s) of authors or organizations in upper case
- Year of publication not enclosed in parenthesis.

However, institutional variations have emerged. Some institutions, in their referencing guidelines to students, follow British Standard and illustrate author names in upper case, while many others do not; and it is almost universal practice in UK institutions now to illustrate author–date (Harvard) references with the year shown in parenthesis.

What appears to have happened is that Harvard and APA styles, because of their similarities, have merged gradually into a referencing hybrid. There are still differences between Harvard and APA to be observed – as this book shows – but these are akin to parents knowing the difference between their identical twin children. Pity then the poor student asked to use both Harvard and APA styles on a combined studies degree and who has to work out the differences between them!

So, faced with the myriad subtle institutional versions of Harvard and a lesser number of numeric referencing guidelines to choose from, which one does this author choose? Like most guides to referencing, this one is somewhat of a hybrid too, in that I have followed the BS order of elements in references, but deviated by using the widespread practice of placing the year in parenthesis for Harvard referencing.

On the other hand, I have followed the British Standard examples by using upper case with author or organizational names, as this tends to distinguish and highlight the author from other elements in the source. I have also followed the recommendation of British Standard to keep capitalization in the title to a minimum, as this in line with the advice in many contemporary writing style guides.

So, and this is where the impertinence in my opening sentence comes in; it is probably impossible to produce a definitive and 'true' guide to referencing that embraces the Harvard and British versions of the numerical styles, given the subtle variations that abound. The guide is, therefore, as 'complete' as a mortal being can make it in the face of these differences.

What I have done, however, is to try and explain why you should reference in the first place, explain the main differences in referencing style, and give examples of the most commonly used assignment sources in Britain today – plus a few that are uncommon. Once the principles of referencing are understood, and with some examples to guide them, you should be able to work out how to reference the sources you are likely to encounter on most courses.

But surely a book on referencing is an anachronism when today you can use referencing management software to find sources and organize your bibliographies? You would think so, but it is not yet the case. As I argue in Chapter 3, although the software is often freely available to students within their own institutions, it can be time consuming to use and to master, and many simply do not bother. The available software does not yet solve all information retrieval, citation and referencing problems, and a universal, easy to use referencing software management system has yet to arrive on the scene. It undoubtedly will arrive in due course, but for the moment, and perhaps even then, this book has some modest expectations of life. For, despite the advance of software, the book and other printed forms still retain the advantages of their flexible, easy to use formats. However, I would say that, wouldn't I?

Sources and influences

The sources for referencing examples presented in this book are based on guidelines and recommendations from the following:

- For author–date (Harvard) and British Standard numerical referencing styles (Numeric and Running-notes): British Standard Institution (BS) guidelines: 5605: 1990: *Recommendations for citing and referencing published material*; BS 1629:1989: *Recommendation for references to published materials*; BS 5261–1:2000: *Copy preparation and proof correction – part 1: design and layout of documents*; BS ISO 690–2:1997 *Information and documentation – bibliographic references – part 2: Electronic documents or parts thereof*
- For variants on the British Standard Numeric referencing style, the following sources were used: IEEE: Institute of Electrical and Electronics Engineers *Transactions, journals, and letters: information for author* (2006); for the Vancouver style numeric system, the International Committee of Medical Journal Editors *Uniform requirements for manuscripts submitted to biomedical journals: sample references* (2006); and for MHRA: Modern Humanities Research Association, the 2002 edition of the *MHRA style guide: a handbook for authors, editors and writers of thesis*
- For author–date (APA): American Psychological Association (2005), *Concise rules of APA style*
- For author–page (MLA): Gibaldi (2003), *The MLA Handbook for Writers*.

I have also drawn on the guidelines on referencing legal sources produced by the Oxford Standard for Citation of Legal Authorities, produced by the Faculty of Law, University of Oxford. Other useful sources have been the British Standard BS 6371:1983 *Recommendations for citation of unpublished documents*; and the guidelines suggested by Li and Crane in their book, *Electronic styles: a handbook for citing electronic information* (1996). Other publications also consulted and found to be particularly helpful were Pears and Shields (2005) *Cite them right: the essential guide to referencing and plagiarism*;

Levin (2004) *Write great essays*; and Maimon, Peritz and Yancey (2007) *A writer's resource*.

This guide to referencing then, offers advice and examples of referencing that will help you to reference sources in a consistent way – and in a way that connects recognizably and conscientiously with a particular and identifiable referencing style.

Acknowledgements

I am grateful to the following for allowing me to use extracts from their publications:

- Pearson Education for allowing me to adapt a table from *Research Methods for Business Students*, shown in Chapter 7 of this book
- Dr Deli Yang at the University of Bradford, School of Management, for her permission to use an extract from her article, shown in Chapter 4. My grateful thanks also to Deli for her consistent support and encouragement generally and, in particular, for her useful comments and advice on sections of the book
- Professor Michael Keniger, Deputy Vice-Chancellor (Academic), University of Queensland for his permission to use his institution's online example of common knowledge in referencing, shown in Chapter 1
- Dr Celia Thompson, University of Melbourne, for her permission to use the referencing example from her article, shown in Chapter 8.

Thanks too, to colleagues who contributed to the Learner Development in Higher Education Network (LDHEN) Discussion Board debate on referencing. In particular: John Hilsdon, Co-ordinator Learning Development, University of Plymouth; Pauline Ridley, Centre for Learning and Teaching, University of Brighton; David Donnarumma, Teaching and Learning Development Unit, Brunel University and Dr Len Holmes, University of Luton Business School.

A grateful word also to my colleagues on the *LearnHigher* Steering Group at the University of Bradford, particularly Professor Peter Hartley, Vikki Illingworth, Becka Currant, Frances Dowson and Adam Birch. This book has grown out of a project to develop a national Centre for Excellence in Teaching and Learning (CETL) *LearnHigher* referencing website and the support and positive encouragement of these colleagues has been very important to me generally, and, in particular, with this book and with the development of the website.

Finally, my sincere thanks to Wendy, my wife, for supporting and tolerating my disappearance for hours as I researched and wrote the book, and for helping me proof-read the chapters. Surely, the person who will willingly do this is the best of partners!

Colin Neville
Bradford, November 2006

1

Referencing

How the book will help you • The roots of referencing • Referencing and society •
Witch-hunts? • What else is to come?

It is an expected academic practice that students will refer to (or cite) the **sources** of ideas, data and other evidence in written assignments. Referencing is the practice of acknowledging in your own writing the intellectual work of others; work that has been presented in some way into the public domain.

As you progress through different levels of study in higher education, you are expected to be increasingly more critical of ideas and theories, and their application in models and practices, and how this criticism includes an awareness, and acknowledgement, of the source of ideas. Ideas are often a product of a particular period of history and of the social, economic, and cultural norms and values of that time. Therefore, your sources inform and alert the reader to the origins of the ideas, theories, models or practices under discussion.

Education needs ideas, arguments and perspectives to thrive, but these have to be tested rigorously and subjected to the critical scrutiny of others. This is done by researching, preparing and presenting work to the public domain. This is a formidable task for any writer or commentator, and one that can take years to achieve. Referencing is, then, about respecting and honouring the hard work of writers and commentators – by acknowledging them in your assignments.

Referencing can also help you to find your own voice in assignments, by helping you write essays and reports that project or reflect the way **you** see or perceive things. Evidence presented and correctly referenced supports and strengthens your opinions – and converts them into arguments.

But despite all these worthy reasons, many students find referencing a pain, a mechanistic chore and a complete bore. Referencing styles adopted may vary from one department to another within the same institution, and even then there may be inconsistencies among tutors in how these styles are interpreted and applied. You may find that, even if a particular style has been adopted, some tutors do not seem to pay much regard to **how** you present evidence, as long as you do, and it generally seems in line with the adopted style; while others will swoop on mistakes, if the adopted referencing style is not applied correctly and precisely.

Some students on combined studies course have to adapt to the required referencing styles of different departments, which may mean getting to grips with two or even three styles of referencing, plus all the varieties of interpretation and application among teaching staff.

How the book will help you

This book presents an overview of the main referencing styles currently applied in British schools, colleges, and in higher education. It is aimed at students, pre-degree, undergraduate and on postgraduate courses, and will explain:

- The **why** of referencing – the academic rationale for all styles of referencing and the principles underpinning the practice
- The **when** of referencing – when to reference, and when it is not necessary
- The **how** of referencing. The main differences between referencing styles in Britain will be described, and illustrated with examples of the types of sources that you will undoubtedly want to refer to in your assignments.

It will also discuss the thorny issue of plagiarism, and how important referencing is to avoid accusations of cheating.

The roots of referencing

Referencing is not a new idea. Grafton (1997) provides us with a history of footnote referencing and has traced the origins of this practice back to Roman jurists who 'provided very precise references to the earlier legal treatises they drew upon' (p.29–30). In other early manuscripts annotation, glosses or explanations were included to connect the finished work to its sources.

However, it was the invention of printing in the late fifteenth century that made ideas more accessible and established the notion of an author. The growth of printing encouraged people to write and to make a living from their ideas and talent for writing. It also encouraged the cult of personality, and the emergence and promotion of artists distinguished by their style of writing (Eisenstein 1983).

However, it also made ideas more vulnerable, and authors became increasingly concerned that others were stealing their work and passing it off as their own. The Statute of Anne, passed into law on 10 April 1710, was the first Copyright Act in the world; it established both copyright for the authors of books and other writings, and the principle of a fixed term of protection against piracy for published works. The Act also included provision for depositing nine copies of a book to principal libraries in Britain. Subsequent copyright laws extended the range of work and the terms and provisions of protection involved.

The development of printing also standardized the practice of annotation into printed footnotes. These appeared within scholarly works from the eighteenth century onwards, and served a dual purpose for an author. They provided a way for an author to identify his sources in a work, as well as insert radical, witty or ironical personal comment, but outside the main text (Grafton 1997, p.229). Authors could thus parade their credentials of erudition and wit to the increasingly educated world.

References appeared in textbooks in footnotes and were referred to in the text by printers' symbols, including asterisks and daggers. Other referencing styles evolved from this, including an in-text author–date (Harvard) style that does indeed appear to have its modern origins at Harvard University. It appears to have emerged from a referencing practice developed by Edward Laurens Mark, professor of anatomy and director of Harvard's zoological laboratory, who in turn appears to have been inspired by a cataloguing system in the Library of Harvard's Museum of Comparative Zoology (Chernin 1988). However, Grafton trumps this, by identifying a thirteenth-century example of in-text source referencing (1997, p.31)!

The development and growth of universities in the nineteenth century in Europe and the USA resulted in the mass examination of student knowledge by way of essays and examinations. There was a rigorous testing of knowledge and, as part of this, students were expected to cite the origins of ideas and offer detailed analysis and interpretation of sources. Citing and analysing the works of authors became a way for students to demonstrate their scholarly engagement with a text.

In the twentieth century, a range of referencing styles has developed, all building on these earlier foundations. Most universities allow for a variety of referencing styles to be used, although there may be attempts, sometimes fiercely resisted, to impose one style on to all disciplines. These adopted styles usually flow from historical associations of disciplines to particular referencing styles or flow from the recommendations of professional associations, who represent the copyright interests of their members.

Copyright laws today in Britain protect the manifestation of ideas into print or other tangible forms. It is not the ideas themselves that are protected, but the expression of these in tangible and publicly accessible work. Referencing represents the formal recognition of this work. In effect, you are saying to the author or creator: 'I recognize that you and your publisher have presented this idea in a particular and public way to the world'.

Referencing and society

The importance given to referencing in Britain is not universal, and students studying in Britain from other countries are often surprised by the emphasis attached to it by institutions. This emphasis can, however, be understood in relation to the type of society that exists here: arguably, one characterized by a democratic form of individualism. In countries characterized by individualism, which includes competition, self-interest, self-reliance and personal achievement, the respect for copyright is usually strong (Hampden-Turner and Trompenaars 2000).

However, other countries have societies that can be seen as ideologically more collective, and where people are more willing to sublimate their individuality to the benefit of the community as a whole. In this context ideas are regarded as being more in the public domain: to be shared and used for self or community improvement. Copying is widely practised as a legitimate form of sharing ideas with others, without the necessity to refer continually to a named originator (Yang 2005, p.286, citing Kuanpoth 2002). While this may be generally true, there appears to be, even within this cultural context, variations on the practices (see Ha 2006, discussed in Chapter 4 of this book).

Referencing in Britain, has to be seen, not just in an academic, but also in a social and political context. It is part of a societal value system that vigorously supports the idea of the intellectual property rights of others. It is this support for intellectual property that is a significant driving force in Britain to tackle what is seen as a growing problem of plagiarism in education.

Witch-hunts?

Plagiarism: even the word is ugly, with its connotations of plague and pestilence. Chapter 4 deals with this issue in more depth, but suffice to say at this point that plagiarism is currently an issue of major concern in higher education, and has been since the mid-1990s. However, the intense focus on the issue has also resulted in some cynicism, resistance or counter-blast to what is regarded as an overzealous hunt for plagiarists by academics and institutions. Levin (2003), for example, refers to the 'witch-hunts' within British universities to root out plagiarism.

The concern about plagiarism has led to more attention being focused on the importance of careful referencing practice as the antidote to plagiarism. But this is not without its critics. Angélil-Carter (2000), for example, refers to tutors who regard over-emphasis on referencing, as 'a fetish which is engaged in to substitute thinking' (p.130). And Levin feels that requiring students to cite every source they have drawn on is akin to, 'insisting they learn to dance with their shoes tied together' (2003, p.7). He argues, 'It's high time that academics and administrators recognised that some unconscious plagiarism in students' work is inevitable and perfectly reasonable' (p.9). Levin's point is that students can get bogged down by the responsibility of tracing sources to back-up their assertions, to the detriment of their ability to write independently. Subsequently they do not progress beyond the 'stages of selecting/copying and translating' in their assignments (p.7).

It can be argued that all imitative learning is plagiarism. We use ideas from other people all the time, weave them into our working and academic lives, gradually taking ownership of them until we eventually forget who influenced us in the first place; referencing becomes difficult, if not impossible, in some situations (see Angélil-Carter 2000; Pennycook 1996; Lensmire and Beals 1994). However, plagiarism, in an academic context, refers to a deliberate decision not to acknowledge the **work** of others in assignments – or deliberately ignoring an obligation to do this. But more later on plagiarism (see Chapter 4).

What else is to come?

The remainder of the book has this to offer:

Chapter 2 Why reference? This looks in more detail at the principles of, and rationale for, referencing that were touched on in this chapter.

Chapter 3 What, when and how to reference. This chapter advises you when referencing is necessary, and when it is not. It also includes advice on effective note-making strategies to help you organize your sources, and a quiz is included to test your knowledge of when to reference.

Chapter 4 Plagiarism. This picks up the points made earlier in this chapter and looks in more detail at the issue of plagiarism and its relationship with referencing. The chapter advises you how to avoid plagiarism and includes two exercises: one to test your understanding of plagiarism; the other to look at the issue of copy and paste from the Internet.

Chapter 5 Referencing styles. This presents the range of referencing styles you may encounter on courses in Britain and looks at the differences between them. The chapter also includes a survey, undertaken by the author, of the predominant referencing styles in UK higher education.

Chapter 6 Harvard style of referencing. This chapter looks in detail at the Harvard style, and includes referencing examples. It also includes an undergraduate essay illustrating Harvard in action, and presents a postgraduate essay with citations removed, to test your understanding of when and how to reference within this style. More attention has been given to this style in response to the survey result, outlined in Chapter 5, and because the benchmark guidelines for using this style in Britain tend to be more ambiguous, compared with the others featured in later chapters.

Chapter 7 American Psychological Association (APA) and Modern Languages Association (MLA) referencing styles. These styles will be discussed and examples of references presented. The differences, often small, between Harvard and APA styles will also be highlighted.

Chapter 8 Numerical referencing styles. The British Standard numerical styles – Running-notes and Numeric – and variants on these – Vancouver style, IEEE and MHRA – are discussed and examples presented.

Chapter 9 Frequently asked questions. Common questions about referencing are answered here. These include the difference between references and a bibliography; how to reference secondary sources; referencing multiple authors; and how to use punctuation within referencing.

Chapter 10 Referencing in action. This chapter presents examples of referencing. You are presented with a range of sources and comparative examples of how to reference within the Harvard, APA, MLA and British Standard numerical styles.

This may prove useful if you are having to use different referencing styles within the same institution or as you progress through education and encounter different referencing styles along the way. To illustrate a range of particular evidence examples, the chapter includes sources from a range of disciplines, including science and technology, social sciences and the humanities. However, for students using MLA, or APA, some source examples, e.g. from technology, are unlikely to fall within their province of study. I hope, however, they will take the point that the examples are illustrative of referencing style differences generally, and they can be adapted to suit their own disciplines. The chapter also touches on yet another referencing style for students on law courses: the Oxford Standard for Citation of Legal Authorities (OSCOLA).

2

Why reference?

Principles of referencing • Why referencing is important

Principles of referencing

Why reference? Walker and Taylor (1998, pp.11–15), argue that all styles of referencing are underpinned by five principles. The first of these establishes a rationale for all referencing styles and the other four establish a framework for referencing practice within all referencing styles.

1 **The principle of intellectual property.** As discussed in the previous section, Western concepts of plagiarism are based on an economic model of capitalism and the notion that someone can claim ownership of an idea if it has been presented in a 'fixed' way, for example, published or presented in the public domain.
2 **The principle of access.** References help readers easily and quickly identify and locate documents referred to in a text. This helps to spread knowledge, as the reader may then be able to use the information for his or her own learning purposes.
3 **The principle of economy.** The references should include as much information as necessary to help readers locate the sources cited. However, they should also be presented in such a way as to reduce the need for lengthy explanations in the text, and to speed up the process of reading.
4 **The principle of standardization.** References should be presented in such a way that allows everyone who has learned the practice to recognize and understand the meaning of codes and formulas presented. Different styles of referencing build a standardized framework for this to happen.
5 **The principle of transparency.** There must be no ambiguity in terms and expressions used.

> **Golden rule of referencing**
>
> The 'Golden Rule' of referencing is to give the reader enough information to help them easily and quickly find the source you have cited. If they wanted to look at your source and check it for themselves, could they find it easily with the information you have supplied?

Why referencing is important

There are at least nine reasons why referencing is important:

1 Tracing the origin of ideas

Academic study involves not just presenting and describing ideas, but also being aware of where they came from, who developed them, why and when. The 'when' is particularly important. Ideas, models, theories and practices originate from somewhere and someone. These are often shaped by the social norms and practices prevailing at the time and place of their origin and the student in higher education needs to be aware of these influences. Referencing, therefore, plays an important role in helping to locate and place ideas and arguments in their historical, social, cultural and geographical contexts.

For example, in 1968, a sociologist, Ken Roberts, argued then that the opportunity structure of a local area was the main determinant of work entered into by most working-class young people. Young people entered work in groups, into local factories or other significant local workplaces. He reached his conclusions at a time when it was possible for groups of young people from the same community to move from school together, to work together in one place close to their homes. Career 'choice' was, according to Roberts, largely an illusion, as it was often circumscribed by the occupational limits of the local community, combined with strong parental and neighbourhood influences.

However, in recent years Roberts has broadened his position in response to the decline of manufacturing industries that once dominated local labour markets. Young people, in theory anyway, have more work 'choices' now within a wider range of service sector jobs. Roberts would still argue, nevertheless, that these so-called choices continue to be circumscribed by boundaries of social class and peer pressures (Roberts 2001).

The year of the original study, 1968, might alert you to the very different economic scene prevailing at the time, and it is likely you would hesitate to advance the 1968 ideas of Roberts as the last word on the subject. It is likely that you would want to trace a developmental path from the original idea to the present time, by linking Roberts' ideas with changes in the economy and changes in social class composition, attitudes and values.

Roberts in 1968, was influenced by colleagues who came before him, and they by those before them, and so it goes on. Learning builds on learning. However, like trying to discover the 'real' source of a mighty river, there are often many contributory networks to knowledge, and it is sometimes impossible to work back to the beginning and to the origin of an idea. This point is pursued in Chapter 4 on plagiarism.

All you can do, sometimes, is to reference **a** source; a source that is immediately relevant to your assignment and particular argument and one that appears to be reliable and valid in relation to the arguments presented by you.

Students as they progress through their studies become more aware that ideas presented by authors are not infallible simply because they are printed, and they learn that the best marks are gained by challenging ideas, looking for flaws in arguments and for exceptions to the rule. They become more aware, as Penrose and Geisler (1994) observe, that:

- Authors present knowledge in the form of claims.
- Knowledge claims can conflict.
- Knowledge claims can be tested.
- This testing is part of the student's role in higher education, particularly at post-graduate level.

2 Building a web of ideas

Knowledge connects and spreads: the past connects with the present and has an impact on the future. As you build your argument in an assignment, it is rather like a spider building its web. You build carefully engineered connections between ideas. You advance an argument in one section, but then counter it with another threaded and connected group of ideas, each supported by its own referenced evidence. But you have at the centre, your own position, your own place in the scheme of things; your point of view.

3 Finding your own voice

Many students when they enter higher education are confused about a gap they perceive between the conventions of academic writing, and the need to make their **own** points in essays. Some tutors will, on the one hand, encourage students to develop their own ideas, while emphasizing the need for them to cite and refer to the work of experts in the particular subject area. Other tutors will encourage personal opinions in assignments, while others will not. This apparent confusion can sometimes result in assignments that are an unsuccessful blend of the personal and the academic.

In written assignments, many of your tutors will expect you to write in an 'academic way', which includes distancing yourself somewhat from the subject, using a third person style of writing, and referencing to support the ideas you present. Whether this style of third person writing is still appropriate today, is an issue I will return to in Chapter 4.

Most lecturers would agree that that their role is to encourage you to develop **your** own opinions and to formulate **your** own arguments, while remaining open-minded and objective. In this way, academic knowledge is advanced as students begin to challenge or adapt existing ideas, theories and practices. Referencing, in this situation is the means to help to build your own personal web of arguments and to give credibility to the information you present in assignments.

You may have to write in a way that is not 'you', in terms of writing style. However, the perspective you take, the idea you present and the conclusion you reach can all be your choice; referencing helps this process. The **selection** of evidence to support your own perspectives is subjective – and is an important way for you to find your own credible voice in higher education.

The process is summarized in the flowchart in Fig. 2.1.

4 Validity of arguments

To be taken seriously, you must present valid evidence in assignments. Aristotle, around 350 BC, argued that persuasive rhetoric included *Logos*: appeals to logic to persuade an audience through sound reasoning. This is done by the presentation of reliable evidence, usually in the form of facts, definitions, statistics and other data that has an appeal to the intelligence of a particular audience. This ageless principle can be applied equally to written arguments. Referencing reliable and valid evidence in assignments has such an appeal to the intelligence of the reader.

Referencing also enables your tutors to check for themselves the accuracy and validity of the evidence presented. In particular, they will want to ensure you are using ideas from the past in a way that is relevant or original to the assignment topic under discussion. Do not assume tutors have read everything on the subject; they may be unfamiliar with the work you cite, so may need to check it themselves.

5 Spreading knowledge

Referencing also presents an opportunity for the tutor and other readers to advance their own knowledge. It gives them the possibility of tracing the sources you cite and using the same evidence for their own purposes. You have probably discovered already how useful bibliographies and lists of references at the end of journal articles can be in identifying other related sources for your own research. Once you start following up sources in bibliographies, it can open up a fascinating trail of knowledge. One source leads to another; you begin to build your own web of learning around a subject.

6 An appreciation

As stated earlier, education needs ideas, arguments and perspectives to thrive. But these have to be tested rigorously and subjected to the critical scrutiny of others. This is done by researching, preparing and presenting work into the public domain, which, as was noted earlier, is a formidable task for any writer, and one that can take years sometimes to achieve. Referencing is then, also about giving appreciation: a modest genuflection to the work of others. It is about showing courtesy and respect, and about honouring the hard work of writers and commentators – by acknowledging them in your assignments.

You can present an argument in an assignment by:

1. Stating your point of view early in the assignment and presenting a clear and consistent rationale to support it.

2. Offering **reliable evidence**, or illustrative examples, to support your argument. This is evidence that you have read in reputable and authoritative texts, articles, newspapers, Internet sites and so on.

3. Showing where this evidence has come from: by citing your sources and listing all your sources in the reference or bibliography section at the end of your assignment.

4. Showing that you are aware of, and have considered, arguments that are counter to your own. You will need to summarize counter-arguments in a clear, accurate and undistorted way.

5. Being able to show why you have decided that the arguments you have chosen to advance are more convincing for you than others.

FIGURE 2.1 Flowchart of argument presentation process

7 Influences

Tutors will be also interested in your list of references or bibliography to identify which authors or sources have been influential in moulding or shaping the direction taken by you in your research. They may, as a result, offer comment on the absence or inclusion of any particular commentator or theorist in an assignment. Your sources may also occasionally help your tutors, by introducing new authors and ideas to them, thus broadening their own knowledge.

8 Marking criteria

The selection of relevant evidence and accurate referencing is an important element in the marking of assignments, particularly at postgraduate level. Accurate referencing can often make the difference between a pass, a credit or a distinction. Accurate referencing is also a tangible demonstration to your tutor of your research, intellectual integrity and the care you have taken in preparing to write the assignment.

9 Avoid plagiarism

Finally, accurate referencing will help you to avoid being accused of plagiarism. There is a grey area between deliberate cheating and carelessness with referencing – or ignorance of it. However, more on this later.

3

What, when and how to reference

References and bibliographies • What to reference • Choosing sources • When to reference • When you do not need to reference • How to reference • Bibliographic software • Quiz

This section of the book is about the range of sources that can be referenced, and about the criteria for evaluating them, particularly Internet sources. It is also about the occasions when you should reference – and when it is not necessary. But first, let us look at the difference between references and bibliographies.

References and bibliographies

What is the difference between a list of 'References' and a 'Bibliography'? The terms are often used synonymously, but there is a difference in meaning between them.

- **References** are the items you have read and **specifically referred to** (or cited) in your assignment.
- A **bibliography** is a list of everything you read in preparation for writing an assignment. A bibliography will, therefore, normally contain sources that you have cited **and** those you found to be influential but decided not to cite. A bibliography can give a tutor an overview of which authors have influenced your ideas and arguments even if you do not specifically refer to them.

At the end of your assignment you will produce a list that is headed either

'Bibliography' or 'References' (Table 3.1), unless you have been asked by your tutor to include both in the assignment. (The MLA style of referencing refers to these lists respectively as 'Works Consulted' and 'Works Cited'.)

Table 3.1 References and bibliographies

Bibliography (or 'Works consulted')	References (or 'Works cited')
If you wish to list the sources you made specific reference to (cited) in your assignment, **and** give details of other sources consulted, (but not directly cited), then you can include all the sources under one sub-heading: **'Bibliography'** However, do not be tempted to include items you have not read in order to impress the tutor. If you, for example, include an item you have not actually read, the tutor may challenge you as to why you have **not** directly referred to a significant author listed or apparently not been influenced by their work in your assignment	If, however, you have cited – made specific reference to – all the sources you consulted in the assignment, your list will be headed **'References'** If you make a point of reading selectively, it is likely that you will make use of everything you read and refer directly to it in your assignment. In that event, it will be perfectly correct to just have a 'References' list instead of a 'Bibliography'; it will certainly not go against you

What to reference

You can cite references taken from a range of sources, e.g.:

- Books written by a single author
- Multiple edited books with contributions from a range of different authors
- Reference books of all types
- Notes supplied by a lecturer
- Legal documents
- Articles from journals
- Newspaper articles
- Reports of various kinds, e.g. official reports from government departments, university working papers, etc.
- Papers presented at conferences
- Internet sources, including weblogs (blogs) and email correspondence (but see below)
- DVD/CD databases
- Radio/television/videos/audio cassette/CD-ROMS
- Interview transcripts
- Cinema films, theatre plays and other creative productions
- Illustrations
- Song lyrics and other original musical works
- Works of art and design

In short, most information that has been written, recorded, filmed or presented in the public domain in some way to others can potentially be used. There is no point in referencing anything that cannot be read, heard or seen by another who wants to find the same source. So personal conversations on the telephone, for example, can be mentioned in the text of an assignment but cannot be referenced, unless there is some audio or written record of the discussion that can be heard or read by others. Emails can be both cited in the text of an assignment and referenced, providing you save them and make them available to your tutor. Interviews you conduct for research can also be cited in the text, and referenced, provided you have evidence that the interview took place. This can take the form of an audio recording, a completed questionnaire, a transcript or notes taken at the time.

Choosing sources

The important thing is to choose **reliable** sources that give credence, authority and support to the ideas and arguments that you present. Your tutor will suggest a range of reliable sources, and this will be your starting point, but you will also be expected to look beyond the recommended reading and search out relevant information for yourself. If you do this, and connect to your assignment relevant evidence gained from additional reading, this can sometimes make the difference between a pass and a distinction grade.

In this respect, you will find that recommended books and other sources will prove – because of the accurate referencing that has gone into them – to be rich veins of additional information. If you read a particular chapter as a starting point for research into an assignment topic, the references or bibliography will often point you in the right direction of other relevant sources.

There are four main sets of questions (see Table 3.2) you can ask of any source, concerning:

1 Relevance and bias
2 Currency
3 Accuracy
4 Coverage.

When to reference

When to reference? There is no referencing practice more likely to confuse students than: 'When exactly should I reference?' This is a recurring question, and one that can produce, unfortunately, a range of different answers from tutors.

Angélil-Carter (2000), for example, found inconsistencies among staff at one higher education institution in South Africa, particularly in the area of what constituted

Table 3.2 Interrogating sources

Relevance and bias
- To what extent is the source relevant and applicable to the assignment?
- Does the information presented give a partial or restricted view of the subject?
- How balanced and objective does the language in the source appear to be?
- Are counter-arguments to the author's own ideas treated with respect? If not, why not?

Authority
- Is the source authoritative enough to be included in the assignment? For example, is the source a credible one, e.g. a reputable publishing company or a peer-reviewed journal?
- Do other authors refer to and discuss this source?
- How credible is the source to you? You can turn your own reservations into a starting point of critical enquiry about it

Currency
- When was the source originally published? You need to ask if the ideas expressed are a product of a particular time and place in history that no longer applies today
- Has the author revised or changed his or her views since the date of the original source? If so, when, why and how?

Scope
- How universal or general are the ideas, models or practices described in the source? Do they have a limited geographical or occupational application?
- Do the ideas in the source span a range of cultures or are they just applicable to particular groups?

common knowledge, which does not need referencing. 'Common knowledge' to one tutor was not always the same to another, even in the same subject area. I will come back to this later in the chapter.

However, Angélil-Carter also noted inconsistencies of approach to assessing students who were regarded as more authoritative (or brighter) than others. Students who wrote well, with confidence, ease and authority, appeared to be shown more latitude with regards to referencing. An example was given of a confident, articulate student, who offered her tutors a 'lubricated journey' through her assignments, which were 'unsnagged by linguistic problems'. This student was granted some latitude and was, 'therefore, not required to reference all her sources', and was also unlikely to be accused of plagiarism (p.86).

Students of apparently high ability were allowed more freedom to present unreferenced summaries and commentaries of their own; and, in particular, they were given more latitude regarding 'common knowledge' and in expressing, ostensibly, their own views on a set essay topic. Angélil-Carter's examples appear to illustrate a 'halo effect', where bright students receive less critical attention from their tutors if their writing is fluent, authoritative and their referencing generally sound. Minor digressions of referencing were overlooked, in comparison with the criticism less able students received for their lack of referencing expertise.

In the Angélil-Carter study, for example, this double-standard appears to originate from the frustration tutors felt when marking assignments they regarded as lacking in credibility due to poor writing style, which included lack of ability with referencing:

let's put it this way. If I thought there was a whole lot of unreferenced stuff . . . I might well, sort of blow my top and sort of say, where the hell is the reference for that? But if it is generally referenced then I'm not going to get upset about that, so I think the context of referencing is probably quite important.

(Tutor quoted by Angélil-Carter 2000, p.86)

This type of tutor frustration is not uncommon in Britain, and is a manifestation of a problem that has surfaced in recent years about falling standards in student writing. A Nuffield Review survey, for example, of 250 academics at 21 UK universities found widespread concern about the writing skills of new undergraduates (Wilde et al. 2006). The Confederation of British Industry (CBI), in the same year, also announced that nearly a quarter of employers (23 per cent) were not satisfied with graduates' basic literacy and use of English (CBI 2006).

The UK government's widening participation agenda of the late 1990s, and early twenty-first century has resulted in an increase in the numbers of students entering higher education. This has increased the teaching and marking workload of teaching staff, and can result in increased impatience of lecturers with marking poorly written assignments. This impatience can extend to criticizing the referencing ability of students, if this is perceived as another contributory factor to an overall poor piece of written work.

Conversely, work confidently written can stand out and is greeted with pleasure by many academics. If an assignment starts well, with a good introduction, written in clear English, the tutor can seek positive reinforcement of this early good impression. If this is forthcoming, and the student can demonstrate early in the assignment that he or she knows how and, generally, when to reference, the tutor may overlook minor lapses in referencing that they might not tolerate from a less able writer.

The important point in all of this is that students need to demonstrate they know generally when to reference and how to reference. This can establish their credibility with the tutor, particularly in the early stages of an assignment. Knowing when to reference is, then, as important as understanding how to reference.

When to reference: six scenarios

You should reference evidence in assignments in the following situations:

1 To give the reader the source of tables, statistics, diagrams, photographs and other illustrations included in your assignment
2 When describing or discussing a theory, model or practice associated with a particular writer (this links specifically to the next two items)
3 To give weight or credibility to an argument supported by you in your assignment
4 When giving emphasis to a particular theory, model or practice that has found a measure of agreement and support among commentators
5 To inform the reader of sources of direct quotations or definitions in your assignment
6 When paraphrasing another person's work, which is outside the realm of common knowledge, and that you feel is particularly significant or likely to be a subject of debate. This can also include definitions.

Examples (in the Harvard style of referencing)

Example: To inform the reader of sources of tables, photographs, statistics or diagrams presented in your assignment (either copied in their original form or collated by you)

The surface temperatures in the world have increased by 1 degree Fahrenheit, or 0.6 degrees Celsius, since the mid-1970s, and the highest surface temperature ever recorded by the National Aeronautics and Space Administration (NASA) was in 2005. Climatologists generally agree that the five warmest years since the late nineteenth century have been within the decade, 1995–2005, with the National Oceanic and Atmospheric Administration (NOAA) and the World Meteorological Organization (WMO) ranking 2005 as the second warmest year, behind 1998 (Hansen 2005).

Example: When describing or discussing a theory, model or practice associated with a particular writer (you may, for example, compare and contrast the views of established authors in the field)

A major study of British school leavers by Maizels (1970) concluded that parents had a major influence on the kind of work their children entered. The children were influenced over a long period of time by their parents' values and ideas about work. A later study (Ashton and Field 1976) reached the same conclusion and showed a link between the social and economic status of parents and the work attitudes and aspirations of their teenage children.

Example: To give weight or credibility to an argument presented in your assignment

Handy (1995) has argued that federalism is a way of making sense of large organizations, and that the power and responsibility that drives federalism is a feature of developed societies and can be extended into a way forward for managing modern business. In relation to power, Handy argues that 'authority must be earned from those whom it is exercised' (p.49). Respect from employees must be earned, and not expected simply because of one's rank.

Example: When giving emphasis to a particular theory, model or practice that has found a measure of agreement and support among commentators

As the behavioural response of communication apprehension (CA) is to avoid or discourage interaction with others, it is not surprising that CA has been linked to feelings of loneliness, isolation, low self-esteem and the inability to discuss personal problems with managers or others (Daly and Stafford 1984; McCroskey and Richmond 1987; McCroskey et al. 1977; Richmond 1984; Scott and Rockwell 1997).

In the above example, the student cites five sources, all saying much the same thing, to emphasize and give credibility to an important point summarized in the assignment. The use of multiple authors can add weight to a summary, particularly if the idea is a controversial one. However, citing six authors is the suggested maximum for this purpose, and citing two or three is the more usual practice.

Example: To inform the reader of sources of direct quotations or definitions in your assignment

Cable (2001) argues that Freeman became ever more resentful of the way he was treated by publishers. It appears he felt that his Oxbridge education should have accorded him more respect from his contemporaries. He talked 'bitterly of a certain titled young gentleman who treated him as an equal on The High in Oxford but who, on Saxmundham railway station, refused to acknowledge him' (p.5). However, Cable argues that this snobbishness was also in Freeman's own character, so he was particularly sensititve when the snubs were directed at him!

If the quote is taken from a printed book or journal, you always need to include the page number in the citation so the reader can go straight to that page to find it. If it is an electronic source the Uniform Resource Locator (URL) address, which will be listed in the full reference, should take the reader to the relevant web page or screen.

Example: When paraphrasing another person's idea or definition that you feel is particularly significant or likely to be a subject of debate

We all perceive the world around us, in ways that are often unique to us, through a series of personal filters, and we 'construct' our own versions of reality (Kelly 1955).

Note: In this example the student paraphrases an idea that Kelly originally outlined in 1955. The inverted commas around 'construct' suggest this is a significant word used by Kelly to describe a key concept. By citing the source the student is, in effect, saying 'this is **Kelly**'s idea; I am just paraphrasing it'.

When you do not need to reference

However, there are four situations when you do not need to reference sources. These are:

1 When presenting historical overviews
2 When presenting your own experiences

3 In conclusions, when you are repeating ideas previously referenced
4 When summarizing what is regarded as 'common knowledge'.

1 Historical overviews

You do not need to reference information drawn from a **variety of sources** to summarize what has happened over a period of time, when those sources state much the same things and when your summary is unlikely to be a cause of dispute or controversy.

In the example that follows, the student summarizes the topic generally, and has used for this purpose a number of different and reliable sources, which all agreed on the reasons for the growth in call centres.

> The growth in call centres in the West was encouraged by economic and technological factors. From the late 1970s the growth of the service sector focused the attention of large organizations on communication with customers in more cost-effective and streamlined ways. This growth of a service sector economy connected with advances in telecommunications and changes in working practices in Western companies. The logic of call centres was that a centralized approach and rationalization of organizational operations would reduce costs, while producing a standard branded image to the world.

However, if the student had used just one source for the summary, this should be cited and referenced.

2 Your own experiences and observations

You do not need to reference your own experiences or observations, although you should make it clear that these are your own. For example, you could use the first person term 'I' to do this, although not all tutors encourage this style of personal writing. If you are discouraged from writing in the first person, you could say something like, 'it has been this author's (or this writer's) experience that . . .'. If, however, you have had your work published in a journal, book or other source, you could cite your own published work in support of your own experiences.

3 Summaries or conclusions

You do not need to reference again if pulling together a range of key ideas that you introduced and referenced earlier in the assignment. For example, it can be good practice in writing, particularly in a long assignment, to summarize ideas before moving on to another line of discussion. Also, when you reach the concluding sections of your assignment and begin to draw your arguments together, you would not need to cite sources previously referenced, unless you were introducing new material or introducing a new perspective drawn from previously cited sources.

4 Common knowledge

This is the most problematic of the four, as there can disagreement among academics on what constitutes common knowledge. One definition is:

Information that is presumed to be shared by members of a specific 'community' – an institution, a city, a national region, the nation itself . . . a particular race, ethnic group, religion, academic discipline, professional association, or other such classification.

(Hopkins 2005)

Common knowledge has two main elements. First, there is knowledge in the public domain. You are using common knowledge when sharing and expressing generally undisputed facts circulating freely, publicly and without the restraint of copyright, and when there is unlikely to be any significant disagreement with your statements or summaries of this information. This would include undisputed information found in reference books and encyclopedias.

However, note the following differences between fact and opinion:

- Thomas Hardy wrote *Tess of the d'Urbervilles*: **Fact**.
- Thomas Hardy wrote *Tess of the d'Urbervilles*, and the poetic beauty of his language raises it above other novels in the rural tradition (Winchcombe 1978): **Opinion**.

The first sentence contains an undisputed fact. However, the second concludes with an opinion, and an author is cited to support the assertion. The wise student would also look for, and include, **other evidence** to support this opinion, by paraphrasing or quoting Winchcombe's reasons for making this assertion, and by seeking evidence from other literary critics to support (or dispute) the view.

Common knowledge also includes general descriptions of folklore and traditions, although specific author comment on these would be referenced. For example, you might talk generally about the traditions in a particular area, but would need to reference what a particular author had to say about, for example, the deeper meanings or origins of these.

Common knowledge would also cover commonplace observations or aphorisms on the world, for example, that the dark winters can have a depressing impact on our moods, although if you produced any specific evidence to that effect, this would be cited.

The University of Queensland include the following six examples of common knowledge when referencing would not be required:

1 That Neil Armstrong landed on the Moon in July 1969 (common fact of history).
2 That Alexander Fleming discovered penicillin (common fact of history).
3 The definition of photosynthesis (common knowledge in the discipline).
4 That humans need food and water for survival (commonsense observation).
5 That Count Dracula lived in Transylvania (accepted folklore).
6 'Life wasn't meant to be easy' (aphorism).

(University of Queensland 2006)

Second, the second element of common knowledge, as noted in the third of the six examples just listed, is common knowledge within a **subject area or discipline**. Every subject has its own set of commonly agreed codes, assumptions, jargons and symbols. At university level, there are assumptions made that students starting on courses where there are particular subject prerequisites, for example, sciences, mathematics and

English literature, will already have begun to connect with these common points of reference. So, although many individual members of the general public might be hard pushed to give the visitor from Mars an accurate summary of the difference between a simile and a metaphor, a student of English literature should be able to do this fairly easily! The point here is that there will be common points of reference and understanding between you and your tutors, and that you will not need to define, explain and continually cite the origins of this knowledge. These common points of understanding may be implicit, soon become clear or be negotiated early in courses between tutors and their students.

How to reference

It can be incredibly frustrating to discover halfway through writing an assignment that you have not taken a full note, or any note at all, of a particular source that you belatedly decide you need to use. It may be that you read something, thought 'that's useful' and meant to take note of it, but did not! You then have to start searching for the source, and if it is on the Internet, or buried in the depths of a book, it can be very time consuming to track it down. The moral is that if you think a source might be useful to a particular assignment or examination, then take an immediate note of it.

Note taking and note making serves a number of purposes. Notes act as a summary or reinforcement of the main points of what you saw, heard or read. However, for referencing purposes, notes are also an essential **record** of information sources. They also remind you of other things you should do, for example, other sources to check. You need to organize a system of note making that suits you, although filing notes away by author, particularly for the author–date or author–page referencing styles, or by topic, tend to be the best approaches. Your notes can then be used to both remind you of the topic for revision purposes and help you compile a list of references or a bibliography. This can be done either manually or with the help of bibliographic software (see end of this chapter).

The difference between taking and making notes is about the transition from a passive to an active process.

Level 1: Note *taking*

Summarizing the main points from a lecture or other sources.

Level 2: Note *making*

Can include one or more of:

- Review and reorganization of notes
- Connecting and synthesizing ideas
- Adding your own personal comments and reflections on the ideas summarized.

Table 3.3 Note taking and note making

Note taking	Note making
A process that involves writing or recording what you hear or read in a descriptive way. This is the first stage of the process of producing effective notes	An advanced process that involves reviewing, synthesizing, connecting ideas from the lecture or reading and presenting information in readable and creative ways, and in ways that will help you revise more effectively

Examples of note taking/making

An example of a manual note-taking/making sheet is shown in Fig. 3.1. Although electronic note making is an important alternative to using manual notes, it is not always convenient to use a personal computer. Manual notes are still an important way of recording information, particularly in lectures and tutorials or in other situations when it is inconvenient to use electronic note-making systems.

The top lines record the full source detail and the source topic. The notes can be filed away thematically by subject or alphabetically by author. In the right-hand column of the sheet, the main points are summarized. The left-hand column can be used to remind you of any key points or questions that occur to you about the source. The Comments/Summary section provides additional space for your comments, for example to remind you of any follow-up work you could do to explore the topic further.

This process converts note taking into something more active – into note *making*.

Bibliographic software

There is now a wide range of referencing management software systems on the market, designed to help students manage referencing, and more appear each year. Many universities provide these free for students to use within the institution or enable students to purchase the software themselves, often at a discounted price. Features of this software include:

- Searching the Internet for references and importing to your database
- 'Cite while you write' features, which includes organizing information retrieved into a particular referencing style, including all the styles featured in this book
- Linking the citation in the text with the full reference, and a facility for ensuring that any citation featured in the text corresponds with a full reference entry
- Editing features – easy addition to references already entered
- Keyword sorting alphabetically of references.

Source: *Brown, J. (2000) The Future: we are on our way. London: Future Inc.*	
Subject: *Future trends: what the world will look like in 2050.*	
Topic & issues raised	Main points:
Smaller families?	*Individual choice – more important; Internet more prominent – for individual lifestyles; women big+ role in the workplace.* *Flexible learning = more important, particularly post-grad. quals; distance-learning opps. will increase + distance learning courses material = big business*
what about quality of life – Alzheimer's Disease?	*Longevity will increase in the developed world to 100+ years We will increase our use of electronic systems to communicate with others, e.g. three-dimensional video systems; growth of electronic communications will encourage more home working, – but will still be a need to meet colleagues socially*
But this is an ageing society – people die= houses come on market	*The trend toward home working will result in less work-related mobility and will encourage the development of community life. However, the lack of mobility may result in fewer houses coming on the market for sale or rent Service sector work will expand and result in a shortage of skilled labour.*
Won't this means less security?	*Employers will need to make work attractive to their employees in order to retain them; a movement away from working in large multi-national companies, to more individual forms of working/self employment*
Comments/Summary *Much more emphasis on personal choices & individuality. This might explain reason for movement away from working in large companies to self-employment– although there will always be a trade-off between security and independence, particularly if you have kids.*	

FIGURE 3.1   Example of a note-making sheet

There are obvious advantages for students in using this software, in both information retrieval and in organizing the citation and full referencing in an assignment. However, the software does have its limitations and, arguably, no one system appears yet to offer completely all that students need for fully integrated information search and easy transfer of information into citation and full reference forms. With some systems, for example, the search facility may be limited; with others there may be particular problems, such as confusion in distinguishing between primary and secondary authors or problems with referencing certain types of uncommon source (Shapland 1999).

The cost of these systems is also a factor and this is a major determinant of which system an institution finally adopts. Most institutions allow students to use the systems free when they are on site. However, the software can be expensive for a student to purchase and use privately, and students must decide if the cost is justified in terms of the use they will make of it. It also takes time, effort and practice before students can use the software proficiently. However, there is no doubt that the effort to learn can be repaid by the consistent referencing entry that is given. Students should talk to the librarian at their institution and find out what referencing management software is available and what training is offered in its use.

Quiz

To test your understanding of when to reference, try answering the questions in the quiz in Fig. 3.2. Look at the following situations that can occur when writing assignments and decide if a citation is needed.

1   When you include tables, photographs, statistics and diagrams in your assignment. These may be items directly copied or a source of data collation which you have used ☐

2   When describing or discussing a theory, model or practice associated with a particular writer ☐

3   When you summarize information drawn from a variety of sources about what has happened over a period and the summary is unlikely to be a cause of dispute or controversy ☐

4   To give weight or credibility to an argument that you believe is important ☐

5   When giving emphasis to a particular idea that has found a measure of agreement and support among commentators ☐

6   When pulling together a range of key ideas that you introduced and referenced earlier in the assignment ☐

7   When stating or summarizing obvious facts, and when there is unlikely to be any significant disagreement with your statements or summaries ☐

8   When including quotations ☐

9   When you copy and paste items from the Internet and where no author's name is shown ☐

10 When paraphrasing or summarizing (in your own words) another person's work that you feel is particularly significant, or likely to be a subject of debate ☐

FIGURE 3.2 Quiz on understanding when to reference

Now check your answers against those in Appendix 1.

4

Plagiarism

Plagiarism? • Three main forms of plagiarism • Levels of plagiarism • Why do students plagiarize? • International students • Patchwork writing • Discouraging plagiarism • How to avoid plagiarism • Plagiarism exercise

> I was not sure about what to do in terms of reference and that sort of thing when I came to university. A student does not have much rich knowledge background; they have to learn other people's opinions in order to write something. . . . This is only due to the student's lack of experience and knowledge . . . but not plagiarism.
> (International student in her final undergraduate year,
> in conversation with author)

You will no doubt be aware that plagiarism is a hot topic of discussion in higher education. But it is certainly not a new phenomenon. And you can find all colours of opinion among lecturers: from those who seize on plagiarism as a symptom of slipping academic standards, devaluation of higher education and an erosion of everything they believe higher education should be, to those who feel that there is more than a little intolerance, hypocrisy and inconsistency around the issue.

There are many academics, probably the majority, who oscillate between both positions, genuinely confused – about whether what they read in front of them in an assignment is plagiarism, carelessness, ignorance, misunderstanding, confusion or poor referencing practice. They can be driven to fury when they encounter blatant and wholesale copying, particularly if it comes during a particularly heavy and exhausting period of marking. Yet, when faced with the individual student, explaining his or her case for apparently plagiarizing a text, can understand why it has happened.

It is an issue that runs parallel to a debate with recurring questions about the purpose of higher education in the twenty-first century. Is an insistence on referencing about supporting a system and a process of learning that is a legacy of a different time and society? Are universities enforcing upon you an arcane practice of referencing that you will probably never use again outside higher education? Or is there something deeper in the practice of referencing that connects with behaving ethically, properly, decently and respecting others – ageless societal values that universities should try to maintain? Plagiarism, from this latter perspective, can be viewed as an attack on these values.

Plagiarism?

But what is plagiarism? There is certainly no single universally agreed definition in Britain. Every institution develops its own definitions and even within these there can be a range of interpretations of what it is – and is not.

In general, plagiarism is one of a number of practices deemed by universities to constitute cheating, or in university-speak: 'a lack of academic integrity'. These include:

- Collusion without official approval between two or more students, with the result that identical, or near identical work, is presented by all those involved
- Falsification – where content of assignments, e.g. statistics, has been invented or falsely presented by a student as their own work
- Replication – where a student submits the same, or very similar piece of work, on more than one occasion to gain academic credit
- Taking unauthorized notes into an examination
- Obtaining an unauthorized copy of an examination paper
- Communication with other students in an examination in order to help, or be helped, with answers
- Impersonation of another person in an examination (Jones et al. 2005).

Plagiarism, specifically, is a term used to describe a practice that involves knowingly taking and using another person's **work** and claiming it, directly or indirectly, as your own.

As stated earlier, this 'work' is usually something that has been produced by another person, 'published' in some tangible way and presented formally in the public domain. It is not the ideas that are being plagiarized, as ideas can occur to people all the time; it is the manifestation of those ideas, in print, Internet, audio-visual, theatrical, cinematic, choreographic or other tangible form. It can also include assignments either ready written or written to order, and sold from Internet sites, which are then presented to an institution by the buyer as his or her own original work.

Three main forms of plagiarism

As already stated, each institution develops its own interpretation of plagiarism, and it is likely your college or university has already made you aware of theirs. But in general, there are three main forms:

1 Copying another person's work, including the work of another student (with or without their consent), and claiming or pretending it is your own
2 Presenting arguments that use a blend of your own and a significant percentage of copied words of the original author without acknowledging the source
3 Paraphrasing another person's work, but not giving due acknowledgement to the original writer or organization publishing the writing, including Internet sites. The exceptions to this would be in relation to common knowledge (see Chapter 3).

It sounds straightforward and – at its most blatant form of simply copying great chunks of someone else's work into your own work with or without any form of acknowledgement of the originator – it can be. As Angélil-Carter puts it, 'the true plagiarist writes to conceal the sources' (2000, p.22).

Levels of plagiarism

But life is not that simple, nor students so blatant, although a minority appear to be reckless enough to plagiarize regularly and deliberately in this way (see Carroll 2005). Howard (1995) has tried to unpick the forms of plagiarism that can occur: cheating, non-attribution and patchwork writing. The first is done deliberately, while the second usually results from the inexperience of the student with referencing or from misunderstanding about academic conventions. The third results when a student tries to put together bits of assorted, copied text to make up an unsatisfactory whole; what Barrett and Malcolm (2006) call 'omission paraphrasing', which is when a student copies from a single source and selectively changes words and sentences to make it fit the assignment. This latter practice moves them into a grey area between paraphrasing and plagiarism and can lead to criticism or, worse, loss of marks.

The issue of non-attribution, Howard's second point, is a tricky one, as although misunderstanding can certainly be a cause, there is evidence that students do understand that they should cite their sources but do not always do it, for a variety of reasons. A significant number of students, faced with a heavy workload, easy opportunity plus pressure to succeed on degree courses, appear to be willing to copy from a printed source or paste from the Internet into their assignments in the hope they will not be noticed.

A study by Jones et al. (2005), for example, found one in five of 171 students from both Engineering and Psychology undergraduate degree courses admitting to copying and pasting material from a website into an assignment without crediting the source. Another study, by Dennis (2005), of 80 undergraduate and postgraduate students on Computer Science degree programmes produced a similar result, with a quarter of respondents admitting to activities the institution regarded as plagiarism, which was largely about copying, or partial copying, from printed or web-based sources.

When students are asked what proportion of their peers are engaged in plagiarism, the estimates tend to be high. For example, a survey of 140 students and staff at Northumbria University suggested that 70.9 per cent of students believed that copying a few paragraphs from a book or Internet without citing the source was a common practice.

Although this survey dealt with perception, this is important, as perception can transfer into discussion among students, and discussion into action. However, the same survey found only around 6 per cent of students who thought that downloading or buying whole essays from cheat sites or ghost writing services was common practice (Dordoy 2002).

Why do students plagiarize?

So why do students do it? One reason may be that they have always done it – maybe to the point when it becomes ritualized behaviour, and because it is easier and more tempting now than it ever has been.

Hart and Friesner (2004) point out that studies of cheating behaviour in the USA date back to the 1940s. They cite studies from the early 1940s, which suggested that, even then, nearly a quarter of students admitted to some form of cheating behaviour. Twenty years later a study by Bowers in 1964 suggested that three-quarters of a sample group of 5000 students had admitted some form of academic cheating. They may have written on the palms of their hands then, or in dictionaries, prior to their examinations, but now there is the Internet and a vast, open orchard of ideas just waiting to be picked and downloaded.

You now invest a significant amount of your own or your parents' money into higher education and high grades are important to secure interviews at big companies. Higher education is now increasingly viewed by many students as a commodity, and the process of learning as part of a 'commercial transaction'. Dordoy (2002) quotes one student as saying: 'If the University sells itself as a business and people only come to get a bit of paper – then plagiarism will always be a problem' (p.5). The potential challenge and intellectual stimulation of learning at this level gives way to the more expedient business of getting the all-important bit of paper, so screw the rules! Politicians and corporations do it, best-selling authors do it, even Shakespeare is supposed to have done it, so why shouldn't I?

Some students blame the pressure of writing to strict word limits:

> We're expected to cite as many references as possible to gain maximum marks but keep our word limit to 1500. Well, it is almost impossible to use so many references as well as our own words, without it looking like a copy-and-paste job.
>
> (THES 2006, p. 9)

Dordoy found the most common reasons cited by students for cheating were related to grades, poor time management and ease of opportunity:

- To get a better grade: 59 per cent
- Because of laziness or bad time management: 54 per cent
- Because of easy access to material via the Internet: 40 per cent
- Because they did not understand the rules: 29 per cent
- Because 'it happens unconsciously': 29 per cent (Dordoy 2002).

Dordoy also found that nearly 16 per cent of students felt that it happened because they did not think they would be caught. Students were aware of the pressure staff were under to teach large number of students and to mark hundreds of assignments, and were simply taking the chance. Some were also disillusioned about the lacklustre approach to teaching and student support taken by hard-pressed staff and saw plagiarism as a form of retaliation: 'students are extremely proud when they "get one over" on lecturers' (p.5). Other studies (Aggarwal et al. 2002; Culwin et al. 2002; Introna et al. 2003) suggest that students regard copying small amounts of material without citing the source as a trivial, or not particularly serious, breach of academic integrity.

Dennis (2005) also found a similar range of reasons given by students for why **others** cheated. The reasons given by 80 students were ranked as follows, with the most frequently cited at the top:

1 They started too late and ran out of time.
2 They simply could not do the coursework otherwise.
3 They did not think it was wrong.
4 They have to succeed. They got higher marks this way.
5 They did not need to learn that material, just pass the module.
6 They could not keep up with the work.
7 They wanted to see if they could get away with it.
8 They felt the tutor did not care, so why should they.
9 They thought paraphrasing would be disrespectful (Dennis 2005).

International students

This last point about 'disrespectful' paraphrasing is likely to be made by some international students. It is clear there are many different interpretations from one country to another on the practice of referencing in academic writing. What is unacceptable practice in Britain is quite legitimate, and even encouraged, elsewhere. What is regarded in Britain as plagiarism, for example, quoting from sources extensively without referencing them, can be regarded as perfectly normal in other countries, even within Europe (Sherman 1992). There may also be differences in experience among students from the same country. Lake (2004) found differences among Chinese students studying in Britain, with more than half having no previous experience of referencing in academic writing, but with a third having had some previous experience of referencing in essays written in their own language.

Ha (2006), responding to suggestions that Asian culture contributes to acts of plagiarism, points out that in Vietnam simply copying other people's work is not acceptable and that it is usual practice for Vietnamese students to give a full bibliography at the end of essays, but not to cite individual authors in the main body of the assignment. Vietnamese universities do not regard this as plagiarism, as all the sources featured in the assignment are mentioned in the bibliography. Many teachers in Vietnam do not require students to cite and reference lecture notes given out in class, as there is an implicit understanding of where the notes came from between teacher and student.

However, both these practices in Britain could result in the student being criticized, and probably penalized, for plagiarism.

Therefore, there are cultural differences in referencing practice for the international student to adjust to – and most do quickly if they are shown how and it is explained why. A more significant issue for international students is how to cope with the pressure of writing six or more assignments in any semester, work with others in groups, read and take notes, listen to lectures and contribute their ideas in tutorials – all in English, a language that many are still struggling to cope with.

They may have gained the requisite minimum English qualification to study in Britain, but these qualifications do not prepare many students for listening to a babble of regional British accents and understanding all the subtle nuances and by-ways of the English language. It does not help either that they have to wade through baffling jargon, pomposity and the often ludicrous 'academic-speak' in textbooks on recommended reading lists that have been written by some authors more for their academic chums than for students.

Add to this the small fortune they or their parents spend on paying for a British education, and the economic and social shame that flows from failure, then the pressure is really on them to succeed, and to succeed at any cost. Failure is not an option. They are told they should summarize or paraphrase in their own words, not copy text from books or paste in from the Internet. They may be given, if they are lucky, some practical instruction in referencing. But they are often faced with a task of paraphrasing something that they only half understand. And they have to do it in a second language, in the best English they can muster, and by tomorrow. So it is no surprise some resort to copying text and patching together copied ideas, rather than risk the shame of failure and exposure of their still partial understanding of ideas and the meanings of words: 'taking a bit here and there helps with getting the meaning across. Paraphrasing, if you are not a native speaker, is difficult' (Greek student quoted in Introna et al. 2003, p.25).

Patchwork writing

Putting the issue of plagiarism aside, many academics discourage this form of patchwork writing by arguing that the process of summarization and paraphrasing helps students to gain a deeper level of understanding about a topic. By converting the ideas into a choice of one's own words, you have to think hard about them and thus gain a deeper level of knowledge. This may be true, but some of you may not see it like this.

Students, and not just those from overseas, argue that to put together an argument by patchwork copying does require an understanding of the topic. It requires the ability to select and connect ideas, and this cannot be done successfully if the student does not have a grip on the main arguments and counter-arguments around a topic:

> If you take all the sentences/paragraphs from other authors – then you have to do the work to put it together – you have learned and need a certain understanding of the topic, it is not just blatant copying.
>
> (UK student quoted in Introna et al. 2003, p.24)

This has found some sympathy among some academics. Some commentators, notably Howard (1999) and Introna et al. (2003), have argued that patchwork writing can be viewed as a transitional writing phase for inexperienced students as they struggle to come to terms with the demands and expectations of a subject and particularly, but not exclusively, if they are trying to do this in a second language.

The entry standard for English language for international students to study in Britain tends to lie between score six and seven in the International English Language System (IELTS), which is somewhere between 'competent user' (band 6) and 'good user' (band 7) of English (Table 4.1).

So a score of 6.5 is somewhere between 'competent' and 'good'. Students in both bands can fall prone to 'misunderstandings', are still only at the stage of understanding 'fairly complex' to 'complex' language (of which there is much in education) and are in a situation that is new, rather than 'familiar'. Given this, patchwork writing can be viewed as part of this transition of developing the skill to communicate using formal language and in a detached, third-person way acceptable to the expectations of academics. But is the style of third-person writing still a valid expectation, and if so, why?

The convention of academic writing in higher education is still largely one where you are encouraged to step back from the assignment topic and look down at it, as if from afar, and to describe the scene in an objective way. In Britain, students are still largely discouraged from writing in the first person. 'I think' is discouraged, and 'It can be argued' encouraged instead (even though in reality it means the same thing). Teachers expect students to present an impression of objectivity (even though this is an illusion), where arguments can be selected to fit the chosen perspective: 'objective subjectivity', may be the best way to describe what is expected by tutors of students in academic writing.

The able, experienced student has learned the art of selecting material to suit his or her own viewpoint, but presenting it in a way that gives the impression of objectivity to the reader – thus satisfying the conventions and traditions of academic writing. The postgraduate student, and certainly one with his or her first degree experience in the UK, has usually learned how to do this. However, the undergraduate and international postgraduate student can both struggle with this, not really knowing what is expected.

This reflects an apparent contradiction: on the one hand, the promise of higher education is that you will develop your own 'independent voice' while on the other, you are expected to conform to norms of writing that seem strangely out of tune with this aim. You are expected to imitate the style of writing of the commentators you read,

Table 4.1 IELTS scores 6 and 7

Band 6: Competent user	Band 7: Good user
Has generally effective command of the language despite some inaccuracies, inappropriacies and misunderstandings. Can use and understand fairly complex language, particularly in familiar situations	Has operational command of the language, though with occasional inaccuracies, inappropriacies and misunderstandings in some situations. Generally handles complex language well and understands detailed reasoning

(Source: British Council 2006)

but these commentators are likely to have a strong command of English and have learned to present their material in a sophisticated way.

Angélil-Carter (2000) argues that permitting the use of the first person 'I' in assignments is an important way of encouraging students to present openly their own words, supported with referenced evidence. Patchwork writing can occur because students feel discouraged about expressing their own views in their own words in the more analytical parts of the assignment. Yet they run the risk in this practice of being accused of plagiarism. The exercise later in this chapter shows examples of patchwork writing that can lead students easily into trouble with their institutions.

Writing in the third person can be an entirely appropriate way of presenting information in the more descriptive and background parts of an assignment. However, the more analytical parts – where the student is expected and encouraged to weigh up arguments – can be considerably more difficult to present when writing in the third person, even for the student with a strong command of English.

Discouraging the use of the 'first person' expression in writing, particularly when engaging with the more discursive parts of an assignment, arguably encourages students to patch together the words of others in the hope of appearing objective. But endorsing a change of writing style, from third to first person, could arguably encourage students to take ownership of the material they introduce into assignments and be more forward with their own ideas. Why not test this argument out on your tutors to see what their response to it is?

One response from them might be that writing in the first person encourages opinionated responses to set questions. But arguably, writing in the first person does not necessarily equate with polemic; one's own view can be presented formally and professionally, and supported with properly cited and referenced evidence. This would be an important way of helping students find their own voice in assignments. Students could be encouraged to seek relevant material that fits the direction they wish to take in an assignment (which happens now), but then to present ideas as their own, in the first person, and in the process take responsibility for them. 'With no authorial voice', writes Angélil-Carter, 'writing is inhibited' (2000, p.128). What do you think? You are part of this debate, too.

Discouraging plagiarism

Plagiarism prevention, rather than prosecution, tends to be the approach adopted by most British universities, although some have been driven to take action to discipline, and even expel students, for worst-case plagiarism, which are usually cases involving repeated incidences of copying wholesale from texts without any attempt at acknowledgement of the original source. Attention has also turned to schools and colleges in an attempt to discourage pupils (and parents) from plagiarism, so that by the time students enter higher education they would have learned effective referencing and techniques of summary and paraphrasing.

Universities are also using software to detect where copied text has been slotted into assignments. Software, such as Turnitin and Ferret can compare submitted assignments with a database of billions of web pages and highlight passages that are directly copied. Some institutions are also encouraging students to check their assignments against the software, to highlight and change copied areas before they submit the work. This seems to be producing some positive results.

Barratt and Malcolm (2006), for example, report on a study involving 182 mainly postgraduate International Masters students on Computer Science, Automotive Engineering and Electronics courses. The students were asked to summarize a number of research papers in an essay, and their assignments were submitted to Turnitin and Ferret with a view to giving feedback on how original their words appeared to be. A threshold of 15 per cent of matching text was used, as it is inevitable that some words and sentences will recur. It was found that 41 per cent of students had submitted work that exceeded this threshold, although on closer inspection a number of these, for a variety of reasons, could not be regarded as plagiarism. However, over a quarter (26 per cent) of assignments was above the threshold, and these students were shown their work with the copied passages highlighted and given an opportunity to resubmit it. On resubmission, the incidence of plagiarism had dropped to 3 per cent overall.

Universities are also looking at the assessments they set, and making these more individual and project based, or written under supervised conditions. They are also looking more critically at the way referencing is taught, and are reinforcing the message that good referencing is 'an indication of worthy membership of the academic community' (Hart and Friesner 2004, p.93). They are also regulating their own teaching, typically by peer evaluation, so that lecturers do not implicitly promote plagiarism by giving lectures accompanied by handouts and PowerPoint slides that do not cite the sources for the ideas presented or discussed with students.

They are doing this largely because they feel that they have to and want to. They have to because the Quality Assurance Agency (QAA) – a watchdog of quality in higher education – seeks assurance from institutions that they are maintaining the quality of higher education, which will attract students, particularly those from overseas, in the first place. They want to because most academics in higher education are interested in, and proud of, their work; they want students to be stretched intellectually and to gain careers where they can take responsibility and use their talents.

If higher education is devalued by a view from the outside that the degree is not worth the paper it is printed on, then this will do no good for either the morale of teachers or your morale – and career prospects. It is likely that you recognize the importance of this debate. If high standards of integrity are expected of you – and exemplified by the conduct of your tutors – it is likely you will respond positively to this. Who, after spending thousands on a degree programme, wants a qualification that others will sneer at?

How to avoid plagiarism

So, how to avoid plagiarism?

Applying, analysing, criticizing or quoting other people's work is perfectly reasonable and acceptable providing you always:

- Attempt to summarize or restate another person's work, theories or ideas and give acknowledgement to that person. This is usually done by citing your sources and presenting a list of references

or

- by always **using quotation marks** (or indenting lengthy quotations in your text) to distinguish between the actual words of the writer and your own words. Once again, you should cite all sources and present full details of these in your list of references.

Summarizing and paraphrasing

The way to avoid accusations of plagiarism is to try to summarize or paraphrase what you read, choosing words that seem to do this best for you. You will need to ask your course tutor what style of writing is expected of you. Can you use the first person for the more analytical parts of it? If not, why not?

So what is the difference between paraphrasing and summarizing? Summarizing is about the general; paraphrasing is about the particular (Table 4.2).

Table 4.2 Summarizing and paraphrasing

Summarizing	Paraphrasing
Summarizing involves writing an account, in one's own words, of the main, broad and general meanings of a text	Paraphrasing involves close attention to a **particular section** of a text and attempting, in one's own words, to capture the essence of the original

It can be sometimes difficult, if not impossible, to avoid using some of the author's original words, particularly those that describe or label phenomena. However, you need to avoid simply copying out what the author said, word for word. Choose words that you feel give a true impression of the author's original ideas or action. There is an exercise later in the chapter that looks at the issue of paraphrasing and plagiarism. However, before you look at that, try the exercise on plagiarism awareness that follows.

Exercise

Remind yourself of the definition of plagiarism earlier in this chapter. Then look at the scenarios in Fig. 4.1 and decide whether the situation described amounts to plagiarism. Tick the appropriate column.

See the answers in Appendix 2.

1 You see a quotation in a book and copy the quotation out word for word into your assignment and do not cite the source ☐

2 You see a quotation in a book or Internet site and copy some of the words and add some of your own words and do not cite the source ☐

3 You see something on an Internet site, for example, an article from a named journal with a named author. You copy, or copy and paste, from the site into your assignment without citing the source ☐

4 You see an interesting and different way of looking at a particular subject on an Internet website. No author's name is shown. You cut and paste the idea into your assignment and do not show the source, i.e. name of website, in your assignment ☐

5 You find some interesting photos or other illustrations on a website. You copy the photos or illustrations and paste them into your assignment. You do not cite the artist, photographer or website ☐

6 You read a range of interesting summaries of different approaches to a subject on a number of Internet websites. You do not copy and paste, but you paraphrase in your own words the summaries into your assignment. You do not mention the website sources in your assignment ☐

7 You are part of a study group of four or five and you all discuss an assignment that all are required to submit individually. You all agree on the approach and arguments to use in the assignment. One of the students, with a little help from another, writes the assignment that all the members of the group submit individually ☐

8 You want to give a historical overview of something that has happened over a long period, for example, general employment trends. You read three or four general textbooks on the topic. They all say much the same thing so you summarize in your own words and do not cite the sources ☐

9 You see some statistics in a magazine that are relevant to a report you are writing. There is no author cited. You use the statistics in your assignment and do not give a source, e.g. the magazine ☐

FIGURE 4.1 Plagiarism quiz

10 You find an article summarizing a particular model, theory or practice associated with a particular theorist Mr X. It is a secondary source, which means the writer is summarizing him or herself what Mr X has said. You like this summary, as it says what you believe Mr X has accurately written. You cannot think of a better way of summarizing Mr X yourself, so you copy out this summary without referring to the secondary source author

11 Your friend is better than you at writing assignments; your strengths are with statistics and mathematics and you have always find writing reports and essays difficult. You discuss a particular assignment together and you help your friend gain a better knowledge of the subject. Your friend is grateful for making things clearer and offers to write the assignment for you both. Your friend writes the assignment and you copy it. You both submit it as an individual assignment

12 You have an assignment to write and you do the research for it. In the process of writing the assignment, a new way of looking at the subject suddenly occurs to you, which you feel is unique. You put forward this 'unique' perspective on the subject and submit the assignment. However, you discover a day or two later that someone else has already published the same idea and perspective a few years earlier

FIGURE 4.1 (contd.)

Plagiarism exercise

Is it plagiarism?

This exercise contains a number of examples of attempts to transfer the information from the original journal extract shown below into seven essay introductions. Read each example and decide whether the attempt amounts to plagiarism of the original journal article.

Original extract

For thousands of years, outsiders have regarded China as a xenophobic country. However, the stereotypes have been changing since China opened up its economy in 1979. Now, the encouragement of foreign direct investment (FDI) and international technology transfer (ITT) lies at the heart of economic relations between foreign countries and China. The international flows of capital, information and technology facilitate the economic growth of China and the influence of multinational enterprises (MNEs). The boom in FDI and ITT has brought to the fore the issue of intellectual property rights (IPRs) as a major topic in the economic development of China. Although a historical review shows that the germination of the concept of IPRs in China goes back more than 100 years, in reality no effective system of intellectual property protection (IPP) existed until very recent times.

Source: Yang and Clarke (2004, p.12).

Now comment on the following extracts from student assignments. Do they amount to plagiarism – or not?

Example 4.1

This essay is about intellectual property (IP) in general and about the situation in China today, and about China's relationship with the West in relation to this issue. For thousands of years, outsiders have regarded China as a xenophobic country. However, the stereotypes have been changing since China opened up its economy in 1979. Now, the encouragement of foreign direct investment (FDI) and international technology transfer (ITT) lies at the heart of economic relations between foreign countries and China. The international flows of capital, information and technology facilitate the economic growth of China and the influence of multinational enterprises (MNEs). The boom in FDI and ITT has brought to the fore the issue of intellectual property rights (IPRs) as a major topic in the economic development of China. Although a historical review shows that the germination of the concept of IPRs in China goes back more than 100 years, in reality no effective system of intellectual property protection (IPP) existed until very recent times.

Plagiarism?   Yes   No   Not sure

Example 4.2

This essay is about intellectual property (IP) in general and about the situation in China today, and about China's relationship with the West in relation to this issue. For thousands of years, outsiders have regarded China as a xenophobic country. However, the stereotypes have been changing since China opened up its economy in 1979. Now, the encouragement of foreign direct investment (FDI) and international technology transfer (ITT) lies at the heart of economic relations between foreign countries and China. The international flows of capital, information and technology facilitate the economic growth of China and the influence of multinational enterprises (MNEs). The boom in FDI and ITT has brought to the fore the issue of intellectual property rights (IPRs) as a major topic in the economic development of China. Although a historical review shows that the germination of the concept of IPRs in China goes back more than 100 years, in reality no effective system of intellectual property protection (IPP) existed until very recent times (Yang and Clarke 2004).

Plagiarism?   Yes   No   Not sure

Example 4.3

This essay is about intellectual property (IP) in general and about the situation in China today, and about China's relationship with the West in relation to this issue. For thousands of years, outsiders have regarded China as a xenophobic country. But since China opened up its economy in 1979, and with the encouragement of foreign direct investment (FDI) and international technology transfer (ITT), economic relations between foreign countries and China have improved. The international flows of capital, information and technology now facilitate the economic growth of China and the influence of multinational enterprises (MNEs). The boom in FDI and ITT has brought to the fore the issue of intellectual property rights (IPRs) as a major topic in the economic development of China. Although history shows that the germination of the concept of IPRs in China goes back more than 100 years, in reality no effective system of intellectual property protection (IPP) existed until very recent times.

Plagiarism?   **Yes**   **No**   **Not sure**

Example 4.4

This essay is about intellectual property (IP) in general and about the situation in China today, and about China's relationship with the West in relation to this issue. Outsiders have long regarded China as a xenophobic country. However, the stereotypes have been changing since China opened up its economy in 1979. Yang and Clarke (2004) argue that now the encouragement of foreign direct investment (FDI) and international technology transfer (ITT) lies at the heart of economic relations between foreign countries and China. They state

> The international flows of capital, information and technology facilitate the economic growth of China and the influence of multinational enterprises (MNEs). The boom in FDI and ITT has brought to the fore the issue of intellectual property rights (IPRs) as a major topic in the economic development of China (p.12).

Although a historical review shows that the germination of the concept of IPRs in China goes back more than 100 years, in reality no effective system of intellectual property protection (IPP) existed until very recent times.

Plagiarism?   **Yes**   **No**   **Not sure**

Example 4.5

This essay is about intellectual property (IP) in general and about the situation in China today, and about China's relationship with the West in relation to this issue. China has long been regarded as a closed and rather xenophobic country. But things have been changing fast since China opened up its economy in 1979. Some commentators, like Yang and Clarke (2004) argue that the encouragement of foreign direct investment (FDI) and international technology transfer (ITT) lie at the heart of economic relations between foreign countries and China. The flow of capital, information and technology between countries has pushed the economic growth of China forward. Also, the influence of multinational enterprises (MNEs) and boom in FDI and ITT has focused attention on the issue of intellectual property rights (IPRs), and this is now seen as a major topic in the economic development of China. Although the idea of IPRs in China goes back more than 100 years, in reality no effective system of intellectual property protection (IPP) existed until recently.

Plagiarism? Yes No **Not sure**

Example 4.6

This essay is about intellectual property (IP) in general and about the situation in China today, and about China's relationship with the West in relation to this issue. For centuries China has been regarded by the outside world as a rather closed and insular country. However, Yang and Clarke (2004) argue that now things are changing, and particularly so since 1979, when China decided to open up its economy. Since then, foreign direct investment (FDI) and international technology transfer (ITT) are important connecting links between China and the rest of the world. Now the flows of capital, information, technology and the influence of multinational enterprises MNEs have stimulated the Chinese economy. But these developments have also caused attention to focus on the issue of intellectual property rights (IPR). Although the concept of IPR goes back more than a hundred years, there has been no effective system of intellectual property protection (IPP) until recently.

Plagiarism? Yes No **Not sure**

Example 4.7

This essay is about intellectual property (IP) in general and about the situation in China today, and about China's relationship with the West in relation to this issue. For centuries China has been regarded by the outside world as a rather closed and xenophobic country. However things are changing. Since 1979, China has loosened and stimulated its economy by foreign direct investment (FDI), international technology transfer (ITT), and from the influence of multinational enterprises (MNEs). However, these developments have also focused attention on the issue of intellectual property rights (IPR) and until recently in China there has been no effective system of intellectual property protection (IPP).

Plagiarism? Yes No **Not sure**

See Appendix 3 for comments.

5

Referencing styles

Which reference styles predominate in Britain? • Relationship of referencing style to subject discipline • Discussion • 'Horrible hybrids'

Which referencing styles predominate in Britain?

In autumn, 2005, I attempted to gain an answer to this question by contacting a representative number of learner support units and librarians within UK universities, via discussion email sites for these practitioners, and asking them to complete an online questionnaire.

I wanted to learn:

- What referencing systems are currently used in their institutions
- What referencing systems predominated in their institutions
- What was the relationship of referencing systems to subject disciplines in their institutions.

From the total of 25 replies, 24 were from separate institutions of higher education, and one reply came from an educational research foundation.

The survey suggested that among the responding institutions five main referencing styles were to be found:

1 The author–date (Harvard) style
2 The British Standard Running-notes numerical style, including the Modern Humanities Research Association (MHRA) variant on this
3 The British Standard Numeric style, and the variants on this presented by the International Committee of Medical Journal Editors (commonly known as the 'Vancouver' style), and by the Institute of Electrical and Electronic Engineers (IEEE)
4 The American Psychological Association (APA) style
5 The Modern Languages Association (MLA) style.

Three of these, the author–date (Harvard), APA and MLA, use citations in the text that mention the name of authors or originators of sources; while the Running-notes and Numeric styles use superscript or bracketed numbers in the text that connect with footnotes or endnotes (Fig. 5.1).

It was found that the Harvard style of referencing had been adopted by nearly 80 per cent of schools and departments within the responding institutions. The range was from 40 per cent to 100 per cent, but 18 of the 25 replies indicated that Harvard had been adopted by approximately 80 per cent of the discipline areas. Two institutions had adopted Harvard for all its courses, but in the majority of institutions, although Harvard style was dominant, most of the other styles mentioned in this chapter were also in active use within relevant schools and departments.

Relationship of referencing style to subject discipline

The relationship of adopted styles to subject disciplines was a little ambiguous, with science areas and computing/information technology (IT) in particular showing the most inconsistency.

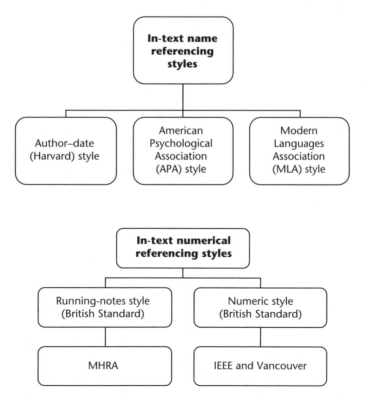

FIGURE 5.1 Flowchart of referencing styles

The author–date (Harvard) and author–page (MLA) styles were consistently linked by respondents with:

- Business and management studies
- Most social sciences (except Psychology)
- Health education
- Many of the humanities areas
- Sciences, particularly life and environmental
- Most computing and IT
- Languages.

The 'Running-notes' style (including MHRA) with:

- Law
- Humanities, particularly History, Classics, Philosophy and some English departments
- Art and Design
- Architecture
- Some social sciences.

(Computer Science was also mentioned by some respondents.)
The Numerical style with:

- Medicine and related areas (Vancouver style)
- Applied science areas
- Engineering and technology areas
- Journalism and media studies.

(Again, Computer Science was mentioned by some respondents.)
The APA style with:

- Psychology
- Some health studies areas, e.g. Occupational Therapy.

Discussion

At the time of the survey there were 325 institutions, including universities, colleges of higher education (HE) and further education colleges that offered HE courses and participated in the Universities and Colleges' Admissions Service (UCAS). So 24 replies (one from a research foundation) to the questionnaire represented only 7 per cent coverage, so the results should only be seen as a reflection of the situation in those institutions, and not as a general picture of higher education.

Nevertheless, the respondents were all in a good position to give an overview of referencing practices within their institutions, and the results were remarkably similar in both the separate waves of responses received from the librarians and learner support professionals. A similar survey in Australia in 2004 among 10 universities found that most major referencing styles were in active use, but that Harvard predominated (CSU 2004).

'Horrible hybrids'

Some respondents in the UK survey took the opportunity to comment on what they regarded as a confusion of styles prevailing in their institutions:

> The combinations of styles had, however, produced, in some instances, 'horrible hybrids' . . .

> Different lecturers recommend different styles of Harvard to their students; it is difficult to get consistency across Schools let alone the University!

> The non-Harvard system used in one of our faculties is described as MLA but uses numbered notes.

> Students who take psychology and sociology modules, usually 1st and 2nd years, do get confused between the two systems (Harvard and APA) that they are asked to use. They are very similar but the psychologists get upset if their system (APA) is not used.

> Systems running in parallel can cause confusion especially on combined courses running across two departments.

It is clear that some colleagues in library or learner support areas had tried to rationalize a confusion of referencing styles within their institution, but had found this difficult, if not impossible to achieve:

> We tried to get the university to agree to just two systems but the academics concerned were unshiftable!

Although at one institution the discussion was ongoing:

> [There is a] Referencing working group attempting to move towards an institutional policy of guidance (rather than prescription).

At two of the institutions, one referencing system had been introduced:

> It is extremely useful to have one standard for the whole institution.

Two institutions in the survey had adopted the Harvard style of referencing for all their schools or departments, although it is clear there was, and probably still is, resistance from some departments who preferred other styles:

there is an issue for us because Harvard is the approved style, but it is not the dominant style in art and design publications! I have answered the questions on what I think happens in practice, rather than the 'official position', which is that we are '100 per cent Harvard'!

It can be argued that adopting one style for the whole institution has distinct advantages, in terms of consistency, advice to students, student induction and ongoing learner support. It can, for example, help learner support, library staff and lecturers to address the 'why' and 'when' questions about referencing that trouble students the most, particularly international students. If more than one referencing system exists within an institution, the teaching or advising of mechanistic 'how to' issues can become more of a priority in learner support areas. One referencing system could, in theory anyway, lead to more unified institutional focus on the principles underpinning the use of the adopted style and make it easier for students to work out how to reference, based on a set of guidelines clearly built on one style.

However, the situation where at least two referencing styles prevail within institutions appeared to be the norm in most of the responding institutions. It is clear that particular referencing styles can become adopted by departments for historical reasons, or because of affiliation to a style guide produced by an organization representing the interests of a professional group or discipline. For example, before 1978 there were over 250 different styles of reference in scientific literature alone. To standardize referencing practice Gustavii describes how, in 1978, editors of major biomedical journals worked out a uniform referencing style: the 'Vancouver' numeric style, which is still favoured by the influential medical and related science disciplines within universities (Gustavii 2003, p.74).

Other reasons for the adoption of a particular style include gradual change over time; departments imitating departments across institutions; arbitrary past decision by someone in a department, probably now long gone; or institutional or departmental decision in an attempt to standardize practice for students.

Arguably, any difficulties this might cause could be minimized if individual schools and departments issued clear guidance to students on the 'why', 'when' and 'how' of referencing, and related and contextualized the adopted style to their own discipline areas. However, it would appear that they would also need, in parallel, to issue clear guidelines and educate their own teaching staff that all must endorse these, and not condone, or even promote, eccentric variations of their own.

What appeared to happen, however, was that because the library or learning support units had produced information that attempted to cover the variation of styles found within the responding institutions, the teaching of referencing was often also left to them as well, usually at induction, or in mainly optional learner support workshops during the year.

This led to a situation where teaching staff never really engaged with the issue, and might even condone variations on a particular 'house' style or not understand the adopted style themselves. This can happen, for example, on hybrid degrees, such as business and management studies, when academic staff from a range of subject disciplines, with different previous experiences of referencing, are brought together.

However, part of the problem is also in the lack of a real benchmark for using Harvard and both numerical styles in Britain. Although a benchmark for using these styles are the British Standard guides, these are not as detailed as the style guides issued by APA and MLA, and are limited in the range of source examples they give. British Standard recommendations are not primarily aimed at student readership, and so have been interpreted and rewritten for students by learner support staff at universities, usually librarians. This can result in a lack of consistency in referencing guides produced by institutions across Britain on the application of these styles, particularly in relation to electronic sources, and the Harvard style.

Referencing guides on Harvard and numerical styles produced by different institutions – and often within institutions – will show differences in the way different sources are presented. Indeed, the relative flexibility of interpretation it allows may be also one of the main reasons for this style's popularity, compared with the detailed prescription of APA, MLA and other referencing style guides. However, on a more negative note, it also encourages the idiosyncrasies and eccentricities of staff who feel they have the academic freedom to insist on the inclusion of little twists and flourishes of their own. As one survey respondent put it:

> From a student perspective, however . . . it would be much better if the institutional, disciplinary and other powers and communities in HE could a) come to a greater level of agreement about the most effective conventions to use; b) be more consistent in ways that these conventions are communicated to students; and c) open up the debate about the 'value' of these practices in relation to their implications for assessment, grading etc. at various 'levels' of HE study.

Not all the respondents agreed, however, with a common referencing style for institutions. A number of them argued that students could learn to adjust to a number of referencing styles, providing they understood the principles that underpin all referencing and have learned the basic format for each style.

> As long as students are encouraged to think about why the conventions have evolved (rather than just trying to follow rules without understanding them), they can usually grasp the basic features of the two main systems, and then learn to use whichever is required on their course.

In relation to this argument, the handbook produced by the MLA makes an interesting comment on the adoption of particular referencing styles by disciplines. It makes the point that referencing styles are shaped by the kinds of research and scholarship undertaken. In the sciences (and business disciplines), the author–date referencing style is often used to given prominence to the year and general timeliness and currency of the research; whereas with the humanities it is often more important to guide the reader to exactly the right author and page, so a telling detail can more easily and speedily be found (Gibaldi 2003, p.143).

The numerical-related styles of referencing are often favoured by visual disciplines, such as art and design and architecture, because they are more subtle, less intrusive and pleasing aesthetically on the page, compared with the relative 'clutter' produced by the Harvard, APA and MLA styles.

Referencing styles, therefore, can sink their roots deep into disciplines and these can prove stubborn ground in their resistance to change from university departments and disciplines. However, the problems for students can occur when they move between departments on combined studies programmes, or choose elective modules from outside their main subject area. They may have to adapt to two or more referencing styles, and this can be aggravated by teaching staff who, as noted earlier, advance their own idiosyncratic ideas about referencing practice within a particular style.

See Table 5.1 for an overview of the main features of each referencing style.

Table 5.1 Overview of main features of each referencing style

Author–date (Harvard) style
Cites name(s) of author(s) or organization, with year of publication, in the text, e.g. Handy (1995). All sources are listed alphabetically at end of an assignment and labelled 'References' or 'Bibliography'.

American Psychological Association (APA) style
Relatively small differences exist between Harvard and APA style, and in practice, they often merge into a hybrid. The main noticeable differences tend to be with citation punctuation, the way multiple authors are cited and referenced, and with referencing electronic sources.

Modern Languages Association (MLA) style
This differs from Harvard and APA in that the page number, instead of year of publication, is cited in the text, e.g. (Handy 149). The full list of references at the end of the text is also labelled 'Works cited', or 'Works consulted'. Proper words in the titles of works cited are capitalized and underlined. The last name of an author is followed by the full first name(s), for example:
Handy, Charles. *Beyond Certainty: The Changing Worlds of Organisations*. London: Hutchinson, 1995.

Running-notes style
This style uses superscript (or bracketed numbers) in the text, which connects with a reference in either footnotes or chapter endnotes. A bibliography is included at the end of the assignment, which lists all the works referred to in the notes. This system uses a different number for each reference in the text.

Numeric style
Uses bracketed (or superscript) numbers in the text that connect with a list of references at the end of the text. The same number can recur, e.g. if a source is mentioned more than once in the text.

6

Harvard style of referencing

Pros and cons of Harvard style • Examples of the Harvard style of referencing
• Harvard style in action

A benchmark for using the Harvard style of referencing in Britain is British Standard (BS) and the following BS publications: *Recommendations for references to published materials*: BS 1629:1989; *Recommendations for citing and referencing published material*: BS 5605:1990; and *Copy preparation and proof correction – part 1: Design and layout of documents*: BS5261–1:2000.

Although British Standard is mentioned by most UK universities on referencing advice booklets for students as their benchmark for Harvard, there tend to be minor variations in practice from one institution to another. British Standard recommendations are helpful for their guidelines on the sequence of source elements in a reference, and most institutions stick to these. However, there are variations between institutions in relation to stylistic presentation of sources. British Standard, for example, illustrates full references showing:

- Name (s) of authors or organizations in upper case
- Year of publication not shown in parenthesis
- Titles in italics.

However, there are institutional variations in this. Some institutions follow British Standard and illustrate names in upper case, while others do not; it is almost universal practice in UK institutions now to present author–date (Harvard) references with the year shown in parenthesis; and most institutions advise that titles can be shown in italics or underlined, with the proviso that the student adopt one practice and be consistent with its application.

This book has followed the common practice of placing the year in parenthesis for Harvard referencing and with the titles shown in italics. For Harvard and both numerical referencing styles, it presents the names of authors and others named in sources in upper case as this is in line with British Standard recommendations and can help distinguish author and other names from other elements in the source. However, students need to follow the recommendations on these stylistic matters given by their own institutions.

The earlier British Standard recommendations did not mention referencing electronic sources in much detail, but in 1997 they issued BS ISO 690–2:1997 *Information and documentation – bibliographic references – part 2: Electronic documents or parts thereof*, an international standard for referencing electronic sources. As this is useful for defining terms, but weak on examples of referencing in action, many institutions have used Li and Crane's 1996 book, *Electronic styles: a handbook for citing electronic information*, as benchmark for student advice guides produced by them on citing and referencing electronic sources. However, as this book advises on referencing in the APA style, which is close to Harvard style but with some differences, particularly in relation to electronic sources, a hybrid version of both styles can often result.

Pros and cons of Harvard style

The **pros** are:

- Most useful when all sources are printed, and these have one or more designated authors
- Easy to follow the chronological progress of a particular debate
- Easy to add or subtract in-text citations and references (particularly useful for last minute assignments!)
- Easy to learn; easy to teach
- Familiar – recognizable from many book and journal articles
- No distraction from the text to look at footnotes or endnotes.

The **cons** are:

- Less useful when citing and referencing sources without authors and/or dates, and particularly Internet references
- Awkward for citing television, radio and other audio-visual sources
- Long-winded for citing secondary sources
- In-text citations are normally counted in assignments on most degree courses, as the student takes 'ownership' of evidence cited. This can add significantly to the word count.

Harvard style: basic idea

The basic idea of the Harvard style is to:

1 Use citations (a partial reference) in the text, by citing the last name of the author(s) and the year of publication in the text of an assignment
2 List all references in full and in alphabetical order at the end of an assignment.

Using citations in the text

In the text of your assignment, you give a partial reference (called a **citation**). This is the last name of the originator, followed by the year of publication. An originator is an author or, if no named author(s), the name of an organization, newspaper, journal, etc. If there is no obvious name of an originator, the title or part of a title can be used instead.

Citing the source as you write involves giving a partial or shortened reference (last name of author(s) and year of publication) in the main body of your written assignment and then giving full details of the source in full at the end of the assignment in a 'References' or 'Bibliography' section. You can abbreviate lengthy organizational names in the citations providing you explain the citation in the full reference; see the example that follows (YHES 1998).

Example (Citations are shown in bold)

Although **Handy (1994)** has argued that education is the key to economic success for individuals, organizations and nations, a majority of adults in the UK have yet to be convinced or persuaded of this argument. In 1999 only 40 per cent of adults had participated in any sort of formal learning in the previous three years. Of these, a significant majority was from social class groups A, B and C. Only a quarter of adults from semi-skilled or unskilled work backgrounds had involved themselves in formal education **(Tuckett 1999)**. The consequences for people without qualifications who lose their jobs are often serious. A study of long-term unemployed people in Yorkshire found that 61 per cent had no educational qualifications, and a significant number of these had special learning needs **(YHES 1998)**. There would appear to be a link too, between lack of qualifications, poor health and a disengagement from participation in political or civic life, and which could aggravate the situation of unemployment for the people concerned **(Hagen 2002)**.

The full list of references at the end of the assignment for just these four citations would be in alphabetical order and look like this:

References

HAGEN, J. (2002). *Basic skills for adults*. Birmingham: The Guidance Council.

HANDY, C. (1994). *The empty raincoat*. London: Hutchinson.
TUCKETT, A. (1999). Who's learning what? *The Guardian*, 18 May 1999, p. 13.
YHES: YORKSHIRE AND HUMBER EMPLOYMENT SERVICE (1998). *Survey of clients aged 25+ unemployed for two years or more*. London: Department for Education and Employment.

Punctuation

In relation to Harvard, the BS 5261–1 advice is to 'be as simple as is consistent with clarity'(2000, p.17, 14.7), and it presents examples that show sentence stops after each distinct part of the full reference, for example:

HANDY, C. (1994). *The empty raincoat: making sense of the future*. London: Hutchinson.

For full discussion on punctuation for all referencing styles, see Chapter 9, 'Frequently asked questions', question 8.

Citations in the text

You can introduce citations into the text in a variety of ways, for example:

1 There would appear to have emerged by the end of the twentieth century two broad approaches to the management of people within organizations (Handy 1996).

This introduces a point of view and the student points to Handy as a major proponent of this perspective. The citation here is at the end of a sentence. However, this is not the only way of citing the author. The student could have started with the citation, as follows:

2 Handy (1996) argues that by the end of the twentieth century two broad approaches to the management of people within organizations had emerged.

Or, (if wanting to include Handy as an exemplar of this proposition):

3 Some commentators, for example, Handy (1996), have argued that by the end of the twentieth century two broad approaches to the management of people within organizations had emerged.

Or

4 It has been argued, (Handy 1996; see also Brown 1999 and Clark 2000), that two approaches to the management of people within organizations had emerged by the end of the twentieth century.

In the example above, a major source, Handy, has been advanced, with two (in this case, fictitious) supporting sources, which are presented in alphabetical order. Or

5 Charles Handy, among others, has argued that by the end of the twentieth century two broad approaches to the management of people within organizations could be observed (Handy 1996).

There is no one 'right' way of citing authors. It depends on the context of the sentence and the style of writing adopted at any particular point in the assignment. The important points to note are the importance of giving credit to authors who have influenced your ideas and arguments, and placing the citation in the sentence in a way that makes clear the authorship or origin of the source.

If there is no specific author name, or the term 'Anon.' is not shown in lieu of a name, look for the name of an 'originator', particularly an organizational name, in the case of websites. In printed material, if no author's name is shown, you can cite the title of the work, or an abbreviated version of this.

List references in full at the end of an assignment

In the References or Bibliography section at the end of an assignment the **basic format** for listing references in the Harvard style is shown, as follows.

- All sources are listed in alphabetical order by last name or name of originator; the citation connects with the alphabetical item in the reference.
- Where there is a named author, start with the surname/last name/family name, followed by the initials of the author's first names. Where there is more than one author, the initials of the first name of the second and subsequent writers precede the last name, for example:
  COLEMAN, A. and A. CHIVA (1991). *Coping with change – focus on retirement.* London: Health Education Authority.
- The forename(s) can be reduced to initials, as shown above, provided that the identity of the person is not obscured by doing this. It is common practice in the Harvard, APA and numerical styles to use initials only of forenames for printed material, although British Standard examples of Harvard and numerical referencing show the full forenames of originators of most audio-visual material and public performances of creative work.
- Alphabetize the prefixes Mac, Mc, and M' in that order: MacDougall, comes before McAllister, which comes before M'Cardy.
- When alphabetizing names in languages other than English, you should treat the last name in accordance with the conventions that apply in the country of origin. However, here are some recommendations for the most common European languages that are featured in citations and references:
  French: the *de* following a first name is not normally used with the last name for referencing purposes. However, there are some exceptions, as follows: when *De* is normally used or associated with the name, e.g. De Quincy; or when the last name has only one syllable, e.g. *de Gaulle*; or when the name begins with a vowel, e.g. *d'Arcy*; or when the prefixes *Du* and *Des* are applied.
  German: the prefix *von* is usually not used with the last name in references, unless it has become associated by tradition and convention with a particular person.
  Italian: Renaissance or pre-Renaissance names are cited and alphabetized by first

name, e.g. Leonardo da Vinci. Post-Renaissance and modern Italian family names are often prefixed with *da, de, del, della, di* or *d'*, which should be included in the reference, although the alphabetization should be with the last name, e.g. *De Sica*, placed in the alphabet under 'S'.

Spanish: last names should be shown in full, e.g. García Márquez; García Lorca. The prefix *Del* is capitalized and used with the last name for referencing purposes.

- If the name of author is shown as 'Anon.' this goes alphabetically into the list. If there is no author or originator's name shown, and 'Anon.' is not presented in lieu of an author's name, a title for printed material (as used as a citation) can be substituted. The first letter of the first proper title word can be the guide to placing it alphabetically in the list of references.
- If you are including several works by the same author, they are listed in chronological order, with the earliest work first.
- If you have references with the same first author, but different second and third authors, arrange these alphabetically by the surnames of these subsequent following authors.
- As stated earlier, if you do not have the name of an author, start with the name of the originator. This can be an organization name, e.g. BBC, or the name of a website, e.g. Bized.
- Author name is followed by the **year of publication**. Although British Standard does not show the year in brackets, it has become common practice now in the author–date Harvard style to do this. The year of publication should be easy to find on printed documents; just look at the printer's imprint and copyright page, which usually follows immediately after the main title page. All the information you need should be there, including name of publisher, where published, when first published and edition. Always show the edition number for the source you looked at. The edition is different from the impression or reprinted number. Look for the year of the edition and ignore the impression number years. So, 'Seventh edition by Oak Knoll in 1995. Reprinted 1997, 1998, 2000, 2002' would be shown as (1995) in your reference – you ignore the reprint years.
- However, in some older books the date of publication may be missing. In this event, put either (n.d.) or (no date). With Internet sources, look for the year the item was placed on the site, or in the absence of this, the year when the site was last updated or, if unsuccessful with either of these two, the year you looked at the information.
- This is followed by the title of the main source consulted. The main source is usually emphasized in some way, e.g. underlined or italics. The main source would be, for example, the title of a book, name of the magazine, journal or newspaper, item title from an Internet site, broadcast production source, title of video or CD-ROM, etc. Whichever mode of emphasis you choose – underlining or italics – keep it consistent throughout.
- If your source is a chapter from an edited book, you then give the name or names of the **editors** of the book, followed by the title of the edited book, underlined or in italics. To distinguish the name of the editor(s) from the writer, the initials of the editor(s) should precede the last name (see the example that follows).
- In most printed items, you would give details of the publisher. You first give the

name of the town or city where the source was published, followed by the name of the publisher.
- In the case of a journal article, you finish with the reference details of volume, edition/issue number (if shown) of the journal and the page numbers of where the article can be located within the journal.

Examples of the Harvard style of referencing

1 Book (one or more authors)

- Start your full reference with the last name of the author so it connects with the citation, then give initials of writer
- Followed by year of publication
- Followed by title of book: in italics or underlined
- Finally, the place of publication and name of publisher.

Example

In-text citation: (Wilmore 2000)
(Just cite the last name(s) of writer(s) and the year the book was published.)
Full reference:
WILMORE, G.T.D. (2000). *Alien plants of Yorkshire*. Kendall: Yorkshire Naturalists' Union.

2 Chapter from an edited book

- Start with the full reference entry with the last name of the chapter's author, followed by initials, then state year of publication
- Then give name (s) of editor(s). The last name of an editor precedes his or her initials, to distinguish editor(s) from the name of the writer of the chapter. Indicate single editor by an abbreviation: (Ed.), or editors: (Eds.)
- State full title of book – in italics or underlined. It is helpful to then give a chapter number
- Finally, give place of publication and name of publisher.

Example

In-text citation: (Nicholls 2002)
(Cite the name of the writer of the chapter or section in the edited book.)
Full reference:
NICHOLLS, G. (2002). Mentoring: the art of teaching and learning. In P. JARVIS (Ed.) *The theory and practice of teaching*, chap. 12. London: Kogan Page.

3 Referencing journal articles

- Start with the last name of the author of the article and initials of author
- Year of publication
- Title of article (this can go in inverted commas, if wished)
- Name of the journal or magazine (in italics or underlined)
- Volume number and part number (if applicable) and page numbers.

References to journal articles do not include the name of the publisher or place of publication, unless there is more than one journal with the same title, e.g. International Affairs (Moscow) and International Affairs (London).

Example

> **In-text citation:** (Bosworth and Yang 2000).
> **Reference:**
> BOSWORTH, D. and D. YANG (2000). Intellectual property law, technology flow and licensing opportunities in China. *International Business Review*, vol. 9, no. 4, pp.453–477.

The abbreviations, 'vol.' (for volume), 'no.' (for number) and 'pp' (for page numbers) can be omitted. However, for clarity and to avoid confusing the reader with a mass of consecutive numbers, they can be included. Note how, in the example above, the initials of the first author follows his last name (Bosworth, D.), but precede the second named (D.Yang). This is common practice with Harvard and both numerical referencing styles.

4 Example of referencing an electronic source

> **In-text citation:** (Dixons Group 2004)
> **Reference:**
> DIXONS GROUP PLC (2004). *Company report: profile*. [Accessed online from Financial Analysis Made Easy (FAME) database], 13 Dec. 2005.

Note: If access to the database is password protected, there is no point in giving a URL address. Web addresses are given if access to the source is freely accessible to others. More information on referencing electronic sources will come later, in Chapter 10.

Harvard style in action

The following report illustrates the Harvard style of referencing in action. It is a report that contains a range of sources, including from the Internet. Note where, when and how references are used to support evidence.

CALL CENTRES IN THE UK: IS THERE A FUTURE FOR THEM?

Introduction

This report will examine the future for call centres in Britain. It will look at current call centre work trends and conditions generally in the UK, will use the Yorkshire region of Britain as an exemplar of trends and will discuss predicted work opportunities over the next decade.

Call centres are collective forms of teleworking, where a group of people work on non-domestic premises controlled by a third party. These premises may be called 'satellite offices', 'call centres', 'computer resources centres', and may use workers employed by the parent company or may use subcontracted workers for particular tasks (Huws 1999).

> This detail contained in the last sentence of the introduction would not be generally known, so is outside of 'common knowledge'. The source, therefore, should be acknowledged, i.e. (Huws, 1999)

The rise of call centres

The growth in call centres in the West was encouraged by economic and technological factors. From the late 1970s the growth of the service sector focused the attention of large organizations on communication with customers in more cost-effective and streamlined ways. This growth of a service sector economy connected with advances in telecommunications and changes in working practices in Western companies. The logic of call centres was that a centralized approach and rationalization of organizational operations would reduce costs, while producing a standard branded image to the world. The approach naturally lent itself to large companies with large, distributed customer bases.

> The student presents a historical overview, drawn from a range of sources and where there is unlikely to be any dispute about the facts summarized. Referencing is not essential in this situation. However, if all the facts came from just one source, this should be cited and referenced.

Currently in Britain 800 000 people are employed in 4000 call centres, but it was predicted that, despite a loss of jobs to India and elsewhere, by 2005 this would have grown to a million workers (DTI 2004). As a result, there is still a future for the UK call centre sector.

> Statistics are presented, so source must be cited, i.e. DTI.

Call centres in Yorkshire

The Yorkshire region of the UK is an example of how call centres can flourish. In South Yorkshire, there has been large investment in call centre development, encouraged by EU regional development. Around 6000 operators are already employed with companies such as Ventura (3750 staff), Selflex (1000) and One-2-One (300); in Doncaster, BT Cellnet employs 900 staff at its call centre (PSU 1996).

> Statistics presented, so source must be cited, i.e. PSU.

In West Yorkshire, 25 call centres had been established in Leeds by 2000, employing around 15 000 people and occupying 10 per cent of office space available in the city. Around a third of the Leeds call centres are within traditional single company financial services and the remainder offer a range of services to their clients, including retail sales, mobile phones services and road breakdown services (*Yorkshire Post* 24.9.98. p.3.). In Bradford, by 2004, around 7000 people were employed in call centres, and this is expected to rise to 10 000 by 2007 (Bradford *Telegraph and Argus* 21.06.04. p.4).

> Here an unattributed newspaper item is cited. If there is no named writer, an in-text citation with details of newspaper, date of publication and page number is usually enough; a full reference entry is not normally required by tutors.

Work opportunities and working conditions in call centres

Studies by Huws (1993; 1996; 1999) of teleworking in Britain have described and analysed the evolution of call centre operations. Types of calls are often divided into outbound and inbound. Inbound calls are calls that are initiated by the customer to obtain information, report a malfunction or ask for help. This is substantially different from outbound calls where the agent initiates the call to a customer, mostly with the aim to sell a product or a service to that customer.

> The beginning of this section makes it clear that a number of studies by Huws over a six-year period will be the main source of evidence for the information presented.

Call centre staff are often organized in tiers, with the first tier being largely unskilled workers who are trained to resolve issues using a simple script. If the first tier is unable to resolve an issue, the issue is escalated to a more highly skilled second tier. In some cases, there may be third or higher tiers of support.

A trend originally observed in the USA is also becoming apparent in Britain: of a 'high' and a 'low' end to the services provided. The characteristics of employment at both ends of this spectrum can be summarized, as shown below:

Table 6.1 'High' and 'low' end call centres

'High end' call centre services	'Low end' call centre services
• Usually involving detailed financial services advice, information and sales • Staff recruited for their knowledge and expertise in these areas • Training of staff a high priority • Emphasis on retaining staff • Staff reasonably well paid	• Operators require little technical knowledge • Generally perform a customer service role, typically within travel, retail and leisure industries • May involve 'cold selling' • Staff not particularly well paid • Turnover of staff as high as 80 per cent

(Source: Huws 1999)

> We are reminded at the end of this boxed summary of the main source for the preceding section, i.e. Huws.

However, all is not well in call centres, particularly regarding working conditions. A report from Income Data Services (IDS 1998) found large variations in pay and work in UK call centres. This was emphasized in a 2004 report commissioned by the Health and Safety Executive that suggested some UK call centres should be compared to Victorian 'dark satanic mills'. The research found that employees at the worst call centres felt powerless and tied to their desks. Many complained that low wages, poor working conditions and repetitive tasks led to poor job satisfaction and high levels of depression (Management Issues 2005).

> Evidence is presented to support the opening sentence, i.e. IDS.
>
> Additional evidence is also cited to back up the main point of the section, i.e. Management Issues.

It would seem, from the evidence cited so far, that where the dominant focus in any call centre is on answering calls as quickly as possible, the stress levels rise. The complaints by customers about call centre services include those of the length of time in queues, automated menu systems, premium rate lines, having to 'communicate' with staff confined to scripts and the lack of continuity of contact with operators between calls.

> Note how the student starts this section by pulling together some key points from the evidence cited in the preceding paragraph.

According to a BBC website, these quality-related problems appear to have risen for a number of reasons:

- The call centre industry is unregulated and no independent body exists to represent the views of consumers.
- Call centres often try to match the number of available operators with the volume of calls coming in, but often the number of calls exceeds this, which results in long queues.
- Some call centres judge operators on the number of calls they take, and set unrealistic targets so customer service suffers.

> Important information is presented in bullet point form to enable the reader to understand why problems have occurred. The source is introduced at the start of the section and cited at the end of the list, i.e. BBC.

- Call centre operators are often given a script, which is meant to cover all possible scenarios, so are unable to give an answer to an unscripted query.
- Operators at offshore call centres do not necessarily have the knowledge of UK culture and language to answer every customer query (BBC 2004).

However, there appears, from the evidence cited so far in this section of the report, to be an increasing recognition of the need for UK call centres to improve the quality of customer experiences. For many businesses the call centres become the yardstick by which they are judged. In a competitive situation, a customer who has had a poor experience is likely to take his or her business elsewhere.

> The student takes the opportunity to summarize some key points from the sources previously cited. Therefore, there is no need to repeat the citations.

The future for call centres

At one time in the recent past, the call centre industry in Europe was dubbed a 'bubble market' after a study into the future of call centres by the London-based economic consultants, Business Strategies, warned that the growth of Internet and automatic voice response technology would make call centre operators redundant (Business Strategies 2000). Another communications company, the OTR Group, suggested around the same time that one in five jobs in all call centres in Europe would disappear over the next decade (Financial Times 1999). The increasing use of automatic voice response technology (AVR) was thought to reduce the need for direct operator interventions, and that the growth of Internet sales would reduce the number of operator–customer contacts.

> Source of the study mentioned is cited, i.e. Business Strategies, and other evidence cited to back up the opening points.

However, in recent years this prediction has been revised (Huws 1999; Business Strategies 2000). Automated voice response technology is currently unpopular with many callers, who often prefer more human interaction. In Britain, the Yorkshire and Tyneside accents are popular with callers from within the UK and from other countries, and call centres report that customers from other countries, particularly the USA, are noticeably inclined to lengthen their call times in order to engage Northern British operators in friendly discussion. British Asian call centre operators are particularly in demand to communicate with customers who speak no English. The relative low cost of commercial property and lower wages, compared with those in the South of England, is also cited as attractive factor with employers, and particularly with the public sector.

> The student makes it clear who has revised the prediction, i.e. Huws 1999, and Business Strategies 2000.

As mentioned earlier, another more serious potential threat to many UK call centre jobs comes with the increasing 'globalization' of work and where multinational companies have subcontracted work to English-speaking countries in South East Asia. In July 2003, the market intelligence company, Key Note, predicted that by 2008 the UK would lose 97 000 call centre jobs to the Indian sub continent (E-Logistics 2003). British Telecom currently has much of its data entry work done in India, and British Airways has established a call centre in Bombay to handle its bookings (The Observer 2003).

> Sources of the statistics (E-Logistics) and the example (The Observer), are cited.

It is certainly true that UK call centre jobs have been lost as employers look to cut costs and relocate overseas. However, USDAW, one of the main trade unions in the call centre industry, has drawn attention to differences in the levels of service between UK and overseas call centres. Referring to studies conducted by a research firm, ContactBabel, of 290 UK call centre directors and managers, and of 44 Indian call centre operations, they highlighted that:

> Our attention is drawn to the source for the data and information to be presented, i.e. USDAW.

- On average, UK agents answer 25 per cent more calls each hour than their Indian counterparts, and resolve 17 per cent more of these calls first time

- UK call centre workers tend to stay with their company for well over three years, while the 'burn out' rates in this £1 billion a year industry in India are extremely high, with an estimated one in three workers quitting within a year
- More than a third of callers to India have to ring back at least a second time (UK has a first-time resolution rate of over 90 per cent)
- Almost a third of Indian call centres do not measure customer satisfaction, while very few perform any proactive quality checking (USDAW 2004).

> The source (USDAW), was introduced at the start of the section and is cited at the end.

It does appear then, that the call centre industry in India appears now to be encountering some of the same problems that emerged in the West and the sector is finding it harder to retain workers as the Indian economy strengthens and career options for well-qualified workers increase. Operators working at a distance from customers are also likely to feel remote from them, physically, socially and culturally. There is no shared understanding of place and society that often underpins discussion between people from similar geographical backgrounds (The Observer 2003).

> A reputable UK Sunday newspaper, i.e. The Observer, is cited. The specific page number is given in the full reference.

The recent DTI report suggests that the expansion of call centre services in the UK is likely to be in the realm of more specialization, with UK call centre operators offering a more informed advisory and information services. UK operators are also likely to be expected to use, at least in the short to medium terms, a wider range of communication technology than operators in other countries (DTI 2004).

> Cites a UK government report (DTI). The abbreviation is explained in the full reference.

We can conclude from the evidence cited and discussed in this report that a likely scenario for the future of call centres globally is one where call centres use a mixture of Internet and operator services. The DTI estimates by 2010 that 900 million people worldwide will be using the Internet and already a quarter of UK call centres have staff dealing with email communications from customers (DTI 2004). Developments, such as computer telephony integration (CTI) and Internet provision enable call centres to diversify their products and services. Computer telephony integration enables call centres to offer support services to the online retail market. Although only a small percentage of sales in the UK are currently conducted through the Internet, this market is growing rapidly. Call centre staff will need to develop more advanced computer skills in the future, and are likely to communicate both by email and verbally with customers.

> The student attempts to pull together points emerging from the sources cited, but is careful to cite any new statistical information that is presented, i.e. DTI.

Conclusion

The future for call centres in Britain is certainly not as gloomy as predicted in the late 1990s, provided that call centres respond to the need for more personal, more responsive and bilingual modes of contact with customers. There is a particularly need in Britain to offer more specialist bilingual services to customers and particularly Asian language services in multi-ethnic areas.

> It is uncommon for citations to appear in conclusions. An exception to this rule might be if a quotation is used for final effect.

Bibliography

ASIA BUSINESS TODAY (2006). *Outsourcing: is India to be blamed? http://www.asiabusinesstoday.org/ briefings/* [Accessed 11/01/2006].

BBC (2004). Brassed-off Britain: call centres. *http://www.bbc.co.uk/bob/callcentres/* [Accessed 09/08/ 2004].

BUSINESS STRATEGIES (2000). Tomorrow's call centres: a research study. *www.business-strategies.co.uk* [Accessed 02/01/2001].

DTI: DEPARTMENT FOR TRADE AND INDUSTRY (2004) *The UK contact centre industry: a study.* London: Department for Trade and Industry.

E-LOGISTICS (2003). Call centres – an inexorable flight? *http://www.elogmag.com/magazine/29/ call-centres.shtml* [Accessed 20/6/04].

HEALTH AND SAFETY EXECUTIVE (2004). *Psychosocial working conditions in Great Britain in 2004.* London: Health and Safety Executive.

HUWS, U. (1993). *Teleworking in Britain: a report to the Employment Department.* Research Series No 18, Oct 1993. London: Department of Employment.

HUWS, U. (1996). *eWorking: an overview of the research.* London: Department of Trade and Industry.

HUWS, U. (1999). *Virtually there: the evolution of call centres.* Report: Mitel Telecom Ltd.

IDS: INCOME DATA SERVICES (1998). *www.incomesdata.co.uk/index.html* [Accessed 20/06/2004].

MANAGEMENT ISSUES (2005). Call centres are modern day satanic mills. *http://www.management-issues.com/display_page.asp?section=researchandid=1063* [Accessed 20/07/2005].

THE OBSERVER. *Bombay calling . . .* 07/12/2003, p.19.

PSU: POLICY RESEARCH UNIT (1996) *Shaping the future: an economic and labour market assessment of Yorkshire and Humberside.* Leeds Metropolitan University/ Leeds Training and Enterprise Council.

USDAW (2004). Indian vs UK call centres: new reports find faults in both. *www.publictechnology.net/modules.php?op=modloadandname=Newsandfile=articleandsid=442* [Accessed 20/06/2004].

A **bibliography** has been presented, as not all the sources listed were cited in the report. The student, however, wants to present to the tutor the totality of reading done in preparation for writing the report.

Now try the exercise that follows. It invites you to think about where to cite references in an essay on the topic of managing change.

Exercise

Now look at an example of an essay, written by a postgraduate student, that follows. The author–date (Harvard) style in-text citations have been removed. Before you start, you may want to quickly re-read Chapter 3 on **when** you should reference.

Read the following essay and mark with an **X** where you think the citations should go.

How can theories of managing change be applied in life planning? Give examples to illustrate your answer

'Change is not made without inconvenience, even from worse to better.' Johnson's observation summarizes a paradox that many people feel: the tension between remaining in a familiar state, or making a change; a change that is likely to cause some 'inconvenience', or more likely, uncertainty. Therein lies the paradox: it is tempting for many people to stay with a situation that has the comfort of familiarity, rather than risk moving into territory for them as yet uncharted. But this assumes a choice over the matter. People are often propelled unwillingly and unexpectedly into situations not of their choosing.

This essay will present and discuss some models for managing change and is aimed at people in three broad categories: first, those who exercise discretionary choice over a given life situation; second, those who are faced with choices they would prefer not to make, but nevertheless have ultimate control of the process; and third, those who have change thrust arbitrarily on them by fate in all its many forms. The examples given will be related to how practitioners charged with the responsibility of managing or supporting others facing change might support the 'change-seekers' or 'change-victims' concerned. In a business context these practitioners are likely to be members of a Human Resources team, but could also include external trainers, management or life planning consultants.

Change is not received or perceived in a homogeneous way. Gerard Egan, for example, draws a distinction between 'discretionary and non-discretionary change'. In the former, the individual has a choice about change to make and makes it willingly. The outcome may be 'inconvenient' or challenging, but the change, nevertheless, is desired and embraced. In the case of 'non-discretionary change', people are faced with situations that are deeply uncomfortable, but they stay in trouble because it is easier to do so than make the emotional effort to change. Egan traces the roots of inertia in emotional passivity, learned helplessness, disorganization or 'vicious circle' self-defeating behaviour. The 'non-discretionary' nature of change is because non-change is likely to result in the person concerned becoming ill or making others suffer. The third form of change is described by Harold Kushner in his book of the same name: *When bad things happen to good people*. These 'bad things' manifest themselves in crisis, misfortunes or traumas in all their malignant shades. These things happen because they happen – but some models of change can at least help in the understanding of process, and support for, those involved.

For those actively wanting and seeking change, Maslow's theory of Hierarchy of Needs offers an explanation as to why individuals seek transition and change in their lives. As basic and intermediate needs (food, shelter, affection) are met, aspirations rise, and people reach out to meet more intrinsic needs, for example, the chance to gain more status at work or opportunity to develop a new interest. In this situation, the 'Managing Change Approach' offers a model for plotting the stages involved. Coleman envisages six steps, including the first trigger step of *'transition'*: a sense of wanting change and being able to identify and articulate the reasons and feelings for this. This is an important first step, as it allows the decision-maker a sense of control over the process and gain 'ownership' of the idea. The decision-maker proceeds then to steps two and three: information gathering, and considering the options available. This leads to a choice (step four), action (step five) and later a process of reassessment and evaluation (step six).

For this model to succeed there are, arguably, a number of assumptions to make about the discretionary decision-makers. Veronica McGivney suggests a number of favourable determinants in adult lives that can motivate them to return to formal learning, and these can be adapted to connect with the Coleman model. The first determinant of success for the Coleman model is that the person concerned has a belief that he or she could cope with the transition and final change desired. The second is that the person concerned knows, or can find out, where to seek the information necessary to make an informed decision. The third and fourth, crucially, are that the person concerned has enough optimism about the future to contemplate change – and feels that he or she **has** some control over their life. These latter points are critical prerequisites for those plotting a life course through the Coleman model of managing change.

The Coleman model connects too, with one advanced in recent years by Bill Law: a 'Career learning theory', although Law has been at pains to point out that the theory is relevant to all life choices, not just vocationally biased ones. Law proposes a four-stage model for managing change: sensing, sifting, focusing and understanding. The first three of these connect with Coleman's middle and latter stages, although Law advances his third stage (focusing) by asserting that this is achieved by a decision-maker engaging with three specific questions: is the choice idea salient; is it valued (in terms of acceptable to self and others); and is it credible (perceived as a sensible or wise decision by self or others)? Law's fourth stage: 'understanding' is explained in terms of an individual's ability to justify overall a particular course of action chosen. This connects with Coleman's first stage, but Law pursues the issue further by arguing 'understanding' also relates to an ability to identify and explain the relationship of past events to future action, which forms the basis for sustainable action. The process of understanding is also about being able to anticipate or visualize the probabilities or consequences of actions.

Coleman's model appears to assume, while Law's is more explicit in this respect, that making choices involves a certain level of risk-taking. Law explicitly points out that action always entails risk, but that risk can be assessed so that probabilities are estimated:

> Autonomous action must involve some such visualization (whether rational or not) of 'this is what will probably happen if I do this . . .' It requires the imagination of possible selves in possible futures.

Perhaps the Coleman and Law models are at their most salient in relation to confident, intelligent people who are faced with relatively straightforward economic-related decisions: career, work, accommodation and money. But perhaps they are less applicable when considering change in the realms of human emotion? The role of practitioners however, in these discretionary choice situations can be one of 'oiling the wheels' of change for the decision-maker; this would include supplying information, listening, encouraging and generally offering support and guidance. The process of change is likely to happen without the practitioner's support, but with it change can happen often faster and more effectively.

However, a common scenario is one where a person is faced with a stark choice, particularly of the emotionally charged variety; the choice is often change or suffer. At one level there is 'choice' but, as Egan has argued, it is of the 'non-discretionary' kind. Egan has noted that people in this situation can vacillate and remain static, rather than face change.

This emotional stasis has been related by some commentators to both lack of confidence – that a particular choice path will lead to certain desirable outcomes, and pessimism about outcomes that might follow from the change. In this scenario, the 'Stages of Change' model offers a way of understanding the process of change – or a relapse back into the 'old habits'. Prochaska and Di Clemente related their model specifically to smoking, but it can be equally applicable to any pattern of behaviour rooted in addiction, habit or compulsion. In this model, the process of change begins with 'contemplation', and the notion that change is for the better. However, there can be an inner voice that warns: change is 'risky', so 'why change?' This can produce oscillation between wanting and not wanting change.

However, whatever the accelerant might prove to be, the person concerned can 'commit' and be ready for change, which propels them forward, and leads to the 'maintenance' stage of maintaining change. The new situation in time becomes the norm, but there is the possibility of relapse, and going back to the stating point of the circle.

The practitioner has a particularly key role to play in helping in the process of reflection at these different stages in the decision-maker's life. Egan suggests six ways of helping people in this situation strengthen self-efficacy to stay on track with a chosen decision. The first is to help people develop any necessary skills to succeed in the belief that self-efficacy is based on ability. The second is to offer feedback on any deficiencies in performance. This helps decision-makers avoid situations of self-delusion, where they rationalize any lapse or diversion from their original goals. The third is to help the decision-maker see how a change of behaviour or direction produces results, which connects with the fourth: about promoting others as role models of success. Steps five and six are related to reducing the anxiety faced by people overly fearful of failure: by encouragement and being generally supportive, and reminding the decision-maker of their original motivations.

The third group (the change victims) requires of practitioners the greatest level of understanding about the anguish of change that people can experience. People are often unwilling victims of change, including redundancy, sudden bereavement and financial disaster. Many of the models of change that are applicable to this situation are similar in tracing a pattern of shock, guilt, bewilderment (or anger), a search for meaning, then gradual acceptance of the change.

Some of the earliest studies that noted this pattern date back to the 1930s with studies of unemployment, particularly the experience of older workers. These noted the impact of shock on the newly unemployed, followed by an active hunt for work, during which the individual is still optimistic. But when all job-seeking efforts fail, the person becomes anxious and suffers depression, which can lead to fatalism and adaptation to a narrower state.

More recent studies have confirmed this pattern still applies today, particularly for the older worker. Two commentators both note that anger is often a feature of the response to sudden changes, as well as guilt, self-doubt and depression. The anger is of the 'why me?' variety, and when there is often no rational answer to this question depression can follow, arising from a realization of the powerlessness of individuals in the path of unstoppable forces.

There is however, a gradual acceptance of and adaptation to the situation. Alvin Toffler suggests that an ability to cope (and recover) from traumatic change depends on the relative security of other aspects of our lives. He argues that we can cope with enormous amounts of change provided at least one area of our life remains relatively stable. He suggests that there are five main 'Stability Zones':

1 **Ideas:** for example, deeply felt religious beliefs, or strong commitment to a philosophy, political ideology or cause
2 **Places:** places that individuals can relate to, on either a large scale (a country) or smaller scale, such as home, street or even office
3 **Things:** favourite, familiar, comforting possessions, and especially things related to childhood or emotional events
4 **People:** particularly valued and enduring relationships with others, especially friends
5 **Organization:** institutes, clubs or societies offering an important source of stability and focus for self-identity.

The role of the change management practitioner in the three situations outlined is to first ascertain whether the person concerned is a discretionary or non-discretionary change seeker, or third a change-victim, as each require different types of help or support. Support for the change-victim can be particularly valuable, and take the form of encouraging the individual to talk through the change experiences and to release feelings of guilt or anger. Understanding these stages can help the practitioner locate a stage the change-victim appears to be in and assist that person to explore relevant new life options and possibilities.

Bibliography

BANDURA, A. (1991). Human agency: the rhetoric and the reality. *American Psychologist*, 46, pp.157–161.

COLEMAN, A. and A. CHIVA (1991). *Coping with change – focus on retirement*. London: Health Education Authority.

EGAN, G. (1994). *The skilled helper: a problem-management approach to helping*. Belmont: Brooks/Cole Publishing Company.

HARRISON, R. (1976). The demoralizing experience of prolonged unemployment. *Department of Employment Gazette*, 84, April, pp.330–349.

KUBLER-ROSS, E. (1970). *On death and dying*. London: Tavistock Publications.

KUSHNER, H.S. (1981). *When bad things happen to good people*. London: Pan Books.

LAW, B. (1996). A career-learning theory, in A. WATTS et al., *Rethinking careers education and guidance: theory, policy and practice*. London: Routledge.

MCGIVNEY, V. (1993). *Adult learners, education and training*. London: Routledge/Open University.

MASLOW, A. (1968). *Toward a psychology of being*. New York: Van Nostrand.

PROCHASKA, J. and C. DI CLEMENTE (1984). Stages and processes of self-change of smoking: towards an integrated model of change. *Journal of Consulting and Clinical Psychology*, vol. 51 (3) pp. 390–435.

SINFIELD, A. (1985). Being out of work, in C.R. Littler (Ed.) *The experience of work*. Aldershot: Gower/Open University.

TOFFLER, A. (1970). *Future shock*. New York: Random House.

See Appendix 4 for comments on this exercise.

7

American Psychological Association (APA) and Modern Languages Association (MLA) styles

American Psychological Association (APA) style of referencing • Full reference/ bibliography detail • Examples of APA referencing • Modern Language Association of America (MLA) style of referencing • Pros and cons of the MLA style

American Psychological Association (APA) style of referencing

Many psychology departments, and psychology-related courses in the UK, require that referencing in assignments be prepared according to American Psychological Association (APA) style. This section gives you foundation information on the APA style, and Chapter 10 will present examples of references in this style. However, for more detailed guidance, and additional examples, you should consult the APA publications *Concise Rules of APA style* or the latest edition of *Publication Manual*. There are relatively small differences between the Harvard and APA styles of referencing, but students asked to use APA referencing should be aware of these.

In-text citations

Saunders et al. (2003, p.463) summarized the main differences between Harvard and APA styles of referencing in relation to citations in the text of an assignment (Table 7.1):

Table 7.1 Differences between Harvard and APA styles

Harvard style	APA	Differences
(Handy 1995)	(Handy, 1995)	Note minor difference in punctuation
(Sherman and Judkins 1995) **or** (Sherman & Judkins 1995)	(Sherman **&** Judkins, 1995)	Note minor difference in punctuation and use of ampersand '&' to connect the names. APA recommendation is to use ampersands; British Standard recommendation offers you a choice whether to use it or not.
Saunders *et al.* (2003)	(Saunders, Lewis & Thornhill, 2003)	Note punctuation, use of ampersand and use of all names in the citation for first occurrence.

With group authors, such as large organizations, government agencies and other bodies, the full official name should be presented in full in citations the first time it is used, e.g. Oxford Standard for Citation of Legal Authorities, but can be abbreviated on second and subsequent usage in the assignment, i.e. OSCOLA, although it should always be shown in full in the list of references.

Full reference/bibliography detail

Authors are listed in the references in the same way as for Harvard (see previous chapter) including the guidelines given earlier for alphabetization of names. However, there are some differences between Harvard and APA, as follow.

Capitalization and use of ampersands (&)

American Psychological Association recommendations on capitalization of titles are similar to the examples shown in British Standard, which is to capitalize only the first letter of a book or article title in the first word and the word following a colon in the title; see the following example in APA style:

Nicol, A.A.M., & Pexman, P.M. (1999). *Presenting your findings: A practical guide for creating tables*. Washington, DC: American Psychological Association.

The exception to this rule would be when naming organizations within a book title, e.g.

American Psychological Association. (2001). *Publication manual of the American Psychological Association* (5th ed.). Washington, DC: APA.

Note also with APA style that the titles of main sources are in italics, e.g. book, name of the magazine, journal or newspaper, domain name of Internet site, broadcast production source, video or CD-ROM, etc. With the Harvard style, titles can be in italics or underlined, providing this is consistent throughout.

As mentioned earlier, British Standard recommendations, on which Harvard style in Britain are based, suggest that ampersands (&) **may** replace 'and' either inside or outside the parenthesis in citations (see BS5261–1 p.16, 13.3), although students need to be consistent in this practice. However, the APA style guide shows the use of ampersands to replace 'and' in both citations and full references (Table 7.2):

Table 7.2 Use of ampersands: Harvard and APA styles

Harvard	APA
Citation: (Saunders *et al.* 2003)	**Citation:** Saunders, Lewis **&** Thornhill (2003), **or** (Saunders, Lewis **&** Thornhill, 2003)
Reference: SAUNDERS, M., P. LEWIS and A. THORNHILL (2003). *Research methods for business students.* Harlow: Prentice Hall.	**Reference:** Saunders, M., Lewis, P. **&** Thornhill, A. (2003). *Research methods for business students.* Harlow: Prentice Hall.

British Standard recommendations present names of authors in upper case in the full reference, whereas in APA style they are shown in lower case. Note how in Harvard the initials of the first name of the second and subsequent writers precede the last name, but not in the APA style, although the initials of an editor or editors precede the last name. The APA style manual also shows references with a hanging indent (indented by five spaces after the first line).

Punctuation

In practice, there is now very little difference between both styles in the way full references are punctuated; for full discussion on punctuation see Chapter 9, 'Frequently asked questions', question 8. Some examples of Harvard style in textbooks and elsewhere show minimum punctuation in references, e.g. no commas between last name and initials. However, British Standard BS 5605:1990 show examples of Harvard style with punctuation similar or identical to APA. Common practice in full references has also now merged to show the year of publication enclosed in brackets in both styles.

Examples of APA referencing

1 Book (one or more authors)

Citation: (Murray, 2005)

Reference:
Murray, R. (2005). *Writing for academic journals.* Maidenhead: Open University Press.

2 Chapter from an edited book

Citation: (Nicholls & Jarvis, 2002)
Reference:
Nicholls, G. & Jarvis, P. (2002). Teaching, learning – the changing landscape. In P. Jarvis (Ed.) *The Theory & Practice of Teaching*. London: Kogan Page.

3 Referencing journal articles

Citation: (Torrance, Thomas & Robinson, 1993).
Reference
Torrance, M., Thomas, M. & Robinson, E.J. (1993). Training in thesis writing: An evaluation of three conceptual orientations. *British Journal of Educational Psychology*, 61: 170–84.

There are, however, more noticeable differences between Harvard and APA in the way electronic sources are referenced (see Chapter 10 for more information and examples).

Modern Language Association of America (MLA) style of referencing

The Modern Language Association of America was founded in 1883 at a time when modern languages were beginning to be established in the curriculum alongside classical languages. This referencing style is still widely used in Britain on language and related studies degree courses. The MLA has developed its own style of referencing and this is outlined in their guide, *MLA Handbook for Writers of Research Papers*. Although this style of referencing also cites the name of the author or originator in the text, it differs from Harvard and APA in the following ways.

Citations

- Although the author(s) name(s) are shown in the text, this is followed by **page number**(s) (instead of year of publication), e.g. (Handy 149) with no punctuation between author's name and page number(s). Where no page number is available, just give the author's name.
- If no author name is shown, the title, or shortened version of a **title**, can be used as a citation.
- If two authors have the same name, you can add initials to distinguish between them in the text, e.g. (K. Smith 53).
- When summarizing an author's ideas made over a number of different pages, this can be done within brackets, as follows (Handy 29, 67, 113).
- If you cite two or more works by the same author, you can include a full, shortened or abbreviated title, depending on its length e.g. (Handy, Beyond Certainty 44–45),

or refer to the specific title in the text of your assignment, e.g. Handy, in 'Beyond Certainty', asserts that . . . (44).

References (or works cited)

- The full list of references at the end of the text is also labelled and presented in a different way to Harvard and APA. It is labelled **Works cited** (equivalent to 'References'), or **Works consulted** (equivalent to 'Bibliography'), and the second and subsequent lines of a reference entry are indented by five spaces (a hanging indent), with double spacing between lines. Sources in Works Cited are listed alphabetically, but with regards to works consulted, MLA allows for either one list of sources in alphabetical order, or sources divided into sections and items alphabetized in each. For example, a works consulted list might be divided into primary and secondary sources, or arranged by subject matter, or different types of source, e.g. books, journals, websites.
- The last name of a single author, or lead author, is followed by his or her full first name(s), and not just the initial letters of these. However, this is reversed if two or three authors are listed. With second and third authors, the first names precede the last; see examples below:

1   Gibaldi, Joseph. <u>MLA Handbook for Writers of Research Papers</u>, Sixth Edition. New York: MLA, 2003.
2   Loach, Ken. (Director) and Sally Hibbin (Producer). <u>Raining Stones.</u> DVD. London: Channel Four Television (FilmFour), 1993.

- If the first name of the writer is not shown on the title page of books or other sources, then just their initials can be used instead. For example, some writers deliberately use their initials in their writing, e.g. A.J. Cronin; T.S. Eliot. However, the MLA handbook (2003, p.48) suggests that you may include first names if you feel the additional information would be helpful, in the following way: Rowling, J[oanne] K[athleen]; as the example shows, the remainder of the name is enclosed in squared brackets.
- The same rules featured earlier in the Harvard style, applying to alphabetization of names, including treatment of non-English names, is applicable also to MLA style.
- After the first works cited entry for this author, the name can be replaced by three hyphens and a stop for other sources by the same author, e.g.
   Handy, Charles. <u>Beyond Certainty: the Changing Worlds of Organisations.</u> London: Hutchinson, 1995.
   —. <u>The Future of Work.</u> Oxford: Blackwell, 1985.
- The MLA Handbook encourages students to 'avoid ambiguity' by underlining main source titles (p.94), rather than italicizing them (see examples above), and to use double quotation marks around titles of articles from the main source (see the 'Referencing a chapter from an edited book' example).
- In the title, first letter in each word is capitalized.
- The publisher's name can be shortened, e.g. W.W. Norton can be shortened to Norton. If the publisher's name is commonly abbreviated, or the abbreviations are likely to be familiar with the readership, they can be used instead of the full title, e.g. MLA, BBC, etc.

- The year of publication usually comes last in the full reference, unless page numbers and essential additional bibliographic information is included, for example, supplementary information about a multivolume work, such as number of volumes, and the dates between which the volumes were published, e.g.:

> Durant, Will, and Ariel Durant. <u>The Age of Voltaire</u>. New York: Simon, 1965. Vol. 9 of *The Story of Civilisation*. 11 vols. 1935–75. (taken from MLA 169)

Additional examples of MLA style references

Referencing a chapter from an edited book

Citation: (Segalen 51)
Reference:
Segalen, Martine. "The Household at Work". <u>The Experience of Work.</u> Ed. Craig Littler. Aldershot: Gower, 1985. 50–71.

The title of the chapter is placed within double inverted commas; 'Ed' is an abbreviation for 'Editor'; the reference ends with details of page numbers of the chapter in the book.

Referencing an article in a journal

Citation: (Murray: 229)
Reference:
Murray, Rowena. "Writing Development for Lecturers Moving from Further to Higher Education". <u>Journal of Further and Higher Education,</u> 26. 3 (2002): 229–39.

The numbers refer to **volume** 26 of the journal, **issue** 3, the year (enclosed in brackets for a scholarly journal) and finally, the page numbers are shown.

Electronic sources

Citation: (Dixons)
If there is no page number to quote, just cite the name of the author or, as in this case, the name of an organization: the originator of the data concerned.
Reference:
Dixons Group PLC. "Company Report: Profile". <u>Financial Analysis Made Easy (FAME)</u> online database, 13 Dec. 2005.

The item is presented within double inverted commas, while the main source (the FAME database) is underlined; the date the information is retrieved from the database completes the reference. In this online example, the URL address is not shown, as the FAME database is password restricted, and so there is no point in giving a URL address that cannot be publicly accessed. More examples of MLA references, including electronic sources, can be found in Chapter ten.

Pros and cons of the MLA style

The **pros** are:

- Helps the reader to find a specific piece of evidence easily in a printed source, particularly in a large-scale work or multi-paged newspaper.

The **cons** are:

- Like Harvard and APA styles, it works less satisfactorily with non-printed sources and can be numerically messy when citing an author or number of authors in the same citation, e.g. 'Huws has argued (1993: 45; 1996: 23–30; 1999: 33–35) that . . .' or 'Commentators on this topic, notably Levin: 93; Raimes: 75–103; Gibaldi: 144, concur that . . .'.

8

Numerical referencing styles

Running-notes styles of referencing • Numeric referencing style

In Britain, there are two main numerical referencing styles, although there are variants within both of these:

1 Numerical referencing linked to footnotes, or end-of-chapter notes. British Standard refers to this as 'Running-notes' style.
2 Numerical referencing, which is linked to a final list of sources. British Standard refers to this as the 'Numeric system' of referencing.

1 Running-notes styles of referencing

The main guidelines for referencing in the Running-notes style are found in British Standard Institution (BS) guidelines, *Recommendations for citing and referencing published material*, BS 5605. The Running-notes style of referencing, as shown in British Standard, uses a superscript (or bracketed) number in the text, for example, in superscript:[1] for the first source,[2] for the second source, and so on. The Modern Humanities Research Association (MHRA) also practises this method of referencing, and MHRA style is still applied in arts and humanities disciplines within higher education in Britain. There are some differences in the way references are presented in both, and students who are asked specifically to follow MHRA style guidelines need to be aware of these differences and should consult the MHRA style guide, *A handbook for authors, editors and writers of thesis*. This type of referencing is also known, but mainly outside Britain, as the 'Chicago', 'Turabian', 'Oxford' or 'Cambridge' style.

This system uses a different number for each note or reference in the text each time it is cited. One source may have many different numbers attached to it, depending on how often it is cited in the assignment.

These numbers connect with citations at the bottom of the page (footnotes), or at the end of the assignment, headed 'Endnotes' or 'Notes'. Both methods are usually acceptable and most university departments allow you to choose which to use, providing you are consistent and do not 'mix and match'. The full reference details of sources are shown against the numbers in the numerical order they appear in your assignment.

A full list of sources, in alphabetical order, usually titled 'Bibliography', normally appears at the end, as this is a way of bringing together all the sources referred to in the assignment.

Pros and cons of the Running-notes style of referencing

The **pros** are:

- There is a long tradition of using footnotes in essays, which, arguably, gives a dignified presence to their appearance in essays and imparts an air of authority, and credibility to the evidence presented. The long history and authority of footnotes can lead to a spirited defence of its continuation in the face of the march of the author–date (Harvard) style across higher education in Britain (see Grafton 1997).
- This referencing style can be used for both authorial notes and to cite sources. Page numbers can be included in these footnotes or endnotes, so the text of your assignment remains uncluttered with source names, dates and page numbers. It is also particularly useful for referencing secondary sources, as details of both secondary and primary source can be given in the notes, rather than in the text.
- The reader can also immediately identify the source on the same page it is mentioned without having to turn to the references or bibliography. Grafton (1997) argues that the use of footnotes enables writers: '. . . to make their texts not monologues but conversations, in which modern scholars, their predecessors, and the subjects all take part' (p.226). They serve, therefore, as an opportunity for the writer to add authorial asides away from the main text. Although footnotes can be used within the author–date (Harvard) and related styles, their use within this style is not always encouraged by tutors, who, in the face of marking a hundred or more scripts, would prefer to zip through the text, without pausing to read too many footnote comments.

The **cons** are:

- In mechanical terms, the main disadvantage of the style is that it can be awkward for a student to format last minute additions and changes, although referencing management software has helped to reduce the problems this once caused.
- Students also need to take care when placing numbers in the text, to ensure it is clear to the reader what source is referred to. Thompson (2005) gives an example of how this can type of referencing ambiguity can occur, with an extract from a student assignment:

> **Example of referencing ambiguity**
>
> These factors (various health, alcohol and drug-related issues), among others, contribute to the lower life expectancy of Aboriginal people (*sic*) to non-Aboriginal people. For males it is 56.9 to 75, respectively. For females, 61.7 to 81.1. **10** Other contributing factors include homicide/purposefully inflicted injury. Aboriginal people 677.1 per 100,000, compared to 28.8.
> Health problems can also be linked to other social problems. The majority of the Indigenous community deemed their housing inappropriate by those living in them 'usually because the dwelling needed repair or did not have enough bedrooms'. **11**
>
> **10** COUNCIL FOR ABORIGINAL RECONCILIATION; Overcoming Disadvantage (2000). Pg. 1–18
> **11** 1994 Aboriginal and Torres Strait Islander Survey, Year Book, Australia, 1996 (ABS Catalogue No. 1301.0).
>
> (Reproduced with permission)

In the example it is not clear if the second paragraph is a continuation of the one preceding it, or whether an additional reference was necessary. If it was from the same source as shown in the footnote, item 10, the student could have given it a number, 11, and in the footnotes stated 'Ibid.' and given the page number (see 'Abbreviations' later in this chapter for an explanation of this).

- But, at another more ideological level, footnotes have been seen by some commentators as supporting poor writing, and more to do with presenting an academic style than with effective communication. Bulley (2006), for example, accuses many academics of poor writing styles: 'A complex style, full of abstraction and footnotes, is the consequence of a misguided desire to appear scholarly . . . the best academic works have always been written plainly and simply' (p.14).
- Some readers also find footnotes distracting from the text. Grafton, citing Hilbert (1989), quotes Noel Coward in his remark that 'having to read a footnote resembles having to go downstairs to answer the door in the midst of making love' (Grafton 1997, p.70 fn.16).

Guidelines for Running-notes styles of referencing

The following extract from an essay demonstrates the Running-notes style of referencing, following British Standard recommendations, and how it is particularly useful for dealing with secondary sources – see reference 2 in the footnote:

This willingness to listen, negotiate, and respond to adult learners is, however, more related to empathy, than 'charisma', a term used by Jarvis[11] to describe the characteristics of inspirational teachers. However, the use of this term: 'charisma', because of the connotations of magnetism or aura that flow from it, may be an attribute hard for many teachers to attain. Empathy with the learner, on the other hand, is attainable by the majority of teachers and in the longer term is, arguably, more durable and appreciated by a wider range of students.

As emphasised earlier, empathy involves listening, negotiation, treating others equally and attempting to equalise the power relationship that can exist between teachers and students. It also requires teachers to be honest with students and to give something of themselves to their students. They need to give this essence of self, paradoxically, in both a humble and bold way. Richard Hoggart asserts that all teachers should be wary of charismatic 'show off' displays, and compares the approach to a 'Pied Piper of Hamlet' teaching style. He points out that shiny-eyed devotion from a class, because of peacock teaching styles, can be addictive for the teacher. But this could also be perceived as an abuse of power, particularly when vulnerable and suggestible adults are involved. He encourages tutors to strive toward assisting students to stand on their own feet and *'be critical or . . . ironic about us and towards us.'*[12]

[11] Jarvis, P. Teaching styles and teaching methods. In P. Jarvis (Ed.) *The theory & practice of teaching.* London: Kogan Page. 2002, pp.22–30.

[12] Hoggart, R. The role of the teacher. Originally published in J. Rogers (Ed.), Teaching on equal terms, BBC Publications, 1969, and cited in Rogers, J. *Adults learning.* 3rd edition. Milton Keynes: Open University Press, 1989, p.81.

As stated earlier, at the end of the essay you are normally also expected to list in a Bibliography all the works referred to in your notes, as well as other works you consulted in preparation for the assignment. Some example references, showing differences between British Standard and MHRA styles, are shown below.

Example of a book written by a single author

British Standard examples show name of author in upper case. With MHRA style, the form recommended is to show the full name of the author, with first name preceding the last, to indent the second line onward of the full reference by five points and to include the place, name of the publisher and year of publication in parenthesis, concluding with page number, if applicable.

The MHRA style also tends to favour commas to separate parts of a reference, ending with a stop. With MHRA, for books in English, the first letter of principal words throughout the title is capitalized, plus the first letter of words after any colon in the title (see Table 8.1). For titles in other languages, follow the way the title is presented on the book, or conform to any known referencing guidelines for the language in question. In addition:

Table 8.1 Single author

British Standard	MHRA
GRAFTON, A. *The footnote: a curious history.* Cambridge, MA: Harvard University Press, 1997. p.71	Anthony Grafton, *The Footnote: A Curious History* (Cambridge, MA: Harvard University Press, 1997), p.71.

- The main source can be in italics or underlined in British Standard, although always italicized for MHRA
- Unless page numbers are shown, the year of publication is the last item in the entry for both British Standard and MHRA styles
- With MHRA, the second and subsequent lines of a full reference entry are indented by five points (a hanging indent).

Example of a chapter from an edited book

British Standard examples of numerical style show names of authors and editors in upper case (Table 8.2). Note how the names are used in full in the MHRA style, and the names of the editors are preceded by the abbreviation for editor. The title of the article is also emphasized with inverted commas. Note that the main source, in both examples, is the book in which the chapter appeared, so the book title is italicized or underlined.

Example of an article in a journal

The title of the journal is the main source, so this is the element in the reference that is italicized or underlined (always italicized with MHRA).

For citing multiple authors, see Chapter 9, 'Frequently asked questions', question 6.

Note how the word, volume and the abbreviation, 'pp' (page numbers), are omitted from MHRA; their omission is optional with British Standard (Table 8.3). However, with MHRA, if you wanted to refer to a specific page number, you could finish with the page number last, prefixed with a 'p' (see 'Example of an Internet source', Table 8.4).

Table 8.2 Edited book

British Standard	MHRA
COLLIN, A. Human resource management in Context. In *Human resource management: a contemporary perspective*. I. BEARDWELL and L. HOLDEN (Eds.). London: Pitman Publishing, 1994, pp. 29–68.	Audrey Collin, 'Human Resource Management in Context', in *Human Resource Management: A Contemporary Perspective*, Ed. by Ian Beardwell and Len Holden. (London: Pitman Publishing, 1994), pp. 29–68.

Table 8.3 Example of an article in a journal

British Standard	MHRA
DELLAVALLE, R.P. et al. Going, going, gone: lost Internet references. *Science*, 2003, vol.302, pp.787–788	R.P. Dellavalle and others, 'Going, Going, Gone: Lost Internet References', *Science*, 302, (2003) 787–788.

Table 8.4 Example of an Internet source

British Standard	MHRA
MEREDITH, S. and T. ENDICOTT. *The Oxford standard for citation of legal authorities*, 2005. p. 17. Available at http://denning.law.ox.ac.uk/ published/oscola.shtml [Accessed 26/04/2006].	Sandra Meredith and Timothy Endicott, *The Oxford Standard for Citation of Legal Authorities*, (2005) <http:// denning.law.ox.ac.uk/published/oscola.shtml> [Accessed 26/04/2006] (p.17).

Table 8.5 Abbreviations

Ibid.	(*Ibidem*) Meaning: in the same book, chapter, passage, etc. and in the previous reference. If used, you should always give the relevant page numbers
Op. cit.	(*Opere citato*) Meaning: in the work quoted. This is used for a further reference to a source previously cited, but not the one immediately preceding it. If you use it, give some means of identifying the previous reference, such as author's name and date of publication;
Loc. cit.	(*Loco citato*) Meaning: in the same place in a work previously cited, i.e. a reference to the same work, the same volume or same page.

Abbreviations

As noted earlier, this referencing style uses a different number for each source in the text. So, the same source used in an assignment at a number of different points will have more than one number allocated to it. Therefore, to save you having to keep repeating the same full reference information in your footnotes or endnotes, abbreviations (Table 8.5) are used to link the references.

Grafton (1997, p.235) in a footnote ending to his book, retells a story appearing in the *New Yorker* in 1996, when singer Harry Belafonte, in search of self-improvement, went into a library with a long list of books to borrow. However, the librarian, who wanted him to cut down on the number of books, challenged him. Taken aback, Belafonte replied testily, 'I can make it very easy. Just give me everything you've got by Ibid.'.

Examples of these abbreviations and how they might appear in a bibliography

1. ALI, L. and S. GRAHAM. *The counselling approach to careers guidance.* S. LENDRUM (Ed.). London: Routledge. 1996.
2. PARSLOE, E. and M. WRAY. *Coaching and mentoring.* London: Kogan Page, 2000.
3. Ibid. p.71.
4. ALI, L and S.GRAHAM. op. cit. p.85.
5. PARSLOE, E. and M. WRAY. loc. cit.

2 Numeric referencing style

The Numeric referencing style uses a bracketed (or superscript) number in the text, which connects with list of references at the end of the text. If brackets are used to enclose numbers, you can use either square [ ] or curved () brackets, providing you are consistent. What makes it different from the Running-notes style of referencing is that the same number can be repeated, for example, if a source is mentioned more than once in the same assignment. A number in the text of your assignment will, therefore, connect with the same number in your final list of references. Your tutors may also require you to include a bibliography, which would list additional sources consulted, but not directly referred to in the text.

There are three variants of this style in use in Britain:

1 The bracketed numbered referencing examples presented by **British Standard** (BS) in BS guides: (BS) BS1629:1989 (*References to published material*) and BS6505:1990 (*Citing and referencing published material*).
2 **Vancouver style**, as outlined by the International Committee of Medical Journal Editors (ICMJE), in their guide *International Committee of Medical Journal Editors uniform requirements for manuscripts submitted to biomedical journals: sample references*.
3 The **Institute of Electrical and Electronics Engineers** (IEEE) also make recommendations on referencing using this style of referencing. These recommendations are adopted by many electrical engineering and related disciplines in the UK. The IEEE produce an information sheet for authors: *IEEE transactions, journals, and letters: information for authors* via their website, although many university libraries produce information sheets on IEEE for their engineering students.

The advantage of this referencing style generally is that only one number is used per source or note and therefore there is no need to use the abbreviations ibid., op. cit. or loc. cit., as is the case with the Running-notes style. If you want to refer to the same source on a number of occasions in the same assignment, but to different pages, you can add the relevant page numbers to the bracketed source reference numbers, e.g. (2: 47) or (2: 47–55).

There are only small differences between the three variants of this referencing style in relation to printed material, although the differences with electronic sources are more marked. The differences with printed sources relate to punctuation and order of elements. Also, titles in the Vancouver style are not italicized or underlined. Nevertheless, students asked to adopt one of these variants need to be aware of the differences; see the following examples.

Book reference

Note minor differences in punctuation, and lack of italicization of title in the Vancouver style example (Table 8.6).

Table 8.6 Book

Vancouver	British Standard	IEEE
Torrieri D. Principles of secure communication systems, 2nd ed. Dedham: MA: Artech House; 1992.	Torrieri, D. *Principles of secure communication systems*, 2nd ed. Dedham: MA: Artech House, 1992.	D. Torrieri, *Principles of secure communication systems*, 2nd ed. Dedham: MA: Artech House, 1992.

Journal reference

Note differences in punctuation, the discretionary use of 'et al.' in the British Standard example, and the quotation marks around the title of the article in the IEEE example (Table 8.7).

Table 8.7 Journal

Vancouver	British Standard	IEEE
Lee C, Eden M, Unser M. High-quality image resizing using oblique projection operators, IEEE. Trans. Image Processing, 1998; 7; May, 679–692.	Lee, C. et al. High-quality image resizing using oblique projection operators, *IEEE. Trans. Image Processing*, vol.7, pp.679–692, May 1998.	C.Lee, M.Eden, and M.Unser, "High-quality image resizing using oblique projection operators", *IEEE. Trans.Image Processing*, vol.7, pp.679–692, May 1998.

Internet reference

You will note with the Vancouver style reference, a wider range of information is included. It starts with the name of the Institute, which is followed by the title of the page and its location (homepage on the Internet). It then includes the place of 'publication' (New Jersey) and publishers name (The Institute). It gives the date the site was visited (cited 2006 Oct. 16), includes the screen title (About the IEEE) and finishes with the URL address (see Table 8.8).

Table 8.8 Internet

Vancouver	British Standard	IEEE
IEEE [homepage on the Internet]. New Jersey: The Institute. 2006. [cited 2006 Oct 16]. About the IEEE; Available from: http://www.ieee.org/portal/site	IEEE. *IEEE Homepage*. Available: http://www.ieee.org/portal/site [Accessed 16 Oct. 2006].	IEEE (2006). *IEEE Homepage*. Available: http://www.ieee.org/portal/site

The IEEE guidelines for referencing electronic information are different from the style recommenced for printed sources and are adapted from both APA referencing style and guidelines from the International Standards Organization (ISO). Unlike printed titles, online titles are not shown in inverted commas, and the punctuation is different. It is not necessary to give the date the information was accessed or retrieved; note the differences between the British Standard and IEEE example in Table 8.9.

Table 8.9 Internet differences

British Standard	IEEE
RONALD, K. et al. Observations of dynamic behaviour in an electron cyclotron maser oscillator. *Journal of Physics, D: Applied Physics*, 7 Feb. 2001, vol. 34, no. 3, L17–22. Available at http://www.iop.org/EJ/article/0022–3727/34/3/104/ d103I4.html [Accessed 16 Aug. 2006].	K. Ronald, A. W. Cross, A. D. R. Phelps and W. He (2001, Feb). Observations of dynamic behaviour in an electron cyclotron maser oscillator. *Journal of Physics, D: Applied. Physics*. [Online]. 34 (3), L17–L22. Available at http://www.iop.org/EJ/article/0022–3727/34/3/104/d103I4.html

Example of an extract from an essay

The following brief extract from a student essay demonstrates how this referencing style works.

Transition and change: the terms are often used interchangeably, and indeed there is a sense of both movement and alteration conveyed in both meanings: from one state of existence to another, or transition. Hopson, Scally and Stafford highlight the movement element implicit in transition, and see it both as a 'passage' (journey) that will last a certain 'period' (of time) and within that time something happens: 'one style is developing into another' (1). So, common within these definitions, is an overall sense that a transition is a cognitive 'journey' of indeterminate length at the end of which change occurs.

However, Bridges (2) argues that 'change' refers to the context or situation itself, whereas 'transition' is aligned to the emotional processes associated with the situational or structural change. Bridges identifies three phases of transition, or emotional change: letting go; passing through 'the neutral zone' (when emotional realignments take place); and emergence into a new situation, when every ending is a beginning.

References

The references are entered at the end of the assignment in the numerical order they appeared (and not in alphabetical order). This is how they would appear in each of the three variants of this referencing style:

British Standard

1. HOPSON, B., M. SCALLY and K. STAFFORD. *Transitions: the challenge of change.* Didcot: Mercury, 1992. p.11.

Alternatively, you could also have put:

1. HOPSON, B. et al. *Transitions: the challenge of change.* Didcot: Mercury, 1992. p.11.

(See Chapter 9, 'Frequently asked questions', question 6, on how to reference multiple authors.)

2. BRIDGES, W. *Managing transitions: making the most of change.* London: Nicholas Brealey, 2003.

Vancouver

1. Hopson B, Scally M, Stafford K. Transitions: the challenge of change. Didcot: Mercury; 1992. p.11.
2. Bridges W. Managing transitions: making the most of change. London: Nicholas Brealey, 2003.

IEEE

1. B. Hobson, M. Scally and K. Stafford. *Managing transitions: making the most of change.* London: Nicholas Brealey, 2003.
2. W. Bridges. *Managing transitions: making the most of change.* London: Nicholas Brealey, 2003.

9

Frequently asked questions

Answers to 15 frequently asked questions

This chapter presents a range of questions that students most frequently ask about referencing. The questions are, as follows:

1 What is the difference between references and a bibliography?
2 When should I use page numbers in my in-text citations?
3 Secondary referencing: the author of the book I read mentions another author. I want to refer to this other author. How do I reference this?
4 How do I cite and reference books or other sources from an author that has been published more than once in the same year?
5 How do I cite in my assignment where an author has written different books, but has made similar points in each?
6 Referencing multiple sources: how do I cite and reference works written and edited by more than one author?
7 I read a book in my own (non-English) language. Do I give you an English translation of the title in the full reference?
8 What punctuation and capitalization style should I use in referencing?
9 The source has no date. How can I reference this?
10 Can I use abbreviations in references?
11 I have noticed that some writers cite more than one author occasionally in support of a particular argument or point of view. When and why should I do this?
12 Are quotations and all the author–date or page citations in the text counted in the word count?
13 How do I cite sources where no author's name is shown?

14 How do I cite sources that are recorded on microfiche/microfilm/microform?
15 I have noticed that both parenthesis () and squared brackets [ ] are sometimes used in references. Why is this?

1 What is the difference between references and a bibliography?

This issue was also discussed at the start of chapter three, but here is a summary of the differences. **References** (or 'Works cited' in the MLA style) are the items you have read and specifically referred to (or cited) in your assignment.

A **Bibliography** (or 'Works consulted' in the MLA style) is a list of everything you consulted in preparation for writing an assignment, whether or not you referred specifically to it in the assignment. A bibliography will, therefore, normally contain sources that you have cited in the assignment **and** those you found to be influential, but decided not to cite. A bibliography can give a tutor an overview of which authors have influenced your ideas and arguments, even if you do not specifically refer to them. You would normally only have one listed, headed 'References' (Works cited) **or** 'Bibliography' (Works consulted), unless your tutor has asked you to provide both.

2 When should I use page numbers in my in-text citations?

Only the MLA style of referencing shows page numbers as an integral part of the citation. With the other referencing systems, the following comments apply.

Single topic books

Many single subject books have a main or dominant message, perspective or argument that forms the essential core or essence of the book. Authors build their arguments around these cores by presenting evidence and examples to back up their perspectives or by challenging counter-arguments. If you wish to offer evidence in your assignment that summarizes these essential core perspectives, then a page number is not necessary. You could, though, include a chapter number if you wanted to isolate a particular feature of the core perspective.

However, if you use and include a quotation from the book, you will need to include a page number in the citation, as shown here using the Harvard style:

Ron Todd of the Transport and General Workers' Union commented, 'we've got three million on the dole and another 23 million scared to death' (quoted by Bratton 1992, p.70).

You can also include a page number in the citation, if you are referring to some specific detail that is secondary or incidental to the book's core point or perspective and which would be hard to find without a page number. These might include, for example:

- Statistics
- Illustrative examples
- Author comments not directly related to the main topic
- Definitions.

You would also give a page number if you are using the book as a **secondary source** – see 'Frequently asked questions', question 3.

Other books and sources

The same comments for books on a single topic apply for other sources. If the reader will struggle to find precisely what you looked at without the benefit of page numbers in the citation, then include them. If it is an Internet source, your full reference will include the complete URL address to enable the reader to go straight to the text that you looked at, or will include search terms to lead the reader from an opening page to the source. You may need, however, to include a section or paragraph sub-heading if the section that encompasses the evidence is a lengthy one.

3 The author of the book I read mentions another author. I want to refer to this other author. How do I reference this?

This is called secondary referencing. Typically, you will be reading a chapter in a book and the author will mention an interesting piece of research done by someone else, or provide a useful fact for your assignment, then give a citation, naming another writer or writers.

You have two choices in this situation. You can find and read the source mentioned yourself and check out the accuracy of the summary given by the secondary source author – this is the recommended option. You can refer directly to this author, as you have then read the source yourself.

However, there are circumstances when it would be appropriate to use the secondary source:

- If you find it difficult to find or gain access to the primary source
- If you are confident the secondary source author is reliable and accurate in the way he or she has summarized, paraphrased or quoted the original author
- If you do not need to go into any great depth of analysis on what the primary author has written.

For example, in the book *Licensed to Work* by Barrie Sherman and Phil Judkins (1995), there is a reference to another writer, Ivan Illich, who refers to 'shadow work': tasks in society that were once the responsibility of extended families and close communities.

If the Sherman and Judkins book was used as a secondary source, your **citation** must make this clear. So, within the author–date (Harvard) referencing systems you could write:

Ivan Illich (1981), as summarized by Sherman and Judkins (1995, p.121), has suggested that 'shadow work', a term he coined, which means . . . .

or

Illich (1981) has coined the term 'shadow work', meaning the tasks in society that were once the responsibility of extended families and close communities (in Sherman and Judkins 1995, p.121).

or

Sherman and Judkins in their book (1995, p.121) refer to the work of Ivan Illich (1981), who coined the term 'shadow work' as being . . . .

Within the **Harvard and APA styles**, it is only necessary to give details of the source you looked at. So your full reference would be for the item you looked at:

SHERMAN, B. and JUDKINS, P. (1995). *Licensed to Work*. London: Cassell.

If anyone wanted to read Ivan Illich's book to pursue in more depth the point he makes, they could look at *Licensed to Work* and find the full reference details there.

However, with the **MLA style**, you can use the term 'qtd. in' (for 'quoted in'), followed by the author or originator name of the source you looked at, e.g. (qtd. in Raimes 78). But like the Harvard and APA styles, you would only reference the source you looked at in your list of works cited.

However, with both the numerical styles of referencing, your tutors may want you to present full information about both sources, as footnotes and endnotes are useful for containing this additional information. For example, with the Running-notes referencing style, your footnote on a secondary source, as shown earlier, could look like this:

Hoggart, R. 'The role of the teacher'. Originally published in J.Rogers (Ed.), *Teaching on equal terms*, BBC Publications, 1969, and cited in J. Rogers, *Adults learning*. 3rd edition. Milton Keynes: Open University Press, 1989, p.81.

4 How do I cite and reference books or other sources from an author that has published more than once in the same year?

Within the author–date **Harvard and APA styles** you use letters a, b, c and onward in your citations to differentiate between the different sources, for example:

> The term 'communication apprehension' was coined by James McCroskey (1976a) and is defined as . . . .

Later in the assignment you might want to refer to the same author, writing in a different source published in the same year, for example:

> Studies suggest that high CA can impact on a person's behaviour, relationships, the perceptions of others, occupational choice and employment opportunities and education (McCroskey 1976b; McCroskey and Richmond 1979 . . . .

In the references/bibliography, you would then link the two different sources to the citation (as shown here in the Harvard style):

> McCROSKEY, J. C. (1976a). The effects of communication apprehension on non-verbal behavior. *Communication quarterly*, vol. 24, pp.39–44.
> McCROSKEY, J. C. (1976b). The problems of communication apprehension in the classroom. *Speech communication journal*, vol. 4, pp.1–12.

Within the author–page **MLA style**, you can (a) either make it clear in your text which book or other source you are referring to; or (b) give a shortened version of the title in a parenthetical citation, e.g.

> (a) McCroskey, in his book 'Problems of Communication Apprehension in the Classroom', argued that . . . (45)
> or
> (b) (McCroskey, Problems 45)

With both numerical styles of referencing, there is less of a problem. With the **Running-notes** referencing style you allocate a different number to each source cited and link these with footnotes and endnotes. With the **Numeric** style of referencing, you allocate a number to the source in question, repeat this number in the text each time you refer to the source, and link the number with the full reference detail at the end of the assignment.

5 How do I cite in my assignment where an author has written different books, but has made similar points in each?

With the author–date **Harvard and APA** styles you might on occasions want to refer to two or more books that an author has written in a single citation – as the author may have presented the same argument on more than one occasion. You can cite the author with the earlier works listed first, e.g. (Handy 1984; 1994; 1997). These are then listed in chronological order in your full list of references, each separated with a semicolon.

With the author–page **MLA** style, if the points made by the author are at the core of the book, i.e. a central recurring theme, it might be easier to refer to the author and years in the text, e.g.:

Handy has argued over nearly twenty years that . . . .

You could then list the sources you have in mind, along with the sources you specifically cite, in a list at the end labelled 'Works consulted', which, like 'Bibliography', indicates that the list of sources is not confined to just those specifically cited in the text. If you did need to refer to specific page numbers, these could be linked to a title or shortened version of book titles concerned, for example:

Handy has argued for over nearly twenty years that . . . (see Future of Work:34; Empty Raincoat: 45; Hungry Spirit: 55).

With the numerical styles of referencing, a specific number can be allocated to each of the sources, e.g.:

Running-notes: 'Handy has argued over nearly twenty years **13, 14, 15**, that . . . .'
The footnotes would show the respective sources:

13. HANDY, C. *The future of work*. Oxford: Blackwell, 1984.
14. ibid. *The empty raincoat: making sense of the future*. London: Hutchinson. 1994.
15. ibid. *The hungry spirit: beyond capitalism; a quest for purpose in the modern world*. London: Hutchinson, 1997.

A **Bibliography**, at the end of the assignment, would also list all sources consulted, including the sources shown in the footnotes.
Numeric: 'Handy has argued over nearly twenty years **(1, 2, 3)** that . . .'
The same sources, as shown in the Running-notes example, would appear in the **References** at the end of the assignment:

1 HANDY, C. *The future of work*. Oxford: Blackwell, 1984.

2 HANDY, C. *The empty raincoat: making sense of the future*. London: Hutchinson. 1994.

3 HANDY, C. *The hungry spirit: beyond capitalism; a quest for purpose in the modern world*. London: Hutchinson, 1997.

Your tutor may also want you to include a bibliography, which will include all sources consulted in preparation for the assignment, included those cited in the text.

6 Referencing multiple sources: how do I cite and reference works written and edited by more than one author?

This depends on the style of referencing. A distinction also needs to be made between what happens in the in-text citation and in the full reference.

Harvard and British Standard numerical styles

In the citation: if a document has one or two authors, both their names should be given in the citation. If there are **more than two** (or three in the case of MHRA style), the name of the first should always be given, but the names of the others may be omitted and replaced by the term 'et al.' (meaning, 'and others'), e.g. *Burchell* et al. 1999 (BS5261–1:2000).

   In the full reference: In British Standard BS 5261–1 (2000) the recommendation is that when a publication is by two authors, the surnames of both should be shown in the reference list or bibliography. When there are three or more authors, the names of all may be given, or the name of the first author only, followed by 'et al.', 'and others' or 'and (specific number) others'.

   So although the first two names should be cited in the text of your assignment, in the full reference it is discretionary whether you add names beyond the first. You may find, however, that institutions often recommend or stipulate in their own referencing guides that up to three authors are listed, and that 'et al.' is only used to substitute beyond the first author if four or more are shown. You need, therefore, to follow your institutional guidelines.

   If you use more than one author's name in the full reference, the initials of second or more authors precede their last names; see example below:

MERRITT, F.S., M.K. LOFTIN, and J.T. RICKETTS (1995). *Merritt's standard handbook of civil engineering*. 4th ed. [CD-ROM]. New York: McGraw Hill.

You could have substituted 'et al.' for the second and third authors, if you preferred. However, as stated earlier, you need to be consistent in what you do.

Vancouver Numeric and IEEE

In the full reference the first six authors are listed, thereafter you can add 'et al.' after the sixth author.

MHRA

In the reference the names of up to three authors should be given in full. For works by more than three authors, the name of only the first should be given, followed by 'and others' (and not 'et al.').

APA style

In the APA citations:

- When a work has two authors, both names should be cited each time the source is mentioned in the text.
- When a work has three to five authors, all of them should be cited the first time the source is mentioned. In subsequent citations only the last name of the first (lead) author is mentioned, followed by et al. (not italicized, and with a stop after 'al', plus the year of publication, e.g. Saunders et al. (2003).
- If the citation is used again in the same assignment, the year can be omitted, e.g. Saunders et al.
- If you have two or more different sources, but with the same lead author, cite the last names of as many of the subsequent authors to distinguish the sources from each other, followed by a comma and 'et al.'.
- If a work has six or more authors, you should cite only the last name of the first author followed by et al. and the year.

In the full APA reference:

- The full name information of the first six authors should be given, but then use 'et al.' for the remaining names.

MLA style

In the MLA citation:

- For a work with up to three authors, include all the names in the in-text citation. For a work with **four** or more authors, use only the first author's name followed by 'et al.'.

In the full MLA reference:

- Give names of the three authors in the order in which they appear on the title page, but put the last name first for the first named author only, e.g. Brown, Jim, Timothy Edwards and Mary Lacy.

- When the work has more than three authors, you can use 'et al.' to replace all the author names, except the first.

See Table 9.1 for a summary of the above.

Table 9.1 Summary

Harvard and British Standard Numerical styles	**Citations:** Cite first two names in full; you can substitute three or more authors for 'et al.' **Full reference:** You can substitute names beyond the first with 'et al.' (but abide by institutional guidelines that differ on this)
Vancouver Numeric and IEEE	First six authors are listed, thereafter you can add 'et al.' after the sixth author
MHRA	Names of up to three authors should be given in full. Over three authors, the name of only the first should be given, followed by 'and others' (and not 'et al.')
APA	**Citations:** • **One or two authors:** always give names for one or both throughout the assignment • **Three to five authors:** give their names the first time mentioned; thereafter use 'et al.' to substitute • **Six or more authors:** just use the first named and substitute 'et al.' for remainder **Full reference:** First six names are listed; 'et al.' to represent the others
MLA	**Citations:** Cite first three names; if more than three, use first name and substitute 'et al.' for rest **Full reference:** If more than three authors, you can substitute 'et al.' after the first

7 I read a book in my own (non-English) language. Do I give you an English translation of the title in the full reference?

You should give details of the source you looked at, which will include the title and author, in the language concerned.

However, it is accepted practice to add an English translation [in square brackets] immediately after the title, particularly if the book was originally published in non-European characters, e.g. Chinese, Arabic and Japanese.

In addition, if the book has also been translated from the original language, the name of the translator should be shown.

British Standard (1989: 6.2) gives an example of this:

GORKI, Maxim. *Delo Artamonovykh* [The Artamonovs]. Translated from the Russian by Alec Brown. London: Folio Society, 1955.

8 What punctuation and capitalization style should I use in referencing?

Punctuation

In all referencing styles, except IEEE and MHRA, stops are usually shown after each integral part of the full reference. In relation to Harvard and both numerical styles of referencing, the BS 5261–1 advice is to 'be as simple as is consistent with clarity' (2000, p.17, 14.7) and it presents examples that show sentence stops after each distinct part of the reference, e.g.:

> HANDY, C. (1994). *The empty raincoat: making sense of the future.* London: Hutchinson.

Capitalization

All referencing styles except MHRA and MLA show all words in the titles of full references, in lower case, apart from the first letters of titles and names of people, organizations and places. British Standard recommend that capitals are limited to proper names, e.g. Victoria, Essex, Britain; this would include the names of journals, magazines, newspapers, films and works of art referenced in the text.

However, you may find institutional variations on this and it is important that you adhere to the referencing style guidelines issued by your institution. Students on science and technology related courses, for instance, are often required to start the main source title in a reference with a capital letter, but then to use lower case for remaining words, as this tends to be in line with referencing styles found in professional journals; for example (in the Harvard style):

> ASHBY, M.F. and K. JOHNSON. (2002). *Materials and design: the art and science of material selection in mechanical design.* Oxford: Butterworth Heinemann.

However, students on other courses, and using the Harvard style referencing, may be advised to start each proper word in the title with a capital letter. This tends to reflect referencing styles in journals for disciplines in these areas, and is an example of how British Standard guidelines merge with other practices to produce hybrids.

As mentioned earlier, the APA style guide shows the capitalization of the first letter of a book or article title in the first word, and the word following a colon in the title; for example:

> Torrance, M., Thomas, G. & Robinson, E.J. (1991). Strategies for answering

examination essay questions: Is it helpful to write a plan? *British Journal of Educational Psychology*, vol. 61, pp.46–54.

The exception to this first rule would be when naming organizations within a book title, e.g.:

American Psychological Association. (2001). *Publication manual of the American Psychological Association* (5th ed.). Washington, DC: APA.

9 The source has no date. How can I reference this?

Older books may not show a date of publication. In that event, state 'no date' in your citation and in the reference, or use an abbreviation, 'n.d.'. You may find other sources, e.g. videos, without apparent production dates, so 'no date' or the same abbreviation can be used with other undated sources.

10 Can I use abbreviations in references?

Abbreviations in the text of assignments are not generally encouraged by tutors, except in scientific and technical writing, in tables, graphs and charts, and in relation to the terms 'ibid.', 'op. cit.' and 'loc. cit.', discussed in Chapter 8 (see 'Running-notes style of referencing'). However, in footnotes and in lists of references or bibliographies they can be used, although clarity always takes precedence over brevity in references. You should use a full word if the abbreviation might confuse readers.

British Standard guidelines, the MLA *Handbook for Writers of Research Papers* and APA style guide all give advice on abbreviations commonly found and acceptable within full references. However, Table 9.2 shows a common list of abbreviations found in most styles of referencing; MLA referencing style exceptions are shown.

Table 9.2 Common list of abbreviations

Term	Abbreviation
abbreviated/abbreviation	abbr.
abstract	abs.
adapted	adapt.
bibliography	bibliogr. (MLA: bibliog.)
compact disc read-only	CD-ROM
cassette	cas.
chapter	ch. or chap.
circa	c. or ca.
Department of . . .	Dept. of . . .

diagram	diagr.
disk	dk.
edition	ed.
(Revised edition)	Rev. edn.
Second edition etc.	2nd ed.
Editor (s)	Ed (s)
electronic mail	e-mail
figure	fig.
folio	fol.
from	fr.
index	ind.
Number/number	No./no.
no date	n.d.
opus (work)	op.
page	p.
pages	pp.
paragraph	par.
part	pt. or part (in music)
plate (as in photographic) or plural	pl.
record(ed)	rec.
series	ser.
summary	sum.
supplement	suppl. (MLA: supp.)
table	tab.
Technical Report	Tech. Rep.
track	tr.
tome	t.
variant	var.
volume	vol.

Abbreviating months

For Harvard, MLA and numerical styles, the months of the year in full reference can be abbreviated, except May, June and July. The APA style shows all the months of the year spelt in full.

11 I have noticed that some writers cite more than one author occasionally in support of a particular argument or point of view. When and why should I do this?

A number of authors can be cited in support of particularly key or important points that you want to make, or to support contentious statements or arguments presented by others. An example was given earlier in the book to illustrate this:

As the behavioural response of communication apprehension (CA) is to avoid or discourage interaction with others it is not surprising that CA has been linked to feelings of loneliness, isolation, low self esteem and the inability to discuss personal problems with managers or others (Daly and Stafford 1984; McCroskey et al 1977; McCroskey and Richmond 1987; Richmond 1984; Scott and Rockwell 1997).

Multiple sources can add emphasis to a specific point – particularly if it is a central one for your assignment, or is the subject of ongoing debate. As stated earlier, you should be careful not to take this practice to ludicrous proportions, and citing five or six authors is a suggested maximum for this practice; see also 'Frequently asked questions', question 12, for other reasons to discourage overuse of multiple citations.

12 Are quotations and all the author–date or page citations in the text counted in the assignment word count?

Normally, yes, although check with your institution on this, as some courses may have decided differently. The general view is that, if you include quotations in your assignment you take 'ownership' of them. You have decided to include quotations for emphasis or to make a particular point, so normally you must include them in your word count, unless your tutor indicates otherwise.

In addition, author–date or author–page citations in the text, e.g. (Handy 1994), are also usually included in the word count on most courses, although footnotes, endnotes and the references, bibliography or works-cited lists are normally excluded from the word count.

13 How do I cite sources where no author's name is shown?

Books

If a book has no author or editor name shown on the title page, you can cite and reference by starting with the title and list the source alphabetically, but ignore any prefix article words: 'The', 'An', 'A'. 'The Hobbit', for example, would be listed under 'H'. However, if the book shows 'Anonymous' or 'Anon.' on the title page, against the author, this can be cited and referenced as such, but only in these circumstances.

Magazine/journals/newspapers

If no author's name is shown, British Standard recommends citing and starting the reference within the Harvard and British Standard numerical styles with the 'originator's' name, e.g. the name of the newspaper. With MLA and APA styles, cite the title, and start the full references or bibliography by letter of alphabet of first significant starting word in the title, again ignoring any article word, e.g. 'The', 'An', 'A'.

Internet sources

- **Never** put a www address as a citation in the text.
- **Never** put the name of a search tool or engine, e.g. 'Google'.

If no author's name is shown, look for the name of an organization that produced the source, or, failing that, the name of the host site, e.g. (Business World 2006) to cite, and this title will connect with your full reference entry.

The **MLA** recommend, however, within this style, to cite and begin the 'Works cited' entry with the title of the document if the author's name is absent. This could be shortened if it is lengthy. For more information and examples on referencing electronic sources, see Chapter 10.

14 How do I cite sources that are recorded on microfiche/microfilm/microform?

Sources that have been photographed and stored on microfilm are referenced as for the original item, e.g. book, journal, map, etc. (see examples in Chapter 10).

15 I have noticed that both parenthesis () and squared brackets [] are sometimes used in full references. Why is this?

Although British Standard does not show the year in brackets, it has become an accepted hybrid practice in Harvard style referencing to enclose the year of publication within round brackets in line with the APA style, e.g. Hardy, T. (1887). *The Woodlanders*. However, whenever you add information that does not appear in the original source, and which is necessary for identification purposes, this should be enclosed in square brackets.

Example (Harvard):

HARDY, T. (1887). *The Woodlanders*. [Online]. (Ed.) M. MONCUR. The Literature Page. Available at http://www.literaturepage.com/read/the-woodlanders.html [Accessed 25 July 2006].

The information about the type of source [Online] and the date when the student found it on the Internet [Accessed] is additional information to help the reader understand the type of source and currency of the information, so is contained within squared brackets.

10

Referencing in action: example references

Examples of references for 19 types of sources

In this chapter comparative reference examples of the four most common referencing styles in Britain are presented. These styles are Harvard, APA, MLA, and the two British Standard numerical styles, which can be combined in the full reference.

Section	Type of source
A	Books
B	Pamphlets, booklets and brochures
C	Journals, magazines and newspapers
D	Occasional papers and reports
E	UK Government publications (non-parliamentary)
F	UK parliamentary publications
G	Legal documents
H	Standards and patents
I	Course manuals and lecture notes
J	Unpublished work
K	Cartographic material: maps and atlases
L	Graphs and charts
M	Visual art and graphics
N	Audio–visual sources
O	Public performances and events (including theatre, dance, music, talks)
P	Referencing course lectures
Q	Interviews and discussions, including telephone conversations
R	Miscellaneous sources
S	Referencing electronic sources

A Books

A book can be a hardback or paperback (or 'soft cover') publication on any subject, with one or more authors and/or editors. The order in which bibliographic elements appear depends on the referencing style, but the following should be included, if applicable.

- **Name(s) of author(s) or originator(s).** If 'Anon.' (anonymous) is shown specifically on the title page, then this should be stated in the full reference entry, but only when this happens. If no author name is given (and 'Anon.' is not shown), you can start with the first proper word of the title.
- **The year of publication.** If no year shown, state 'no date' or 'n.d'., and it may be appropriate to give an approximate indication of when the book was published. This can be done by stating 'circa', or 'c.', and an idea of the period, e.g. 'circa 1920', or 'c.1920'.
- **Main title of the book**, in italics or underlined.
- **Title of a chapter** in an edited collection. This may be contained within single or double inverted commas, depending on referencing style.
- **Name (s) of editor(s)**, if applicable, and indicated as 'Ed'. or 'Eds.'.
- **State edition**, but only if it is not the first edition. This is usually abbreviated to 'ed'.
- **Place of publication and publisher.** The place of publication is the town or city where the publisher is located. If the publisher is outside the UK, state the country, then the town or city, unless this is obvious from the name of the city.
- **Page number or other numeration**, if applicable. The abbreviation 'p.' or 'pp.' can be used for all styles, except MLA.

A1 Book: single author

Table 10.A1 Book: single author	
Harvard KOTRE, J. (1984). *Outliving the self: generativity and the interpretation of lives*. Baltimore: Johns Hopkins University Press.	**APA** Kotre, J. (1984). *Outliving the self: Generativity and the interpretation of lives*. Baltimore: Johns Hopkins University Press
MLA Kotre, John. <u>Outliving the Self: Generativity and the Interpretation of Lives</u>. Baltimore: Hopkins, 1984.	**Numerical** KOTRE, J. *Outliving the self: generativity and the interpretation of lives*. Baltimore: Johns Hopkins University Press, 1984.

A2 Book: two or more authors

(Also see 'Frequently asked questions', question 6.)

Table 10.A2 Book: two or more authors

Harvard	APA
SAUNDERS, M. et al. (2003). *Research methods for business students*. Harlow: Prentice Hall.	Saunders, M., Lewis, P. & Thornhill, A. (2003). *Research methods for business students*. Harlow: Prentice Hall.
MLA	**Numerical**
Saunders, Mark, Philip Lewis and Adrian Thornhill. Research Methods for Business Students. Harlow: Prentice Hall, 2003.	SAUNDERS, M. et al. *Research methods for business students*. Harlow: Prentice Hall, 2003.

A3 Edited book

Table 10.A3 Edited book

Harvard	APA
MCGINTY, J. and T. WILLIAMS (Eds.) (2001). *Regional trends 36*. London: Stationery Office.	McGinty, J. & Williams, T. (Eds.) (2001). *Regional trends 36*. London: Stationery Office.
MLA	**Numerical**
McGinty, Jon & Tricia Williams, Eds. Regional Trends 36. London: Stationery Office, 2001.	MCGINTY, J. and T. WILLIAMS (Eds.) *Regional trends 36*. London: Stationery Office, 2001.

A4 Edited collections of articles (sometimes called 'readers')

It is the title of the book that is underlined or set in italics, not the chapter.

Table 10.A4 Edited collections of articles

Harvard	APA
NORTH, D. et al. (1983). Monitoring industrial change at the local level: some comments on methods and data sources. In M. HEALEY (Ed.) *Urban and regional industrial research: the changing UK data base*. Norwich: Geo Books, pp.111–29.	North, D., Leigh, R. & Gough, J. (1983). Monitoring industrial change at the local level: Some comments on methods and data sources. In M. Healey (Ed.) *Urban and regional industrial research: The changing UK data base*, pp.111–29. Norwich: Geo Books.
MLA	**Numerical**
North, David, Roger Leigh and Jamie Gough. "Monitoring Industrial Change at the Local level: Some Comments on Methods and Data Sources". In M. Healey (Ed.) Urban and Regional Industrial Research: The Changing UK Data Base. Norwich: Geo Books, 1983. 111–29.	NORTH, D. et al. Monitoring industrial change at the local level: some comments on methods and data sources. In M. HEALEY (Ed.) *Urban and regional industrial research: the changing UK data base*. Norwich: Geo Books, pp.111–29, 1983.

A5 Book published by an agency or organization (no specific named author)

The group that produced the book is the originator, so this takes first position in the reference.

Table 10.A5 Book published by an agency or organization (no specific named author)

Harvard	APA
AMERICAN PSYCHOLOGICAL ASSOCIATION (2005). *Concise rules of APA style*. Washington, DC: American Psychological Association.	American Psychological Association (2005). *Concise rules of APA style*. Washington, DC: as author. (If publisher same as author, put 'as author')
MLA	**Numcriool**
American Psychological Association. <u>Concise Rules of APA Style</u>. Washington, DC: APA, 2005.	AMERICAN PSYCHOLOGICAL ASSOCIATION. *Concise rules of APA style*. Washington, DC: American Psychological Association, 2005.

A6 Translated book

Include name of translator, date of publication of source and date of publication of original work.

Table 10.A6 Translated book

Harvard	APA
TURGENEV, I. (1972). *Spring torrents*. (L. Schapiro. Trans.). London: Eyre Methuen. (Original work published 1873).	Turgenev, I. (1972). *Spring torrents*. (L. Schapiro. Trans.). London: Eyre Methuen. (Original work published 1873).
MLA	**Numerical**
Turgenev, Ivan. <u>Spring Torrents</u>. Trans. L. Schapiro. London: Methuen. 1972. Trans. of original work published 1873.	TURGENEV, I. *Spring torrents*. (L. Schapiro. Trans.). London: Eyre Methuen 1972. (Original work published 1873).

A7 Book in a series

Show both the author(s) and editor(s) names. State if the editor is the series editor (Series Ed.) or volume editor: (Vol. Ed.). If both are shown, list series editor first and volume editor second. Note how the initials (or first name with MLA) precede the last name of the editor.

Table 10.A7 Book in series

Harvard	APA
PINES, J. (1997). Localization of cell cycle regulators by immuno-fluorescence. In W. D. DUNPHY (Vol. Ed.) *Methods in Enzymology, vol. 283: cell cycle control*. New York: Academic Press, pp.99–113.	Pines, J. (1997). Localization of cell cycle regulators by immuno-fluorescence. In W. D. Dunphy (Vol. Ed.) *Methods in Enzymology*, (Vol. 283): *Cell cycle control* (pp.99–113). New York: Academic Press.

(Cont.)

MLA	Numerical
Pines, Jonathan. "Localization of Cell Cycle Regulators by Immuno-Fluorescence". <u>Methods in Enzymology: Vol. 283, Cell Cycle Control</u>. Vol. Ed. William D. Dunphy. New York: Acad. Press, 1997. 99–113.	PINES, J. Localization of cell cycle regulators by immuno-fluorescence. In W. D. DUNPHY (Vol. Ed.) *Methods in Enzymology: vol. 283, cell cycle control*. New York: Academic Press, pp.99–113, 1997.

A8 Multivolume work

Give full information on the name(s) of writers of the chapters cited or editor(s) names, plus full information of the main title and volume title of the work concerned. You may also need to add page numbers to isolate a particular section of the chapter.

Table 10.A8 Multivolume work

Harvard	APA
Tsien, T.H. (1985). Paper and printing. Vol. V (1). J. Needham (Ser. Ed.) (1954–1998). *Science and civilisation in China*. Cambridge: Cambridge Univ. Press, pp.32–39.	Tsien, T.H. (1985). [Paper and printing]. Vol. (1). In J. Needham (Ser. Ed.) (1954–1998). *Science & civilisation in China*. (pp.32–39). Cambridge: Cambridge Univ. Press. (If the volume has its own title, as shown above, put this in brackets before the main title of the work).
MLA	**Numerical**
Tsien, Tsuen-Hsuin. "Paper and printing". Vol. V (1) (1954–1998). Joseph Needham (Ser. Ed.). <u>Science and Civilisation in China</u>. Cambridge: Camb. Univ. Press, 1985. 32–39.	Tsien, T.H. Paper and printing. Vol. V (1). J. Needham (Ser. Ed.) (1954–1998). *Science and civilisation in China*. Cambridge: Cambridge Univ. Press, pp.32–39, 1985.

A9 Encyclopedia

It is unlikely that the name of an individual writer or contributor will be shown, but if a name is given then start with this: last name first, then the initials of the writer. However, if no writer's name is shown, start with the title of entry. For well-known general encyclopedias, you can omit the place of publication and name of publisher, but if in doubt, include it.

Table 10.A9 Encyclopedia

Harvard	APA
Goshen. (1975). *New Encyclopaedia Britannica*. Vol. 4. p.642.	Goshen (1975) in *New Encyclopaedia Britannica*. Vol. 4, p.642.
MLA	**Numerical**
"Goshen". <u>New Encyclopaedia Britannica</u>. Vol. 4. 1975. 642.	Goshen. *New Encyclopaedia Britannica*. Vol. 4, p.642, 1975.

A10 Other reference books

If no author is shown for an individual entry, or for the book as a whole, start with:

- the title of the reference book, if referring generally to the book (see example i);
- or title of entry, if that is more relevant to the particular evidence presented in your assignment (see example ii).

Do not cite or reference the name of an editor for a reference work.

Table 10.A10i Other reference books

Harvard	APA
Directory of management consultants and professional service firms in the UK (2004), 15th ed. Centre for Management Creativity. Peterborough: Kennedy Information Inc. p.220.	*Directory of management consultants & professional service firms in the UK* (2004), 15th ed. (p.220). Centre for Management Creativity. Peterborough: Kennedy Information Inc.
MLA	**Numerical**
Directory of Management Consultants and Professional Service Firms in the UK. 15th ed. Centre for Management Creativity. Peterborough: Kennedy, 2004.	*Directory of management consultants and professional service firms in the UK* 15th ed. Centre for Management Creativity. Peterborough: Kennedy Information Inc. p.220, 2004.

Table 10.A10ii Other reference books

Harvard	APA
'Everything has an end'. (1992). *The concise Oxford dictionary of proverbs*. 2nd ed. Oxford: Oxford University Press, p.82.	'Everything has an end'. (1992). *The concise Oxford dictionary of proverbs*. 2nd ed. (p.82). Oxford: Oxford University Press.
MLA	**Numerical**
"Everything has an end". The Concise Oxford Dictionary of Proverbs. 2nd ed. Oxford: OUP, 1992.	'Everything has an end'. *The concise Oxford dictionary of proverbs*. 2nd ed. Oxford: Oxford University Press, 1992, p.82.

A11 Dictionary

If the author (not editor) is shown on the title page, start with this, if not start with the title of the dictionary. If the dictionary has been revised by another writer, then name this person, as shown in the example below.

Table 10.A11 Dictionary

Harvard	APA
BLOM, E. (1988) *The new Everyman dictionary of Music* 6th ed. Revised by D. CUMMINS. London: J.M. Dent.	Blom, E. (1988) *The new Everyman dictionary of music* (6th ed.) Revised by D. Cummins. London: J.M. Dent.

(Cont.)

MLA	Numerical
Blom, Eric. <u>The New Everyman Dictionary of Music</u>. 6th ed. Rev. David Cummins. London: Dent, 1988.	BLOM, E. *The new Everyman dictionary of Music* 6th ed. Revised by D. CUMMINS, London: J.M. Dent, 1988.

A12 Republished book, including book-club or paperback reprint

State both the year and publisher information of the republished book, and the publication year and publisher of the original version.

Table 10.A12 Republished book

Harvard	APA
MASTERS, J. (1970). *Fourteen Eighteen*. London: Corgi (originally published by Michael Joseph 1965).	Masters, J. (1970). *Fourteen eighteen*. London: Corgi (originally published by Michael Joseph 1965).
MLA	**Numerical**
Masters, John. <u>Fourteen Eighteen</u>. London: Joseph: 1965. London: Corgi, 1970.	MASTERS, J. *Fourteen Eighteen*. London: 1970 Corgi (originally published by Michael Joseph 1965).

If the book you are looking at was originally issued under a different title, give the new title first and publication details, and then state 'Reprint of . . .', followed by the original title and original year of publication.

B Pamphlets, booklets and brochures

Pamphlet: a short essay, composition or treatise on a subject, usually printed in paperback.

Booklet: a publication with a limited number of pages, usually printed in paperback on a non-fiction subject.

Brochure: a publication, usually printed in paperback, promoting or advertising a product or service.

What to include in the reference:

- Name s) of author(s) or originator(s). If no author's name is shown, either start with the name of the organization producing the booklet, or if that is not obvious, the title of it (see example B3)
- Year of publication, and edition, if applicable
- Title, in italics or underlined
- Editor(s), if applicable: (indicated Ed./Eds.)

- Place of publication and publisher
- Page number or other numeration, if applicable.

B1 Pamphlet

Table 10.B1 Pamphlet

Harvard	APA
STEFF, B. (1977). *My dearest acquaintance: a biographical sketch of Mary and Henry Webb.* Ludlow: The King's Bookshop.	Steff, B. (1977). *My dearest acquaintance: A biographical sketch of Mary & Henry Webb.* Ludlow: The King's Bookshop.
MLA	**Numerical**
Steff, Bernard. <u>My Dearest Acquaintance: A Biographical Sketch of Mary and Henry Webb</u>. Ludlow: The King's Bookshop, 1977.	STEFF, B. *My dearest acquaintance: a biographical sketch of Mary and Henry Webb.* Ludlow: The King's Bookshop, 1977.

B2 Booklet

Table 10.B2 Booklet

Harvard	APA
HANDS, T. (1992). *Thomas Hardy and Stinsford Church: a brief companion for the visitor.* Stinsford Parochial Church Council.	Hands, T. (1992). *Thomas Hardy & Stinsford Church: A brief companion for the Visitor.* Stinsford Parochial Church Council.
MLA	**Numerical**
Hands, Timothy. <u>Thomas Hardy and Stinsford Church: A Brief Companion for the Visitor</u>. Stinsford Parochial Church Council, 1992.	HANDS, T. *Thomas Hardy and Stinsford Church: a brief companion for the visitor.* Stinsford Parochial Church Council, 1992.

B3 Brochure

Brochures may contain statistical or other information that you might want to include in your assignment. You may need, therefore, to refer to a particular page number so the reader can go straight to this. If no author's name is shown, start with the name of the organization and name the publisher as 'author', or 'as author'. If no date is shown, put n.d., or 'no date', in place of the year. With MLA style, if no author's name is shown, start with the title of the brochure.

Table 10.B3 Brochure

Harvard	APA
UNIVERSITY OF BRADFORD (2006). *Lifelong Education Prospectus 05/06.* Bradford: as author.	University of Bradford (2006). *Lifelong Education Prospectus 05/06.* Bradford: as author.

(Cont.)

MLA	Numerical
Lifelong Education Prospectus 05/06. Univ. Bradford, 2006.	UNIVERSITY OF BRADFORD. *Lifelong Education Prospectus 05/06*, p.6. Bradford: as author, 2006.

C Journals, magazines and newspapers

C1 Journals

You will need to include details of:

- Name of writer
- Title of article
- Name of journal, in italics or underlined
- Volume number, issue number (if applicable) and page numbers. if it is a special edition or supplement to a journal, you need to indicate this, e.g. (Suppl.).

APA

Do not enclose titles of articles within quotation marks.
Both the title of journal and volume number should be shown in italics.
The issue number should be enclosed in brackets.
Do not use pp. before page numbers for academic journals, but this abbreviation should be used with newspaper references.

MLA

Enclose the titles of articles within journals within double quotation marks.
Put the volume number after title of the journal.
If there is an issue number, put this after the volume number, as shown in example ii that follows, e.g. 220:C3.
For academic journals, put the year in brackets and do not use pp. (page numbers) abbreviation.

With the Harvard and Numeric styles the abbreviations vol.', 'no.' (number) and 'pp.' can be omitted. However, for clarity, and to avoid confusing the reader with a mass of consecutive numbers, they can be included.

Table 10.C1i Journal

Harvard	APA
YANG, D. (2005). Culture matters to multinationals' intellectual property business. *Journal of World Business*. No. 40, pp.281–301.	Yang, D. (2005). Culture matters to multinationals' intellectual property business. *Journal of World Business*, *40*, 281–301.

(Cont.)

MLA	Numerical
Yang, Deli. "Culture Matters to Multinationals' Intellectual Property Business". Journal of World Business, 40, (2005): 281–301.	YANG, D. Culture matters to multinationals' intellectual property business. Journal of World Business. 2005, No. 40, pp.281–301.

References to journal articles do not usually include the name of the publisher or place of publication, unless there is more than one journal with the same title, e.g. *Banking Weekly* (New York) and *Banking Weekly* (London).

Table 10.C1ii Journal (special issue)

Harvard	APA
TRENDAFILOVA, I. (2006). Vibration-based damage detection in structures using time series analysis. *Journal of Mechanical Engineering Science* (Special Issue on Chaos in Science and Engineering), vol. 220, no. C3, pp.361–372.	Trendafilova, I. (2006) Vibration-based damage detection in structures using time series analysis. *Journal of Mechanical Engineering Science* (Special Issue on Chaos in Science and Engineering): *220*: (C3), 361–372.

MLA	Numerical
Trendafilova, Irena. "Vibration-based Damage Detection in Structures Using Time Series Analysis". Journal of Mechanical Engineering Science (Special Issue on Chaos in Science and Engineering), 220: C3 (2006): 361–372.	TRENDAFILOVA, I. Vibration-based damage detection in structures using time series analysis. *Journal of Mechanical Engineering Science* (Special Issue on Chaos in Science and Engineering), 2006, vol. 220, no. C3, pp.361–372.

C2 Magazines

The same sequence of referencing academic journals applies to magazines with a general readership. However, if an author's name is shown, start with this.

MLA

For articles in a monthly magazine with a general circulation, show the month and the year. If there is an issue number show this too, and also show the page number(s). Unlike references for academic journals, the year does not need to go in brackets for a magazine with a general readership.

APA

The month of the edition follows after the year for magazines published monthly. For weekly magazines, add the month and the day, e.g. 2006, July 28.

Table 10.C2 Magazines

Harvard	APA
COOPER, S. (2006). Almost tomorrow: the speculative fiction of Edmund Cooper. *Book and Magazine Collector*, July, no.270, pp.51–61.	Cooper, S. (2006, July) Almost tomorrow: The speculative fiction of Edmund Cooper. *Book & Magazine Collector*, 270, 51–61.
MLA	**Numerical**
Cooper, Shaun. "Almost Tomorrow: The Speculative Fiction of Edmund Cooper". <u>Book and Magazine Collector</u> July 2006. 270: 51–61.	COOPER, S. Almost tomorrow: the speculative fiction of Edmund Cooper. *Book and Magazine Collector*, July 2006, no. 270, pp.51–61.

C3 Newspapers

Include the following information:

- Name of writer, if shown
- Name of the newspaper, in italics or underlined
- Day, month and year of publication. for Harvard, MLA and Numerical styles, the months of the year can be abbreviated, except May, June and July. for the APA style spell out the month in full
- Title of article
- Details of any special identifying feature, e.g. late edition, review sections, supplements. if a particular edition is involved, e.g. late edition, this can be shown next to the date, e.g. 4 June 2006 (late edn.)
- Page number(s).

Table 10.C3i Newspaper article (with an author's name shown)

Harvard	APA
MARTIN, L. Top women cheated by pay gap. *The Observer*, 4 June 2006, p.18.	Martin, L. Top women cheated by pay gap. (2006, June 6). *The Observer*, p.18.
MLA	**Numerical**
Martin, Lorna. "Top Women Cheated By Pay Gap." <u>The Observer</u> 4 June 2006.	MARTIN, L. Top women cheated by pay gap. *The Observer*, 4 June 2006, p.18.

Newspaper item (no author's name shown)

Short, snippet-type items in newspapers, without author's name given, can be cited just by giving full details in the text of your assignment (citation only). If it is a local paper, it is helpful to include the city of origin, e.g. (Bradford *Telegraph and Argus* 21 June 2004, p.4). If the item is in a supplement, give information of this after the name of the newspaper, e.g. *Financial Times: FTfm (Fund Management)* 12 Dec. 2005, p.3; or *Financial Times (FT Companies and Markets supplement)* 12 Dec. 2005, p.24.

However, the article is particularly significant, in terms of data provided or for other evidential purposes in the assignment, it should also be included in the references or bibliography list, as follows.

Table 10.C3ii Newspaper item (no author's name shown)

Harvard	APA
FINANCIAL TIMES. Duke does u-turn over spin-off sale, 12 Dec. 2005, p.14.	Duke does U-turn over spin-off sale (2005, December 12). *Financial Times*, p.14.
MLA	**Numerical**
"Duke Does U-turn Over Spin-off Sale". <u>Financial Times</u> 12 Dec. 2005.	*FINANCIAL TIMES*. Duke does u-turn over spin-off sale, 12 Dec. 2005, p.14.

D Occasional papers and reports

For all discussion, occasional or working papers and all types of report you should include:

- Author's name
- If no name of author, start with name of organization
- Year of publication
- Full title of report, in italics or underlined
- Subsection or subtitle information and edition number
- Place of publication
- Name of publisher or originating organization
- Volume, sections, page number(s) if not cited in the text. abbreviations 'p.', or 'pp.' can be used, if required, for all styles, except MLA.

D1 Discussion paper (named authors)

Table 10.D1 Discussion paper (named authors)

Harvard	APA
ANAND, S. and A.K. SEN (1996). *Sustainable human development: concepts and priorities*. United Nations Development Programme (UNDP), Discussion Paper Series. New York: UNDP: Office of Development Studies, p.23.	Anand, S. & Sen, A.K. (1996). *Sustainable human development: Concepts & priorities*. United Nations Development Programme (UNDP): (Discussion Paper Series). New York: UNDP: Office of Development Studies, p.23.
MLA	**Numerical**
Anand, Sudhir and Amartya Sen. <u>Sustainable Human Development: Concepts and Priorities</u>. United Nations Dev. Programme. (UNDP), Discussion Paper Series. New York: UNDP: Office of Development Studies, 1996.	ANAND, S. and A.K. SEN. *Sustainable human development: concepts and priorities*. United Nations Development Programme (UNDP), Discussion Paper Series. New York: UNDP: Office of Development Studies, 1996. p.23.

D2 Occasional paper (with a named author)

Table 10.D2 Occasional paper (with a named author)

Harvard	APA
SYMONDS, M. (1994). *The culture of anxiety: the middle class in crisis*. Occasional Paper No.9. London: Social Market Foundation,	Symonds, M. (1994). *The culture of anxiety: The middle class in crisis* (Occasional Paper No.9). London: Social Market Foundation.
MLA	**Numerical**
Symonds, Matthew. The Culture of Anxiety: The Middle Class in Crisis, Occasional Paper No.9. London: Social Market Foundation, 1994.	SYMONDS, M. *The culture of anxiety: the middle class in crisis*, Occasional Paper No.9. London: Social Market Foundation, 1994.

D3 Annual report: non-commercial organization (no named author)

If no named author, start with the name of the organization. Give full details of the report, plus any information on relevant subsections and pages, if applicable.

Table 10.D3 Annual report: non-commercial organization (as named author)

Harvard	APA
OVERSEAS DEVELOPMENT INSTITUTE (2003). *Annual report 2002/03*: finance: balance sheet summary, pp.30–33. London: as author.	Overseas Development Institute (2003). *Annual report 2002/03*: Finance: balance sheet summary, pp.30–33. London: as author.
MLA	**Numerical**
Overseas Development Institute. Annual Report 2002/03: "Finance: Balance Sheet Summary". London: as author, 2003, 30–33.	OVERSEAS DEVELOPMENT INSTITUTE. *Annual report 2002/03*: finance: balance sheet summary, pp.30–33. London: as author, 2003.

D4 Annual report: commercial organization (no named author)

Company annual reports often involve multiple authors and rarely show the name or names of the compilers or editors. If they do then start with these. If not, start with the company or organizational name, then give the year, full title of report, details of any relevant chapter or section. You can also include page numbers, if applicable, and details of publisher, which is often the organization concerned.

Table 10.D4 Annual report: commercial organization (no named author)

Harvard	APA
CABLE AND WIRELESS Plc (2005). *Annual report 2005: cash flow*, p.80. Bracknell: as author.	Cable & Wireless Plc (2005). *Annual report 2005: Cash flow*, 80. Bracknell: as author.
MLA	**Numerical**
Cable and Wireless Plc. Annual Report 2005: "Cash Flow". Bracknell: as author, 2005.	CABLE AND WIRELESS Plc. *Annual report 2005:* cash flow, p.80. Bracknell: as author, 2005.

D5 Other reports (no named author)

Give as much information as is necessary to identify title, subsection and page numbers of the report concerned.

Table 10.D5 Other reports (no named author)

Harvard	APA
BUSINESS RATIO REPORTS (2004). *Security industry*, edn. 26, section 4: performance league tables: sales: 4–2. Hampton: Keynote.	Business Ratio Reports (2004). *Security industry* (edn. 26, section 4): Performance league tables: Sales: 4–2. Hampton: Keynote.
MLA	**Numerical**
Business Ratio Reports. <u>Security Industry</u>, edn. 26, section 4: "Performance League Tables": Sales: 4–2. Hampton: Keynote, 2004.	BUSINESS RATIO REPORTS. *Security industry*, edn. 26, section 4: performance league tables: sales: 4–2. Hampton: Keynote, 2004.

(See also E, 'Government publications', next entry, for other examples of reports.)

E UK government publications (non-parliamentary)

The publishers for many UK government publications is The Stationery Office (TSO), although documents published before 1996 are usually shown as published by HMSO (Her Majesty's Stationery Office). The Stationery Office was privatized from the HMSO (now the Office of Public Sector Information) in 1996. However, other government departments and agencies also produce their own publications, e.g. Office of the Deputy Prime Minister (ODPM), Department for Transport (DfT) and Health and Safety Executive (HSE). Government-sponsored research may also be published by other bodies or organizations, see example E3.

You need to include the following information:

- Name of author(s) or name of government department or agency. You may also need to mention the country of origin, if it is not obvious from the place of publication
- Year of publication
- Title of article or the title of publication, in italics or underlined
- Place of publication and name of official publisher
- Volume or edition date number, table or page number, if applicable.

E1 Government publication (no named author)

Table 10.E1 Government publication (no named author)

Harvard	APA
OFFICE FOR NATIONAL STATISTICS (2000). *Standard occupational classification: vol. 2: the coding index*. London: The Stationery Office.	Office for National Statistics (2000). *Standard occupational classification: Vol. 2: The coding index*. London: The Stationery Office.

(Cont.)

MLA	Numerical
Office for National Statistics. Standard Occupational Classification: Vol. 2: The Coding Index. London: TSO. 2000.	OFFICE FOR NATIONAL STATISTICS. *Standard occupational classification: vol. 2: the coding index*. London: The Stationery Office, 2000.

E2 Government publication (named author)

Table 10.E2 Government publication (named author)

Harvard	APA
SUDLOW, D. (2003). *Scoping study on motorcycle training*. Great Britain. Department for Transport: Road Safety Research Report no. 36. Wetherby: Dft Publications.	Sudlow, D. (2003). *Scoping study on motorcycle training*. Great Britain. Department for Transport (Road Safety Research Report no. 36). Wetherby: Dft Publications.
MLA	**Numerical**
Sudlow, Diane. Scoping Study on Motorcycle Training. Great Britain. Department for Transport: Road Safety Research Report no. 36. Wetherby: Dft Publications, 2003.	SUDLOW, D. *Scoping study on motorcycle training*. Great Britain. Department for Transport: Road Safety Research Report no. 36. Wetherby: Dft Publications, 2003.

E3 Government-sponsored publications

Government-sponsored reports often have long titles, but become commonly known by the name of the chairman/chairwoman of the committee responsible. You should always give the full official title of the report in a reference, but you can also give the popular title, if you wish. An abbreviated title can be shown in citations in the text, but the full title must always be explained in the reference, as shown in the example that follows.

Table 10.E3 Government-sponsored publications

Harvard	APA
UNWCED: UNITED NATIONS WORLD COMMISSION ON ENVIRONMENT AND DEVELOPMENT (1987). *Our common future* (Brundtland Report). Oxford: Oxford University Press.	UNWCED: United Nations World Commission on Environment & Development (1987). *Our common future* (Brundtland Report). Oxford: Oxford University Press.
MLA	**Numerical**
UNWCED: United Nations World Commission on Environment and Development. Our Common Future (Brundtland Report). Oxford: OUP, 1987.	UNWCED: UNITED NATIONS WORLD COMMISSION ON ENVIRONMENT AND DEVELOPMENT. *Our common future* (Brundtland Report). Oxford: Oxford University Press, 1987.

F UK parliamentary publications

United Kingdom parliamentary publications can be grouped into four main categories:

Table 10.F0 Categories of parliamentary publications

Parliamentary business	Records of debates
• Weekly information bulletins • Sessional information digest • Votes and proceedings (House of Commons: HC) • Minutes of proceedings (House of Lords: HL) • Journals (HC and HL)	• Parliamentary debates (Hansard, abbreviated House of Commons or Lords: HC and HL) • Standing Committees Debates (HC)
Parliamentary papers	**Acts of Parliament**
• House of Commons Bills • House of Commons Papers • Command Papers • House of Lords Bills • House of Lords Papers	• Public General Acts • Local and Personal Acts

(Source: Butcher 1991)

What to include:

- United Kingdom Parliament: The House of . . . (Commons or Lords)
- Year of publication
- Title of publication, in italics or underlined
- Place of publication and name of publisher
- Other identifying features, e.g. details of Paper, Bill, Series, numbers.

F1 Minutes of proceedings

Table 10.F1 Minutes of proceedings

Harvard	APU
UNITED KINGDOM PARLIAMENT. House of Commons (1999). *Order of business, Wed. 11 Nov. 1998*. Oral questions to the Secretary of State for International Development. Norwich: Office of Public Sector Information.	United Kingdom Parliament. House of Commons (1999). *Order of business, Wed. 11 Nov. 1998*. Oral questions to the Secretary of State for International Development. Norwich: Office of Public Sector Information.
MLA	**Numerical**
United Kingdom Parliament. House of Commons. Order of Business, Wed. 11 Nov. 1998. Oral questions to the Secretary of State for International Development, Norwich: OIPC, 1999.	UNITED KINGDOM PARLIAMENT. House of Commons. *Order of business, Wed. 11 Nov. 1998*. Oral questions to the Secretary of State for International Development. Norwich: Office of Public Sector Information, 1999.

F2 Parliamentary debates

Hansard is the collective name of the independent record of debates and speeches in the Chamber of the House of Commons, sub-chamber in Westminster Hall and in Standing Committees of the House of Lords. The impartial recording of parliamentary proceedings dates from the early nineteenth century, but the term 'Hansard' derives from Thomas Curson Hansard, the son of Luke Hansard, a printer in the House of Commons. Thomas Hansard employed reporters to record verbatim parliamentary procedure and their reports rapidly gained public respect for their accuracy and attention to detail.

Today much the same procedure applies, with Hansard reporters in the Press Gallery recording by shorthand, or by sub-editors recording the proceedings of Westminster Hall and the Standing Committees.

Hansard is produced in daily, weekly and bound volume versions of proceedings in the Chamber of the House of Commons. In Select Committees there is no Hansard record published, but instead 'minutes of evidence' are published by the Committee and form part of their report.

There is a fact sheet (ref. G17) that can be obtained from The House of Commons Information Office, London SW1A 2TT, and this give examples of how to reference Hansard entries.

For all styles of referencing the following abbreviations should be used:

HC Deb: House of Commons Debate
W: Written Answers
WH: Westminster Hall
WS: Written Statements
SC: Standing Committee
c: column numbers.

Harvard, APA and MLA citations in the text can show 'United Kingdom Parliament' (or UK Parliament) and the date, e.g. (United Kingdom Parliament 13 Nov 2001), and these can then link to the full references.

Full reference examples:

- United Kingdom Parliament HC Deb 13 November 2001 c345; or cc345–6 or c134W or c101WH or 1WS

For the older versions of Hansard, the volume and series numbers can be quoted. Examples:

- UNITED KINGDOM PARLIAMENT HC Deb 3 February 1977 vol 389 c973
- UNITED KINGDOM PARLIAMENT HC Deb 17 December 1996 vol 596 cc18–19
- UNITED KINGDOM PARLIAMENT HC Deb 4 July 1996 vol 280 c505W
- UNITED KINGDOM PARLIAMENT HC Deb (5th series) 13 January 1907 vol 878 cc 69–70.

In Standing Committees, the citations are, as follows:

- UNITED KINGDOM PARLIAMENT SC Deb (A) 13 May 1998 c345.

Note: the term 'United Kingdom Parliament' has been added to the above references. This term is used on the office website for parliamentary sources in Britain, so has been used here to make it clear which country is referred to.

However, British Standard BS 1629: 1989 offers an alternative version of citing Hansard, as follows:

- GREAT BRITAIN. House of Commons. *Official Report. Parliamentary debates (Hansard)* . . . (then details, as above examples) (see BS 1999 p.18)

Check with your tutor which version is preferred.

F3 Command papers

Command papers are those 'commanded' by the sovereign to be presented to Parliament, including 'White' or 'Green' Papers: policy proposals or consultation documents, or reports of committees of inquiry, responses to Select Committee reports and other important departmental reports or reviews.

References to Command papers should include name of originating department, title, Command paper number and year of publication.

Table 10.F3 Command papers

Harvard	APA
SCOTLAND OFFICE (2006). *Departmental report.* CM 6834. London: The Stationery Office.	Scotland Office (2006) *Departmental report.* CM 6834. London: The Stationery Office.
MLA	**Numerical**
Scotland Office. Departmental Report. CM 6834. London: TSO, 2006.	SCOTLAND OFFICE. *Departmental report.* CM 6834. London: The Stationery Office, 2006.

F4 Select Committee reports

Select Committees examine particular and selected subjects. In the House of Commons they review the running of each of the main government departments and associated public bodies and have the power to take evidence and issue reports.

In the House of Lords, Select Committees examine broader issues, such as the European Union, and Science and Technology.

You should include the name of the Select Committee, title of the report, and HC or HL to indicate House of Commons or House of Lords respectively, and the serial number of the report.

Table 10.F4 Select Committee reports

Harvard	APA
UNITED KINGDOM PARLIAMENT (2005). *The Select Committee on BBC charter review.* HL50–1 [75]. London: The Stationery Office.	United Kingdom Parliament (2005). *The select committee on BBC charter review.* HL50–1 [75]. London: The Stationery Office.
MLA	**Numerical**
United Kingdom Parliament. The Select Committee on BBC Charter Review. HL50–1 [75]. London: TSO, 2005.	UNITED KINGDOM PARLIAMENT. *The Select Committee on BBC charter review.* HL50–1 [75]. London: The Stationery Office,2005.

The numbers in squared brackets indicate paragraph numbers. If you wanted to refer to sequential paragraphs, this can be done by linking them, e.g. [75]–[80].

See also 'Legal documents', next section.

G Legal documents

Students on law degree or related courses will learn a referencing style that is particular to this subject, which is usually the Oxford Standard for Citation of Legal Authorities (OSCOLA). This is the style used by the *Oxford University Commonwealth Law Journal*, which contributed to its development. However, students on other courses, who occasionally have to cite legal cases, may also find this section helpful.

OSCOLA style of referencing

More detailed information on the OSCOLA style of referencing can be obtained from the website of Faculty of Law, University of Oxford, and most institutions of higher education that offer law degrees will offer students summary versions of the OSCOLA guide. Briefly, the OSCOLA referencing style links with the Running-notes style of referencing in that it uses raised or superscript numbers in the text, combined with footnotes. The OSCOLA style is, however, different to the four main referencing styles in the way it is presented.

With books, for example, the first name or initials of the author(s) is presented before the author's last name, without a stop or comma between them. Also, the title is always in italics, and the edition, publisher, place of publication and date are enclosed within brackets. Page numbers can be included, if relevant, as last items in the reference. When there are more than three authors, just state the first, followed by 'and others'.

OSCOLA examples:

- D French, *How to Cite Legal Authorities* (London: Blackstone, London 1996) 33–35
- P Loose and others, *The Company Director* (9th rev edn Jordans, Bristol 2006)

(**Note:** the book mentioned above, *How to Cite Legal Authorities*, is recommended reading regarding citations and referencing for any student studying for a law degree.)

Cite essays and chapters in edited journals, as follows:

- D Cullen, 'Adoption – a (Fairly) New Approach', Child and Family Law Quarterly (Oct 2005) 17 475, 486.

A minimum of punctuation is used, and commas should be used only to stop words running into each other. All words in the title should be capitalized, except prepositions ('of', 'by', 'which'), articles ('the', 'an', 'a') and conjunctions ('and', 'or').

G1 Case citation

Case citation is a frequent occurrence in law course assignments. You need to include:

- Names of the parties
- Year, in square or round brackets (see below discussion for when to do this)
- Volume number
- Abbreviated name of the law report series
- First page of the reference.

Case names should be italicized in assignments, e.g.:

Murphy v Brentwood District Council [1990] 2 All ER 908

When referring to a case for the first time, give its full name exactly as it appears in the report. In subsequent references a case can be referred to by a shortened name, e.g. *Murphy v Brentwood District Council*, and can be referred to as the *Murphy* case.

If you give the full details of the case in the text, you do not need to repeat the information in a list of references.

Examples:

1 Campbell v Mirror Group Newspapers Ltd [2004] 2 All ER 995
2 Rees v United Kingdom (1987) 9 EHRR 56

You could, however, refer to part of the citation in the text, e.g. *Campbell v Mirror Group Newspapers*, and give the full reference details in footnotes.

Square or round brackets?

Square brackets are used when the date is essential for finding the report. Round brackets are used when the date is merely of assistance in giving an idea of when a case was featured in law reports that have cumulative volume numbers.

Abbreviations?

The abbreviations in the examples shown above refer to All England Law Reports (All ER) and European Human Rights Reports (EHRR). A full list of abbreviations in the names of law reports and journals can be found at the Cardiff University 'Cardiff Index to Legal Abbreviations' website at http://www.legalabbrevs.cardiff.ac.uk/searchabbreviation/ or from OSCOLA.

Punctuation?

Use open punctuation – no stops after parts of the abbreviation, e.g. *All ER* (and not All. E.R.)

Specific page references?

When a particular passage is being quoted or referred to, the specific page references must be included, e.g.:

Jones v Tower Boot Co Ltd [1997] 2 All ER 406 at 411

Judge's name?

When the judge's name is being quoted or referred to in a particular passage, the judge's name should be provided as part of the citation, e.g.:

That was the opinion of Lord Mackay LC in *Pepper v Hart [1993] 1 All ER 42 at 47*

G2 UK Acts of Parliament (Statutes)

These are Acts passed by Parliament, which eventually receive royal assent and become law. You would normally list the source in the full reference, as follows:

- Title of Act and year
- The part: pt, and section: s, and/or
- The schedule: sch, and section: s.

Example:

Citation: (Data Protection Act 1998)
Reference: Data Protection Act 1998. pt 1, s2.

Note: the year: 1998, does not appear in brackets in the reference, as the date is part of the title.

For older statutes, the *Oxford Standard* suggests it can be helpful to give the appropriate year of reign and chapter number, e.g. Crown Debts Act 1801 (14 Geo 3 c 90), meaning that the Act was given Royal Assent in the fourteenth year of the reign of George the Third, and was the ninetieth Act given Royal Assent in that parliament, hence c 90).

G3 UK bills

A bill is proposed legislation before Parliament. Bills are cited by their name, the Parliamentary Session, the House of Parliament in which it originated and the running order assigned to it, and any relevant sections or subsections. HC = House of Commons; HL = House of Lords.
Example:

Citation: (Identity Cards Bill 2004–5)
Reference: Identity Cards Bill 2004–5 HC–8, s 9(4).

G4 UK statutory instruments

These are orders and regulations linked to particular Acts and should be referenced by name, date and serial number (where available).

Subsidiary words in long titles within the in-text citation may be abbreviated (see example below), but the full title must be given in the reference.

Example:

Citation: (Telecommunications (LBP) (IC) Regulations 2000)
Reference: The Telecommunications (Lawful Business Practice) (Interception of Communications) Regulations 2000.

G5 EC legislation

European Community (EC) legislation (Regulations, Directives and Decisions), and other instruments (including Recommendations and Opinions) should be referenced by providing the legislation type, number and title, then publication details from the *Official Journal* (*OJ*) of the European Communities. Be warned, these references can be lengthy!
Example:

Citation: (Commission Regulation 1475/95)
Reference: Commission Regulation (EC) No 1475/95 of 28 June 1995 on the application of Article 85 (3) [*now 81 (3)*] of the Treaty to certain categories of motor vehicle distribution and servicing agreements *Official Journal L 145*, 29/06/1995 pp. 0025–0034.

The capital letter 'L' in the example, i.e. '*Official Journal L*', indicates the series stands for Legislation; the C series contains EU information and notices, and the S series contains invitations to tender (see Oxford Standard p.18).

H Standards and patents

Standards

The full reference should include:

- The number and year of standard, e.g. BS 5605:1990
- Year of republishing, if applicable; see example below (shown in brackets for APA and Harvard)
- Title of Standard, in italics or underlined
- Place of publication, and name of publisher.

H1 British Standard

Table 10.H1 British Standard

Harvard	APA
BS 5605:1990 (1999). *Citing and referencing published material*. London: British Standard Institution.	BS5605:1990 (1999). *Citing & referencing published material*. London: British Standard Institution.

(Cont.)

MLA	**Numerical**
BS 4821:1990. <u>Citing and Referencing Published Material</u>. London: BS, 1999.	BS 5605:1990. *Citing and referencing published material.* London: British Standard Institution, 1999.

H2 International Organization for Standardization (ISO)

Table 10.H2 International Organization for Standardization

Harvard	**APA**
ISO 14001:2004. *Environmental management systems.* Geneva: International Organization for Standardization.	ISO 14001:2004. *Environmental management systems.* Geneva: International Organization for Standardization.
MLA	**Numerical**
ISO 14001:2004. <u>Environmental Management Systems</u>. Geneva: International Org. for Standardization.	ISO 14001:2004. *Environmental management systems.* Geneva: International Organization for Standardization.

H3 Patents

The full reference should include:

- Name(s) of inventor(s) or patentee(s)
- Year of publication
- Title of patent, in italics or underlined, with the exception of MLA style, which does not show a title underline for this particular type of source
- Country of origin and serial number
- Date of application and date of acceptance.

Table 10.H3 Patents

Harvard	**APA**
LUND-ANDERSON, B. (2001). *Device for the damping of vibrators between objects.* US Patent 6296238. Appl. 24 June1999. Acc. 2 Oct. 2001.	Lund-Anderson, B. (2001). *Device for the damping of vibrators between objects.* US Patent 6296238. Appl. 24 June 1999. Acc. 2 Oct. 2001.
MLA	**Numerical**
Lund-Anderson, Bernard. Device for the Damping of Vibrators Between Objects. US Patent 6296238. Appl. 24 June 1999. Acc. 2 Oct. 2001.	LUND-ANDERSON, B. *Device for the damping of vibrators between objects.* US Patent 6296238. Appl. 24 June 1999. Acc. 2 Oct. 2001.

I Course manuals and lecture notes

You can also refer to printed course given to you by teaching staff.
   You need to include in the reference:

- Name of the lecturer
- Year of lecture
- Title of lecture or course notes. These can be in italics or underlined, but this is not strictly necessary, unless the notes have been made more widely and publicly available
- Title of course or module
- Level (undergraduate or postgraduate)
- Name of institution, department or school.

These notes may be a **primary source**, e.g. a summary or explanation written by a lecturer, or a **secondary source**, where a lecturer is quoting what someone else has said, or referring directly to a third person.
   To illustrate the difference between primary and secondary sources, the following extracts from two student essays illustrate the use of a course manual as both a primary and secondary source. Harvard style referencing has been used to illustrate both examples.

Primary (Extract 1)

When choosing from the mix of promotional activities available to market a product, the market objectives should be the main driving force. Low (2004) has suggested four main questions: who is your target group? What do you want them to do? When do you want them to act? And how much are you prepared to spend to communicate with them?

Secondary (Extract 2)

Marketing Communications has been defined by Fill as a process *'through which an organisation enters into a dialogue with its various audiences'*. The objective is to influence in a positive way a particular target audience in its awareness, understanding and actions towards that organisation and its products or services (Fill 2002, as cited in Low, 2004, p.2).

The secondary reference for the extract above, in the four main referencing formats, would be presented, as follows:

Table 10.11 Secondary referencing

Harvard	APA
LOWE, C. (2004). *Marketing communications*. MA course manual, 2004/5, p.2, Bradford University, School of Management.	Lowe, C. (2004). *Marketing communications*. MA course manual, 2004/5, p.2, Bradford University, School of Management.
MLA	**Numerical**
Lowe, Chris. <u>Marketing Communications</u>. MA Course Manual, 2004/5. Bradford Univ., School of Mgt., 2004.	LOWE, C. *Marketing communications*. MA Course Manual, 2004/5, p.2, Bradford University, School of Management, 2004.

However, you might want to go to the original source, i.e. Fill (2002), to enable you to expand on the definition presented, or to be critical of it. If you did this, you could then treat it as a primary source and cite and reference Fill instead of Low.

J Unpublished work

You can reference work of scholarly interest that is unpublished, providing it is still publicly accessible in some way. 'Unpublished', in this sense, means that the source has not featured in any publication produced for large-scale public consumption, although it may be available as a limited circulation document, e.g. to delegates, members of a group, internal circulation within an organization. Despite the limited circulation, it is often possible to obtain copies of these documents, although you should be wary of their validity as evidence unless the work has been subject to critical scrutiny in some way; for example, by the delegates at a conference or seminar.

Unpublished work you might want to use could include:

- Dissertations
- Papers presented at conferences and seminars
- Manuscripts and other documents in libraries and archives
- Personal correspondence, if relevant to make particular points
- The minutes of meetings.

The same basic format referencing published work applies for referencing unpublished sources. You should include:

- Author name(s)
- Year
- Title or name of work/conference/seminar, in italics or underlined
- Name of any host institution
- Location of archive material, if applicable
- Any other information to help locate the material.

J1 Dissertation

Table 10.J1 Dissertation

Harvard	APA
COOPER, T. (2003). *Implementing strategic change in the recruitment advertising/ employment communication industry.* Unpublished MBA project report, 2002/3. Bradford: University of Bradford, School of Management Library.	Cooper, T. (2003). *Implementing strategic change in the recruitment advertising/ employment communication industry.* Unpublished MBA project report, 2002/3. Bradford: University of Bradford, School of Management Library.
MLA	**Numerical**
Cooper, Thomas. Implementing Strategic Change in the Recruitment Advertising/Employment Communication Industry. Unpublished MBA project report, 2002/3. Bradford: U. Bradford, Schl. Mgt. Libr. 2003.	COOPER, T. *Implementing Strategic Change in the Recruitment Advertising/Employment Communication Industry.* Unpublished MBA project report, 2002/3. Bradford: University of Bradford, School of Management Library, 2003.

J2 Unpublished conference paper

Table 10.J2 Unpublished conference paper

Harvard	APA
BROADBENT, M. (2005). *Tackling plagiarism: a teaching and learning perspective.* Unpublished paper presented at 'Tackling Plagiarism' Conference. University of Hertfordshire, Business School, 22 Mar. 2005.	Broadbent, M. (2005, March 22). *Tackling plagiarism: a teaching and learning perspective.* Unpublished paper presented at 'Tackling Plagiarism' Conference. University of Hertfordshire, Business School.
MLA	**Numerical**
Broadbent, Mick. (2005). Tackling Plagiarism: a Teaching and Learning Perspective. Unpublished paper presented at 'Tackling Plagiarism' Conf. U. of Hertfordshire, Business School. 22 Mar. 2005.	BROADBENT, M. *Tackling Plagiarism: a Teaching and Learning Perspective.* Unpublished paper presented at 'Tackling Plagiarism' Conference. University of Hertfordshire, Business School, 22 Mar. 2005.

J3 Archive material

If the author of a manuscript is not known, start with the title of the manuscript, or collection of manuscripts (italics or underlined). Include any date or year of the manuscript, if known, plus the name of the collection and any reference number (also in italics or underlined). State the name and place of archive and add any additional relevant information to help others locate the material.

Examples:

- *LNWR plans* at West Yorkshire Archive Service, Kirklees, ref. KX272.
- Deposited Building Plans, no 10, 1 October 1886, West Yorkshire Archive Service, Leeds.

Table 10.J3 Archive material

Harvard
VICKRIDGE, A. *Correspondence of Alberta Vickridge 1917–1965.* Box 2. Letter to Vickridge from Agatha Christie, 12 Feb. 1918. University of Leeds, Brotherton Library.

APA
Vickridge, A. *Correspondence of Alberta Vickridge 1917–1965.* Box 2. Letter to Vickridge from Agatha Christie, 12 February 1918. University of Leeds, Brotherton Library.

MLA
Vickridge, A. Correspondence of Alberta Vickridge 1917–1965. Box 2. Letter to Vickridge from Agatha Christie, 12 Feb. 1918. Univ. Leeds, Brotherton Libr.

Numerical
VICKRIDGE, A. *Correspondence of Alberta Vickridge 1917–1965.* Box 2. Letter to Vickridge from Agatha Christie, 12 Feb. 1918. University of Leeds, Brotherton Library.

J4 Unpublished proceedings of a meeting

Give names of contributors or presenters and full details of the meeting, including name and date of meeting, where it was held and details of any formal contribution made to the meeting by speakers or delegates.

Table 10.J4 Unpublished proceedings of a meeting

Harvard
Bonanni, L. and C. Vaucelle (2006) *A framework for Haptic psycho-therapy.* In Proceedings of IEEE ICPS Pervasive Health Systems Workshop, Lyon, France, 29 June 2006.

APA
Bonanni, L. and Vaucelle, C. (2006, June 29) *A framework for Haptic psycho-therapy.* In Proceedings of IEEE ICPS Pervasive Health Systems Workshop, Lyon, France.

MLA
Bonanni, Leonardo and Cati Vaucelle. A Framework for Haptic Psycho-therapy. In Proceedings of IEEE ICPS Pervasive Health Systems Workshop, Lyon, France, 29 June 2006.

Numerical
Bonanni, L. and C. Vaucelle. *A framework for Haptic psycho-therapy.* In Proceedings of IEEE ICPS Pervasive Health Systems Workshop, Lyon, France, 29 June 2006.

K Cartographic material: maps and atlases

If you wish to use illustrations in any work that will be publicly accessible, you will need to seek permission from the people or organizations holding copyright.

For referencing purposes, treat any illustrated or cartographic material in the same way you would books. If there is any named author, illustrator or photographer, start with this, if not give title of the item.

Atlases

Table 10.K1 Atlases

Harvard	APA
Atlas of the world 12th edn. (2004). Oxford: Oxford University Press.	*Atlas of the world* (12th ed.). (2004). Oxford: Oxford University Press.
MLA	**Numerical**
Atlas of the World. 12th Edition. Oxford: OUP, 2004.	*Atlas of the world* 12th edn. Oxford: Oxford University Press, 2004.

Maps

You should include:

- Name (e.g. Ordnance Survey)
- Year
- Title of map, italics or underlined
- Sheet number and scale
- Series (if applicable)
- Place of publication and publisher.

Table 10.K2 Maps of Britain

Harvard	APA
ORDNANCE SURVEY (1974). *Saxmundham and Aldeburgh* 156, 1:50 000. First series. Southampton: Ordnance Survey.	Ordnance Survey (1974). *Saxmundham & Aldeburgh* 156, 1:50 000. First series. Southampton: Ordnance Survey.
MLA	**Numerical**
Ordnance Survey. Saxmundham and Aldeburgh 156, 1:50 000. First series. Map. Southampton: OS, 1974.	ORDNANCE SURVEY. *Saxmundham and Aldeburgh* 156, 1:50 000. First series. Southampton: Ordnance Survey, 1974.

Maps for countries outside Britain should include the title of map in the language of the country concerned, although a translation could be included if non-European characters have been used.

Table 10.K3 Map outside Britain

Harvard	APA
Wanderkarte Boppard (1996). M1: 25.000. Germany: Boppard, Tourist Information.	*Wanderkarte Boppard* (1996). M1: 25.000. Germany: Boppard, Tourist Information.
MLA	**Numerical**
Wanderkarte Boppard. M1: 25.000. Map. Germany: Boppard, Tourist Information, 1996.	*Wanderkarte Boppard*. M1: 25.000. Germany: Boppard, Tourist Information, 1996.

Table 10.K4 Geological map

Harvard BRITISH GEOLOGICAL SURVEY (1992). *Thirsk* (S&D) E52. 1:50 000. Nottingham: British Geological Survey.	**APA** British Geological Survey (1992). *Thirsk* (S&D) E52. 1:50 000. Nottingham: British Geological Survey.
MLA British Geological Survey. <u>Thirsk</u> (S&D) E52. 1:50 000. Map. Nottingham: BGS, 1992.	**Numerical** BRITISH GEOLOGICAL SURVEY. *Thirsk* (S&D) E52. 1:50 000. Nottingham: British Geological Survey, 1992.

It may be necessary to state the medium, i.e. satellite image.

Table 10.K5 Map from satellite image

Harvard *PLANET OBSERVER* (2006). European map. Satellite image. 1:8.000.000. USA: National Geographic Society.	**APA** *Planet Observer* (2006). European map Satellite image. 1:8.000.000. USA: National Geographic Society.
MLA <u>Planet Observer.</u> European Map. Satellite image. 1:8.000.000. USA: National Geographic Society, 2006.	**Numerical** *PLANET OBSERVER*. European map. Satellite image. 1:8.000.000. USA: National Geographic Society, 2006.

With old maps, give title, date (or c: circa) and where the map is located.

Table 10.K6 Old maps

Harvard *Map of the precincts of St Mary Graces, Tower Hill* (c.1590). London: Guildhall Library.	**APA** *Map of the precincts of St Mary Graces, Tower Hill* (c.1590). London: Guildhall Library.
MLA <u>Map of the Precincts of St Mary Graces, Tower Hill</u>. London: Guildhall Library, c.1590.	**Numerical** *Map of the precincts of St Mary Graces, Tower Hill*. London: Guildhall Library, c.1590.

L Graphs and charts

It is important to cite and reference all sources imported in or used to construct graphs, tables and charts in your assignments. For example with the constructed table, which follows, the source (in Harvard style) is shown below the table. If more than one source has contributed to the compilation, show all these in the citation and list them separately in the references.

Table 10.L1 Population of children in Tanzania (2002)

Age	Both sexes	Male	Female
Total population	18,837,206	9,399,477	9,433,920
0–4 (per cent of total)	16.45	16.82	16.09
5–9 (per cent of total)	14.9	15.29	14.51
10–14 (per cent of total)	12.9	13.27	12.55
15–19 (per cent of total)	10.44	10.47	10.41

(Source: Canadian Cooperation Office 2003, p.6)

The above table would be referenced, as follows:

Table 10.L2 Reference for source of Table 10.

Harvard
CANADIAN COOPERATION OFFICE (2003). *Canadian government support to the education sector in Tanzania*. Dar es Salaam, Tanzania: as author.

APA
Canadian Cooperation Office (2003). *Canadian government support to the education sector in Tanzania*. Dar es Salaam, Tanzania: Author.

MLA
Canadian Cooperation Office. <u>Canadian Government Support to the Education Sector in Tanzania</u>. Dar es Salaam, Tanzania: as author, 2003.

Numerical
CANADIAN COOPERATION OFFICE. *Canadian government support to the education sector in Tanzania*. Dar es Salaam, Tanzania: as author, 2003.

M Visual art and graphics

These can include original paintings and any form of photographic or printed graphic illustration, including cartoons, line drawings, advertisements and postcards. You should state the artist's name, title of work, type of work and where the work can be located or viewed, e.g. book title, name of gallery, etc. If no artist name is shown, start with the title, in italics or underlined, and then give as much information as necessary to help others locate the source. British Standard show full first name(s) of originator for visual sources for both Harvard and Numerical Styles.

M1 Painting exhibited in a gallery

Table 10.M1 Painting exhibited in gallery

Harvard
KLIMT, Gustav. (1898). *Allegory of sculpture*. [Painting]. Salzburg: Galerie Welz.

APA
Klimt, G. (1898). *Allegory of sculpture*. [Painting]. Salzburg: Galerie Welz.

(Cont.)

MLA	Numerical
Klimt, Gustav. <u>Allegory of Sculpture</u>. Painting. Salzburg: Galerie Welz, 1898.	KLIMT, Gustav. *Allegory of sculpture*. [Painting]. Salzburg: Galerie Welz, 1898.

M2 Photographs

You should include

- Name of photographer
- Year photograph taken, or approximate date, e.g. 'circa' or 'c';
- Title of photograph, or description, if no title. Titles should be in italics or underlined
- State medium, and enclose this description in square brackets, e.g. [photograph]
- Publisher or where photograph is to be viewed.

If it is a personal photograph, start the reference with a general description of the subject, but this does not need to be in italics or underlined. Then state the name of the photographer (if known), and the date, or approximate date, the photograph was taken. You also need to state who has ownership of the photographs.

Examples:

- Alberta Vickridge, aged approximately 19 years. Photographer unknown. Circa 1911. In the private collection of Henry Vickridge, Otley, West Yorkshire.
- River Wharfe, near Bolton Abbey, North Yorkshire. Personal photograph by author. 22 June 2006.

Table 10.M2 Photograph in a public collection

Harvard	APA
GRIFFITHS, Frances. (1920). *Frances and the leaping fairy*. [Photograph]. Bradford: National Museum Film and Photography.	Griffiths, F. (1920). *Frances & the leaping fairy*. [Photograph]. Bradford: National Museum Film and Photography.
MLA	**Numerical**
Griffiths, Frances. <u>Frances and the Leaping Fairy</u>. Photograph. Bradford: Natl. Mus. Film & Photo. 1920.	GRIFFITHS, Frances. *Frances and the leaping fairy*. [Photograph]. Bradford: National Museum Film and Photography, 1920.

M3 Book illustration

You should include:

- Name of the artist or illustrator, if known
- Date work originally completed (if known), or the year book was published
- Title of plate (if any)

- Author/editor of book, if different from artist
- Title of book and when published, if not already given. As this is the primary source, show this in italics or underlined
- Where published
- Publisher.

Table 10.M3 Book illustration

Harvard	APA
FORSTER, Peter. (1999). Two illustrations for Romola. In S. Brett (Ed.) *An engraver's globe* (2002). London: Primrose Hill Press.	Forster, P. (1999). Two illustrations for Romola. In S. Brett (Ed.) *An engraver's globe* (2002). London: Primrose Hill Press.
MLA	**Numerical**
Forster, Peter. "Two Illustrations for Romola", 1999. In Simon Brett (Ed.) An Engraver's Globe. London: Primrose Hill Press, 2002.	FORSTER, Peter. Two illustrations for Romola. 1999. In Simon Brett (Ed.) *An engraver's globe*. London: Primrose Hill Press, 2002.

M4 Graphic art: cartoon (artist's name not shown)

If the artist's name is not shown, start with the name of the originator or title of the graphic. If the artist's name was shown, start with this. Make it clear what type of graphic art is referenced, e.g. advertisement, cartoon, poster, where it was publicly shown and give any other identifying information, e.g. title of the work.

Table 10.M4 Graphic art: cartoon (artist's name not shown)

Harvard	APA
VODAFONE (2005). Advertisement on London Transport Underground. *Make the most of now – seize the day.*	Vodafone (2005). Advertisement on London Transport Underground. *Make the most of now – seize the day.*
MLA	**Numerical**
Vodafone. Advertisement on London Transport Underground. Make the Most of Now – Seize the Day, 2005.	VODAFONE. Advertisement on London Transport Underground. *Make the most of now – seize the day*, 2005.

N Audio–visual sources

This section includes any transmitted or produced visual and audio means of communication, including radio, television, music, cinema and other film productions (for live performances, see section O).

Radio and television

References to television and radio programmes should contain the following information:

- Writer of programme, if relevant
- Producer of programme, if relevant
- Title of the programme, in italics or underlined, and name of episode, if relevant
- Title of the series, if applicable
- Name of the radio or television network, e.g. BBC Radio 4
- Place of broadcast, if it is a regional station, e.g. Bradford: Pulse Radio
- Broadcast or transmission date.

British Standard examples of Harvard and Numerical styles of referencing for audio/ visual transmitted or produced sources, show the full first name(s) of presenter(s) or originator(s).

If you miss them at the time of the broadcast, the names of the authors/presenter or producers can normally be found on the websites of the broadcast stations concerned. If you feel the names of authors/presenters and producers are not required, start with the title. It might be, for example, that the points made generally in a radio or television programme are more important to you than the details of people involved in the production.

However, if it is a work of fiction, or where the author/presenter's identity is associated with the programme, then you need to include this information. If someone has been interviewed (see television programme example below), and the interview is the basis for the citation and reference, the reference should start with the name of the person interviewed.

N1 Radio programmes (three examples)

Table 10.N1i Radio programme

Harvard	APA
BBC Radio 4 (2003). *Analysis: future of work*. Broadcast 12 May 2003.	BBC Radio 4 (2003, May 12). *Analysis: Future of work*.
MLA	**Numerical**
BBC Radio 4. "Analysis: Future of Work". Broadcast 12 May 2003.	BBC Radio 4 (2003). *Analysis: future of work*. Broadcast 12 May 2003.

Table 10.N1ii Radio programme

Harvard	APA
RICH, Emma. (2006). Interview with Jenni MURRAY. *Woman's Hour*. BBC Radio 4 broadcast, 4 July 2006.	Rich, E. (2006, July 4). Interview with J. Murray. *Woman's hour*. BBC Radio 4 broadcast.

(Cont.)

MLA	Numerical
Rich, Emma. Interview with Jenni Murray. Woman's Hour. BBC Radio 4 broadcast, 4 July 2006.	RICH, Emma. Interview with Jenni MURRAY. Woman's Hour. BBC Radio 4 broadcast, 4 July 2006.

Table 10.N1iii Radio programme

Harvard	APA
LICHTAROWICZ, Ania. (Presenter). (2006). Hip fractures. BBC World Service. Radio broadcast, 4 July 2006.	Lichtarowicz, A. (Presenter). (2006, July 4). Hip fractures. [Radio broadcast]. BBC World Service.

MLA	Numerical
Lichtarowicz, Ania. (Presenter). Hip Fractures. BBC World Service. Radio broadcast. 4 July 2006.	Lichtarowicz, Ania. (Presenter). Hip fractures. BBC World Service. Radio broadcast, 4 July 2006.

N2 Television programmes (three examples)

Table 10.N2i Television programme

Harvard	APA
PORRIT, Jonathan. (1991). Interview by Jonathan DIMBLEBY on Panorama. BBC 1 television, broadcast, 18 Mar. 1991.	Porrit, J. (1991, March 18). Interview by Jonathan Dimbleby on Panorama. television BBC 1 broadcast.

MLA	Numerical
Porrit, Jonathan. Interview with Jonathan Dimbleby on Panorama. BBC 1 tv broadcast, 18 Mar. 1991.	PORRIT, Jonathan. Interview by Jonathan DIMBLEBY on Panorama. BBC 1 television, broadcast,18 Mar. 1991.

Table 10.N2ii Television programme

Harvard	APA
WOOD, Michael. (Presenter). (2006). Gilbert White the nature man. BBC4 television broadcast, 28 June 2006.	Wood, M. (Presenter). (2006, June 28). Gilbert White the nature man. BBC4 television broadcast.

MLA	Numerical
Wood, Michael. (Presenter). Gilbert White the Nature Man. BBC4 television broadcast, 28 June 2006.	WOOD, Michael. (Presenter). Gilbert White the nature man. BBC4 television broadcast, 28 June 2006.

Table 10.N2iii Television programme

Harvard	APA
The Simpsons (2006). Episode. Bye-bye Nerdy. Channel 4 Television broadcast, 28 June 2006.	*The Simpsons* (2006, June 28). Episode: Bye-bye Nerdy. Channel 4 Television broadcast.
MLA	**Numerical**
The Simpsons. Episode: "Bye-bye Nerdy". Channel 4 Television broadcast, 28 June 2006	*The Simpsons*. Episode. Bye-bye Nerdy. Channel 4 Television broadcast, 28 June 2006.

N3 Audio productions on CD, tape and vinyl LPs

You should include:

- Name of writer, if applicable, e.g. songwriter, composer, poet
- Title of item, in inverted commas or italics
- Specify the medium and (excepting MLA) enclose description within squared brackets, e.g. [CD-ROM]
- Track, side or position on medium
- Give name of producer, speaker, reader or performer(s), whoever is relevant to the evidence presented
- Where produced and publishers/producers of item, e.g. name of record label and any reference number
- Date (year) of copyright or production, if known.

The order in which you include items depends on the desired emphasis. You may, for example, want to call attention to the original writer, or to the performer, or to the title of the item.

Examples:

Table 10.N3i Audio-CD

Harvard	APA
ROBERTS, Roland. (2000). *Passive music for accelerated learning*. [Audio-CD]. Carmarthen: Crown House Publishing.	Roberts, R. (2000). *Passive music for accelerated learning*. [Audio-CD]. Carmarthen: Crown House Publishing.
MLA	**Numerical**
Roberts, Roland. Passive Music for Accelerated Learning. Audio-CD. Carmarthen: Crown House, 2000.	ROBERTS, Roland. *Passive music for accelerated learning*. [Audio-CD]. Carmarthen: Crown House Publishing, 2000.

Table 10.N3ii Audio-tape

Harvard	APA
OWEN, Wilfred. *Anthem for doomed youth: selected poems and letters*. [Audio-cassette]. (1993). Side 2: poem: 'Disabled'. Read by Kenneth Branagh. London: Random House Audiobooks.	Owen, W. *Anthem for doomed youth: Selected poems & letters*. [Audio-cassette]. (1993). Side 2: poem: 'Disabled'. Read by Kenneth Branagh. London: Random House Audiobooks.
MLA	**Numerical**
Wilfred Owen: Anthem for Doomed Youth: Selected Poems and Letters. [Audio-cassette]. Side 2: poem: "Disabled". Read by Kenneth Branagh. London: Random House Audiobooks, 1993.	OWEN, Wilfred. *Anthem for doomed youth: selected poems and letters*. [Audio-cassette]. Side 2: poem: 'Disabled'. Read by Kenneth Branagh. London: Random House Audiobooks, 1993.

Table 10.N3iii Vinyl LP

Harvard	APA
DELIUS, Frederick. (1982). *Delius*. Hallé Orchestra. [LP]. Hayes: Music for Pleasure, CFP 40373.	Delius, F. (1982). *Delius*. Hallé Orchestra. [LP]. Hayes: Music for Pleasure, CFP 40373
MLA	**Numerical**
Delius, Frederick. Delius. Hallé Orchestra. LP. Hayes: Music for Pleasure, CFP 40373, 1982.	DELIUS, Frederick. *Delius*. Hallé Orchestra. [LP]. Hayes: Music for Pleasure, CFP 40373, 1982.

N4 Film sources

These include any film produced, on DVD, VHS or downloaded from the Internet for entertainment, interest or educational purposes. There is no set formula for listing elements, although both the APA and MLA offer examples in their respective style guides. However, in most instances you should include:

- The title, in italics or underlined
- Year of release (or production, if emphasizing DVD or VHS medium)
- Medium, e.g. [DVD] in squared brackets (exception of MLA)
- Volume, part number or episode (if in a set)
- Country of origin (where made)
- Place and name of distributor/movie studio.

The order in which these will appear will depend on the reason or emphasis that you wish to place on their inclusion in your assignment. You may, for example, be discussing the work of the director generally or referring to the playwright, in which case you would want to start with their names. Or, it might be the film itself, the themes, metaphors, dialogue, that interest you, so in this instance the title will feature first. Some examples:

Film: fiction

Table 10.N4i Fiction film

Harvard
LOACH, Ken. (Director) and Sally HIBBIN (Producer). (1993). *Raining stones*. [DVD film]. London: Channel Four Television (FilmFour).

MLA
Loach, Ken. (Director) and Sally Hibbin. (Producer). Raining Stones. DVD. London: Channel Four Television (FilmFour), 1993.

APA
Loach, K. (Director) & Hibbin, S. (Producer). (1993). *Raining stones*. [DVD film]. London: Channel Four Television (FilmFour).

Numerical
LOACH, Ken. (Director) and Sally HIBBIN (Producer). *Raining stones*. [DVD film]. London: Channel Four Television (FilmFour), 1993.

Table 10.N4ii Same film, but different emphasis

Harvard
ALLEN, Jim (Screenplay). (1993). *Raining stones*. [DVD film]. London: Channel Four Television (FilmFour).

MLA
Allen, Jim (Screenplay). Raining Stones. DVD film. London: Channel Four TV (FilmFour), 1993.

APA
Allen, J. (Screenplay). (1993). *Raining stones*. [DVD film]. London: Channel Four Television (FilmFour).

Numerical
ALLEN, Jim. (Screenplay). *Raining stones*. [DVD film]. London: Channel Four Television (FilmFour), 1993.

Table 10.N4iii Fiction film

Harvard
SCHAFFER, Peter. (Playwright). (1977). *Equus*. Motion picture starring Richard Burton. [VHS]. Produced in Britain by MGM/United Artists Home Video.

MLA
Schaffer, Peter. (Playwright). Equus. Motion picture starring RICHARD BURTON. VHS. Prod. Britain. MGM/United Artists Home Video, 1977.

APA
Schaffer, P. (Playwright). (1977). *Equus*. Motion picture starring Richard Burton. [VHS]. Produced in Britain by MGM/United Artists Home Video.

Numerical
SCHAFFER, Peter. (Playwright). *Equus*. Motion picture starring RICHARD BURTON. [VHS]. Produced in Britain by MGM/United Artists Home Video, 1977.

Table 10.N4iv Fiction film

Harvard
HANKS, Tom and Steven SPIELBERG (Producers). (2001). *Band of brothers: part 9: why we fight*. Television film series. Available on VHS. Vol. 4. USA: Warner Brothers· Warner Home Video.

APA
Hanks, T. & Spielberg, S. (Producers). (2001). *Band of brothers: part 9: Why we fight*. Television film series [VHS Set] Vol. 4. USA: Warner Brothers: Warner Home Video.

(Cont.)

MLA	Numerical
Hanks, Tom and Steven Spielberg (Producers). Band of Brothers: part 9: "Why We Fight". TV film series. Available VHS. Vol. 4. USA: Warner Bros: Warner Home Video, 2001.	HANKS, Tom. and Steven SPIELBERG (Producers). *Band of brothers: part 9: why we fight*. Television film series. Available on VHS. Vol. 4. USA: Warner Brothers: Warner Home Video, 2001.

Table 10.N4v Fiction film

Harvard	APA
Twelve angry men. (1957). [Motion picture]. USA: MGM Studios	*Twelve angry men*. (1957). [Motion picture]. USA: MGM Studios
MLA	**Numerical**
Twelve Angry Men. Motion picture. USA: MGM Studios, 1957.	*Twelve angry men*. [Motion picture].USA: MGM Studios, 1957.

Non-fiction film productions

It may be necessary to add postal or Internet contact details to help others locate the smaller, independent production companies.

Table 10.N5 Non-fiction film with postal contact details

Harvard	APA
The presentation: a guide to effective speaking (n.d). [VHS]. Bromley: TV Choice Productions [P.O. Box 597, Bromley, Kent BR2 OYB].	*The presentation: A guide to effective speaking* (n.d). [VHS]. Bromley: TV Choice Productions [P.O. Box 597, Bromley, Kent BR2 OYB].
MLA	**Numerical**
The Presentation: a Guide to Effective Speaking. VHS. Bromley: TV Choice Productions [P.O. Box 597, Bromley, Kent, BR2 OYB], n.d.	*The presentation: a guide to effective speaking*. VHS. Bromley: TV Choice Productions [P.O. Box 597, Bromley, Kent BR2 OYB], n.d.

Table 10.N6 Non-fiction film

Harvard	APA
Guardians of the night (2005). [DVD]. USA: Janson Media.	*Guardians of the night* (2005). [DVD]. USA: Janson Media.
MLA	**Numerical**
Guardians of the Night. DVD. USA: Janson Media, 2005.	*Guardians of the night*. [DVD]. USA: Janson Media, 2005.

O Public performances and events (including theatre, dance, music, talks)

You may want to reference a live event or performance to discuss an aspect of a talk, performance or production, or to use an extract from it to make a particular point. Wherever possible, try to include some printed evidence, e.g. a programme, that you could present as an appendix item in your assignment to support the points you make.

01 Play

The scripts of plays are usually available in printed form, so you should be able to give details of the playwright and the publisher of the script, particularly when referring to dialogue, or to any themes and metaphors underpinning the dialogue. To reference dialogue in plays, start with the name of the playwright, then state year of publication, title of play (in italics or underlined). You also need to state the medium, e.g. 'play', unless it is obvious, and include details of the Act, Scene and/or page number, and publisher information.

If your emphasis is more concerned with the production, you can give more attention to this and less on other details. In this instance, you would start with the name of the play.

With performance arts sources, British Standard examples show full first name(s) of originator for Harvard and Numerical referencing.

Table 10.01i Emphasis on text in published script

Harvard	APA
KEMPINSKI, Tom. (1983). *Duet for one*. [Play]. Act 1, p.21. Script published London: Samuel French.	Kempinski, T. (1983). *Duet for one*. [Play]. Act 1, p.21. Script published London: Samuel French Inc.
MLA	**Numerical**
Kempinski, Tom. Duet for One. Play: Act 1, p.21. Script published London: S. French, 1983.	KEMPINSKI, Tom. *Duet for one*. [Play]. Act 1, p.21. Script published London: Samuel French, 1983.

Table 10.01ii Emphasis on the production and cast

Harvard	APA
Duet for One by Tom KEMPINSKI (1980). [Play]. First produced 13 Feb 1980 at Bush Theatre, London. Performers: Frances de la TOUR, David de KEYSER. Director: ROGER SMITH.	*Duet for one* by Kempinski, T. (1980, February 13). [Play]. First produced at Bush Theatre, London. Performers: Frances de la Tour, David de Keyser. Director: Roger Smith.
MLA	**Numerical**
Duet For One by Tom Kempinski. Play. Perfs. Frances de la Tour, David de Keyser. Dir. Roger Smith. First produced at Bush Theatre, London, 13 Feb.1980.	*Duet for one* by Tom KEMPINSKI. [Play]. First Produced at Bush Theatre, London. Performers: Frances de la TOUR, David de KEYSER. Director: Roger SMITH, on 13 Feb. 1980

02 Dance

As with theatrical productions and film, the emphasis in the reference will depend on the context of the assignment and what is being discussed. The emphasis, for example, might be on the choreography and music, or on the main performers.

However, you would normally include:

- Title, in italics or underlined
- Details of medium (e.g. contemporary dance; ballet) unless obvious from the name of company
- Year of production
- Name of dance troop or company
- Place of company base, or place of performance.

You could include also names of performers, choreographer, musical composer or arranger and other details, as necessary.

Table 10.02i Dance

Harvard	**APA**
Wuthering Heights (2003). [Ballet]. David NIXON (Choreographer). Claude-Michel SCHONBERG (Music). Leeds: Northern Ballet.	*Wuthering Heights* (2003). [Ballet]. Nixon, D. (Choreographer), Schonberg, Claude-Michel (Music). Leeds: Northern Ballet.
MLA	**Numerical**
Wuthering Heights. Ballet. Choreog. David Nixon, Mus. Claude-Michel Schonberg. Leeds: Northern Ballet, 2003.	*Wuthering Heights*. [Ballet]. David NIXON (Choreographer). Claude-Michel SCHONBERG (Music). Leeds: Northern Ballet, 2003.

Table 10.02ii Dance

Harvard	**APA**
Sacred monsters (2006). [Dance: kathak and ballet]. Performers: Akram KHAN and Sylvie GUILLEM. London: Sadler's Wells, 19–23 Sept. 2006.	*Sacred monsters* (2006, September 19–23). [Dance: kathak & ballet]. Performers: A. Khan & S. Guillem. London: Sadler's Wells.
MLA	**Numerical**
Sacred Monsters. Dance: kathak and ballet. Perfs: Akram Khan and Sylvie Guillem. London: Sadler's Wells, 19–23 Sept. 2006.	*Sacred monsters*. [Dance: kathak and ballet]. Performers: Akram KHAN and Sylvie GUILLEM. London: Sadler's Wells, 19–23 Sept. 2006.

---

03 Music

To reference a live music performance, you would normally start with the title of the work (in italics or underlined), followed by name of composer, then give details of the performance, including name of performers and place of performance. Other details can be included, if relevant, including name of conductor or leader, and names of soloists. It may be occasionally necessary to clarify that it is a music performance, if this is not obvious from other details supplied (see also section R: Miscellaneous: music scores).

Table 10.03i Music

Harvard	APA
Double piano concerto. MOZART, Wolfgang (2006). London Mozart Players. Pianists: G. and S. PEKINEL. Leeds: Town Hall, 14 Oct. 2006.	*Double piano concerto*. Mozart. (2006, October 14). London Mozart Players. Pianists: G. & S. Pekinel. Leeds: Town Hall.
MLA	**Numerical**
Double Piano Concerto. Mozart, Wolfgang London Mozart Players. Pianists: Guher and Suher Pekinel. Leeds: Town Hall, 14 Oct. 2006.	*Double piano concerto*. MOZART, Wolfgang. London Mozart Players. Pianists: G. and S. PEKINEL. Leeds: Town Hall, 14 Oct. 2006.

Table 10.03ii Music

Harvard	APA
Jerry Springer, the opera (2006). Musical. Bradford: Alhambra Theatre, 22–27 May 2006.	*Jerry Springer, the opera* (2006, May 22–27). [Musical]. Bradford: Alhambra Theatre.
MLA	**Numerical**
Jerry Springer, the Opera. Musical. Bradford: Alhambra, 22–27 May 2006.	*Jerry Springer, the opera*. Musical. Bradford: Alhambra Theatre, 22–27 May 2006.

Table 10.03iii Music

Harvard	APA
The lark (2006). [Folk song]. Composer/Performer, Kate RUSBY. Chepstow Arts Festival, Chepstow Castle, 8 July 2006.	*The lark* (2006, July 8). [Folk song]. Composer/Performer, Kate Rusby. Chepstow Arts Festival, Chepstow Castle.
MLA	**Numerical**
The Lark. Folk song. Comp./Perf. Kate Rusby. Chepstow Arts Festival, Chepstow Castle, 8 July 2006.	*The lark*. [Folk song]. Composer/Performer, Kate RUSBY. Chepstow Arts Festival, Chepstow Castle, 8 July 2006.

04 Other live public event (e.g. talk, reading, address)

In most instances start with name of speaker, performer or principal person, title or type of event or performance, and the date of event and its location. Add other detail that is relevant to the source and point being made in the assignment. If there was a title given to any speech or talk, this can be shown in italics or underlined.

Table 10.04i Address

Harvard	APA
BENN, Tony. (2006). Speaker. Tolpuddle Martyr's Festival. Dorset: Tolpuddle, 16 July 2006.	Benn, T. (2006, July 16). Speaker. Tolpuddle Martyr's Festival. Dorset: Tolpuddle.
MLA	**Numerical**
Benn, Tony. Speaker. Tolpuddle Martyr's Festival. Dorset: Tolpuddle, 16 July 2006.	BENN, Tony. Speaker. Tolpuddle Martyr's Festival. Dorset: Tolpuddle, 16 July 2006.

Table 10.04ii Reading

Harvard	APA
DUFFY, Carol, Ann. (2006). Poetry reading. West Sussex: Chichester Festival, 22 July 2006.	Duffy, C.A. (2006, July 22). Poetry reading. West Sussex: Chichester Festival.
MLA	**Numerical**
Duffy, Carol Ann. Poetry reading. West Sussex: Chichester Festival, 22 July 2006.	DUFFY, Carol, Ann. Poetry reading. West Sussex: Chichester Festival, 22 July 2006.

Table 10.04iii Talk

Harvard	APA
GREER, Germaine. (2004) Talk: *Shakespeare and sexual difference*. Perth: University of Western Australia, 7 Sept. 2004.	Greer, G. (2004, September 7) Talk: *Shakespeare and sexual difference*. Perth: University of Western Australia.
MLA	**Numerical**
Greer, Germaine. Talk: Shakespeare and Sexual Difference. Perth: Univ. of Western Australia, 7 Sept. 2004.	GREER, Germaine. Talk: *Shakespeare and sexual difference*. Perth: University of Western Australia, 7 Sept. 2004.

P Referencing course lectures

You can reference lectures from course tutors and visiting guest speakers. You can include:

- Name of lecturer
- Year
- Medium (lecture) and details of lecture, e.g. title or topic
- Module and course details, including academic year
- Place and name of institution
- Date of lecture.

You could include evidence from the lecture, e.g. handouts, as appendix items, if relevant.

Table 10.P1 Lecture

Harvard	APA
NEVILLE, C. (2005) *Lecture on academic writing.* Self-development module. First year undergraduate course 2005/6. Bradford: University of Bradford, 25 Nov. 2005.	Neville, C. (2005, November 25) *Lecture on academic writing.* Self-development module. First year undergraduate course 2005/6. Bradford: University of Bradford.
MLA	**Numerical**
Neville, Colin. (2005) <u>Lecture on Academic Writing</u>. Self-development module. First year undergraduate course 2005/6. Bradford: University of Bradford, 25 Nov. 2005.	NEVILLE, C. *Lecture on academic writing.* Self-development module. First year undergraduate course 2005/6. Bradford: University of Bradford, 25 Nov. 2005.

Q Interviews and discussions, including telephone conversations

Personal communications, without supporting data, should be only cited in the text, or footnoted, but are not given a full reference. A citation-only in the text of an assignment might look like this: (Telephone conversation with author 21 Oct. 2006).

However, if data has been collected and can be made accessible to others, e.g. interview notes, transcripts, completed interview questionnaires or recordings made, then a full reference can be given. Written data collected from interviews can be added as appendix items, if appropriate (check with your tutor).

If you include a full reference for this type of evidence, you need to include the family name of the interviewee, initials, year of interview, the purpose of the interview, place of interview, name of interviewer (if you are the interviewer: 'with author'), and date of interview. You could also refer the tutor to the appropriate appendix item, as shown in the first example that follows.

You do not need to underline or italicize the title element of the full reference.

Table 10.Q1i Personal interview

Harvard	APA
BROWN, J. (2005). Personal interview. Marketing survey for MA project. At GKN, Leeds, with Jim CLARKE, 20 Mar. 2005 (see appendix item 2a).	Brown, J. (2005, March 20). Personal interview. Marketing survey for MA project. At GKN, Leeds, with Jim Clarke (see appendix item 2a).
MLA	**Numerical**
Brown, James. Personal Interview. Marketing survey for MA project. At GKN, Leeds, with Jim Clarke, 20 Mar. 2005 (see appendix item 2a).	BROWN, J. Personal interview. Marketing survey for MA project. At GKN, Leeds, with Jim CLARKE, 20 Mar. 2005 (see appendix item 2a).

Table 10.Q1ii Telephone interview

Harvard	APA
WALTERS, M. (2006). Telephone interview with author, 25 July 2006 (see appendix item 3).	Walters, M. (2006, July 25). Telephone Interview with author (see appendix item 3).
MLA	**Numerical**
Walters, Mark. Telephone interview with author. 25 July 2006 (see appendix item 3).	WALTERS, M. Telephone interview with author, 25 July 2006 (see appendix item 3).

You could also reference **published interviews** in journals, magazines or elsewhere. The sequence for this would be:

- Name of person interviewed (last or family name first, then initials)
- Year of interview
- Title of interview
- Explanation of interview
- Interviewer's name
- Title of publication (in italics or underlined)
- Publication details, including full date and page number.

Example of published interview (in Harvard style):

TURNER, N. (2005). Turner's secret: the short-haul factor. Interview with Nigel Turner, BMI's new CEO, by Ben Flanagan. *The Observer (Business Section)*, 22 May 2005, p.18.

R Miscellaneous sources

R1 Music scores

Music scores are treated like books, except that the date of composition appears after the title. If there is no year of publication shown for the score, put 'no date' or 'n.d'.

Table 10.R1 Music score

Harvard	APA
BRUCH, Max. *Concerto in G Minor, Op. 26* (1867). USA: New York: G. Schirmer. (n.d.).	Bruch, M. *Concerto in G Minor, Op. 26* (1867). USA: New York: G. Schirmer. (n.d.).
MLA	**Numerical**
Bruch, Max. Concerto in G Minor, Op. 26 (1867). USA: New York: G. Schirmer. n.d.	BRUCH, Max. *Concerto in G Minor, Op. 26* (1867). USA: New York: G. Schirmer. (n.d.).

R2 Posters or wall-charts

Posters or wall-charts can contain useful information or may be of artistic, social or historical importance. In the text of the assignment you would normally outline your reasons for citing the poster or wall-chart, so the reference detail you give is to help others identify the source. So keep information to a minimum, but supply enough to help others to trace it, if required. Include name of the designer or artist, if known, title or type of poster, year of publication, state medium, e.g. [wall-chart], details of the source or supplier, and exact date of issue if it was issued as a supplement in a newspaper or magazine.

If the poster is on display in a public collection, state the place and name of the museum or gallery. In the example that follows, the poster does not have a title, so the description of the item (recruitment poster) is not in italics or underlined.

Table 10.R2i Poster

Harvard	APA
LEETE, Alfred (1914) Recruitment poster. London: Imperial War Museum.	Leete, A. (1914) Recruitment poster. London: Imperial War Museum.
MLA	**Numerical**
Leete, Alfred. (1914) Recruitment poster. London: Imperial War Museum.	LEETE, Alfred. Recruitment poster. London: Imperial War Museum, 1914.

Table 10.R2ii Wall-chart

Harvard	APA
Whales (2006). [Wall-chart]. Supplement in *The Guardian*, 25 June 2006.	Whales (2006, June 25). [Wall-chart]. Supplement in *The Guardian*.
MLA	**Numerical**
"Whales". Wall-chart. Supplement in The Guardian, 25 June 2006.	Whales. [Wall-chart]. Supplement in *The Guardian*, 25 June 2006.

Table 10.R2iii Poster in series

Harvard	APA
Ethel Waters (2006). [Poster]. In *Stars of the Harlem renaissance* series. USA: Emeryville: art.com.	*Ethel Waters* (2006). In *Stars of the Harlem renaissance* series [Poster]. USA: Emeryville: art.com.
MLA	**Numerical**
Ethel Waters (2006). Poster. In Stars of the Harlem Renaissance series. USA: Emeryville: art.com.	*Ethel Waters*. [Poster]. *Stars of the Harlem renaissance* series. USA: Emeryville: art.com, 2006.

R3 Postal items

First day issues, which are envelopes bearing the cancellation dates of the first day of issue of stamps, can be interesting as historical or design sources. They are usually mailed from the place where the stamp was first put into circulation. You should include country of origin, year, nature or type of first day cover, number (if a limited edition), design features of stamp, if relevant, and any significant markings or postal franking on envelope.

Table 10.R3 First day issue

Harvard	APA
CANADA (1928). *First flight cover via Amos to Siscoe.* 28th Oct. Bearing 'Amos', 'Quebec', 'New York', 'Siscoe' and other postmarks on illustrated envelope.	Canada (1928, October 28). *First flight cover via Amos to Siscoe.* Bearing "Amos", "Quebec", "New York", "Siscoe" and other postmarks on illustrated envelope.
MLA	**Numerical**
Canada. <u>First flight cover via Amos to Siscoe.</u> Bearing "Amos", "Quebec", "New York", "Siscoe" and other postmarks on illustrated envelope. 28 Oct. 1928.	CANADA. *First flight cover via Amos to Siscoe.* 28th Oct. Bearing 'Amos', 'Quebec', 'New York', 'Siscoe' and other postmarks on illustrated envelope. 28 Oct. 1928

R4 Postcards

Postcards can be useful sources for the social or art historian. You would normally describe the features of the relevant postcard in the text of your assignment, so the full reference would just contain enough information to help the reader identify the location of the postcard, e.g. gallery, private collection, plus other relevant identifying features, i.e. reference number or title. These would include the name of the artist or photographer, if known, and date, or estimated date, of first printing. Unless there is a specific title, you do not need to italicize or underline the general description of the item (see first example below).

Table 10.R4i Postcard

Harvard	APA
MCGILL, D. (1927). Seaside cartoon postcard. Ref.115. Holmfirth: Postcard Museum	McGill, D. (1927). Seaside cartoon postcard. Ref. 115. Holmfirth: Postcard Museum
MLA	**Numerical**
McGill, Donald. (1927). Seaside cartoon postcard. 115. Holmfirth: Postcard Museum	MCGILL, D. Seaside cartoon postcard. Ref.115. Holmfirth: Postcard Museum, 1927.

Table 10.R4ii Postcard with specific title

Harvard	APA
Picnic make believe (circa 1930s). Postcard. Photographer unknown. Private collection of Tom PHILLIPS.	*Picnic make believe* (circa 1930s). [Postcard]. Photographer unknown. Private collection of Tom Phillips.
MLA	**Numerical**
<u>Picnic Make Believe</u>. Postcard. Private Collection: Tom Phillips. Photographer unknown (circa 1930s).	*Picnic make believe*. Postcard. Private collection of Tom PHILLIPS. Photographer unknown (circa 1930s).

R5   Sacred or classical texts

Sacred texts

These include the Bible, Talmud, Koran, Upanishads and major classical works, such as ancient Greek and Roman works. If you are simply quoting a verse or extract, you do not need to give full reference entries. Instead, you should include the detail in the text of your assignment, for example:

> The film script at this point echoes the Bible: 'And God looked upon the earth, and, behold, it was corrupt; for all flesh had corrupted his way upon the earth' (Gen. 6:12).

However, if you were referring to a particular edition for a significant reason, it could be listed in full in the references, e.g.

> Good News Bible (2004). Rainbow Edition. New York: Harper Collins.

Abbreviations

Abbreviations can be used in citations, e.g. Gen., for Genesis; Ezek., for Ezekiel. The online Journal of Biblical Studies has a useful website giving abbreviations for all biblical works likely to be cited (Search for 'Journal of Biblical Studies – Abbreviations').

Copies of *New Testament Studies* 34, 3 (1988): 476–79 and *Journal of Biblical Literature* 107, 3, can be consulted for abbreviations and the MLA Handbook also has a section (7.7) on abbreviations for literary and religious works.

Classical texts

Students studying the Classics are often given advice on referencing these texts by their tutors, but the format for citing sources in the text is normally, as follows:

- Name of author
- Title (italics or underlined)
- Details of book/poem
- Line number.

For example, Homer, *Iliad* 18.141–143.

If an author wrote only one work, e.g. Herodotus, you may omit the name of the work, i.e. *Histories*.

Page numbers should be from the translation or edition cited. However, citations to Plato and Plutarch should be included in the text using the Stephanus pagination, when possible. These works are divided into numbers, and each number will be divided into equal sections a, b, c, d and e. The numbers, however, must be used in conjunction with a title to make sense of them, e.g. *Republic*, 344a2.

The works of Aristotle are usually cited using the Bekker system of numbers. These numbers take the format of up to four digits, a letter for column 'a' or 'b', then the line number. These should be shown against the title of the particular work of Aristotle, e.g. Politics: 1252a1 4.

The full details of the book used should be included in the references, bibliography or 'works cited' section.

S   Referencing electronic sources

Electronic sources are very important to students. The Internet is quick, accessible and easy to use, and, if the right keyword searches are made, it can produce useful evidence for assignments.

However, there are drawbacks to using electronic sources, particularly the Internet, and students often experience difficulty in citing and referencing them. The apparent absence of authorship detail, dates and page numbers on some websites, plus the length of URL addresses can cause problems. Citation of sources in the text of an assignment can also cause difficulty, with students often uncertain what to put.

Common mistakes

- You should not put a www address as a citation. You always put the name of an author, or the source organization, but never cite a URL address in the body of an assignment.
- You do not need a separate list of www sites in your 'References', 'Works cited' or 'Bibliography' sections. Internet sites are incorporated, along with other sources, into one list at the end of the assignment.
- Another common mistake is to simply paste in a URL address to a list of references, without any other supporting information, such as the title of item, the name of hosting organization and date the information was viewed.

Examples of a range of electronic sources will be presented later in this section. The examples are, of course, not exhaustive, but do offer examples of sources that students typically use in assignments. If you encounter sources not specifically illustrated in this book, the following 'Basic principles' and 'What to include' sections of this chapter should help you to work out how to reference them.

If you are using APA and MLA referencing styles, you can also consult the respective style guides produced by these organizations, as both include chapters on citing and referencing electronic sources. For Harvard and Numerical styles, the nearest thing to a benchmark guide to referencing electronic sources is the British Standard recommendations: BS ISO 690–2:1997, *Information and documentation – bibliographic references – part 2: Electronic documents or parts thereof.*

Basic principles of referencing electronic sources

There are four main principles or guidelines to referencing electronic sources.

First, and this is common for all types of referencing, the citation should link with the full reference. What appears in the citation will begin the full reference entry. So, in the case of an author–date in-text citation, the citation might be, as follows:

Citation: (Friends of the Earth 2005)
This would then link to the full list of references (in Harvard style):

Reference:
FRIENDS OF THE EARTH (2005). *Corporates: corporate power.* Available at http//
www.foe.co.uk/campaigns/corporates/issues/corporate_power/ [Accessed 13 Dec.
2005].

Second, tutors should be directed as closely as possible to the online information
being cited and referenced. This usually means giving the complete URL addresses to
take your tutors to the same screen you looked at, rather than leading them to just
home or menu pages. However, if the URL is ridiculously long, for example, stretching
over three or more lines, it would be better to give the homepage address and then give
a series of keyword search words to take the reader to the relevant screen. If access to a
particular online database is restricted or password protected, there is no point in supplying a URL address as others will not be able to access the site without a password.
Web addresses are given only in references if the source is freely accessible to others. In
the case of restricted access, you need to state the name and give details of the database
publisher to enable others to gain access to it, if wanted.

Third, ensure you show website addresses that work! There is nothing more frustrating than to type out the URL address given, only to find the address given is incorrect.
Make sure you have copied them or pasted them in correctly.

Fourth, because sites do disappear without warning, it is wise to print out copies of
sources used for citation purposes to show a tutor, if required, and some tutors will insist
you do this. These copies can be included in an appendix, or a note included in the
assignment for the reader to the effect that they can be made available to the tutor, if
required.

What to include

Generally, the following elements are listed in the order in which they appear in a full
reference entry. However, there may be occasional exceptions to this rule because of
particular referencing style guidelines, either because the nature of the source, or the
context in which you want to use it in an assignment.

You can include:

- Main responsibility for message
- Title of work consulted
- Type of medium
- Publisher and place of publication
- Date of publication
- Online address or location within portable database
- Name of database, if applicable
- Other identifying features
- Date you looked at the information.

Table 1O.SOi What do these elements mean in practice?

Main responsibility for message	This means the name of the person, persons or corporate body responsible for writing or editing the document you looked at, including weblog (or 'blog') sites. This can include the name of an online site responsible for hosting the information, if no named author is shown. If a subsidiary company of a larger corporate body is responsible, show the names of both
Title of work consulted	This means the main title(s) and subtitle(s) of the source you are citing or listing. Translations of title may be added, and these are usually enclosed in brackets
Type of medium	The type of electronic medium should be indicated, e.g. CD-ROM; database online; computer program on disk; bulletin board online; electronic mail, etc.
Publisher and place of publication	This would apply particularly to documents on portable databases and refer to the organization responsible for preparing the data and/or the medium, and where they are located. Do not forget, one of the main aims of referencing is to help the reader locate the material, which includes knowing who the publisher is, and where they can be located. In the case of something that originally appeared in print, you need to show the name of the original publishers, as well as details of the online or portable database you looked at
Date of publication	This is any date of publication or copyright shown on original work. For online material, show the last date of update or revision. If no dates are shown, put (n.d.), (no date) or (date unknown)
Online address, or location within portable database	Show full electronic online address and any other commands or methods of access to the document. This information is usually prefixed with a relevant term, e.g. 'Available from . . .' or 'Retrieved from . . .' or by using angle brackets to enclose URL addresses (see MLA examples). In most cases of URL addresses, you would copy and paste in the full address to take the reader straight to the relevant data. In a portable database, give details of how and where to locate the relevant data, e.g. page numbers etc.
Date you looked at the information	Electronic information can disappear or change very quickly, so it is important you state the date you looked at the source. With Harvard, APA and Numerical styles of referencing, you can precede this date with the words 'Accessed . . .' 'Retrieved from . . .' or 'Cited'. As stated earlier, it is advisable to print out copies of online sources cited to prove, if necessary, the material was to be found on the date and on the site stated in the reference
Other identifying features	The principle of helping readers identify location of sources must be kept in mind. This could mean including, for example, page, screen, paragraph or line number (if shown); any labelled part, section, table, graph, chart; any host-specific label or designation. If in doubt – include it

The order these elements will appear in will depend on the referencing style and type of source, but if you include all or most of this information you will not go far wrong.

Table 10.SOii An example of an Internet site, shown in the four main referencing styles	
Harvard	JISC PLAGIARISM ADVISORY SERVICE (2001). *Plagiarism – a good practice guide.* Available at http://www.jiscpas.ac.uk/apppage.cgi?USERPAGE=6296 [Accessed 23 Aug. 2006].
APA	JISC Plagiarism Advisory Service (2001). *Plagiarism – a good practice guide.* Retrieved August 23, 2006 from http://www.jiscpas.ac.uk/ apppage.cgi?USERPAGE=6296
MLA	JISC Plagiarism Advisory Service. Plagiarism – A Good Practice Guide. 2001. 23 Aug. 2006 <http://www.jiscpas.ac.uk/apppage.cgi?USERPAGE=6296>
Numerical	JISC PLAGIARISM ADVISORY SERVICE. *Plagiarism – a good practice guide*, 2001. Available at http://www.jiscpas.ac.uk/apppage.cgi?USERPAGE=6296 [Accessed 23 Aug. 2006].

Some hints

- Many Internet pages do not show an author's name. If this appears to be the case, it might be possible to identify an author by looking at the header of the HTML encoded text. To do this, click on the 'View' option in your browser and then either 'View Source' or 'Document Source'. If you cannot identify an author, cite the originator of the site/site name, or if this is not obvious, cite the title.
- If you find that, for some reason, an Internet URL address is not shown for the source concerned, you need then to give search terms to take others to the same source. The search terms can be entered after the URL address, and before the (Accessed–date) information.
- As mentioned earlier, you should cite the year the document was last updated. You can find this, if it exists, usually at the foot of the page.

Evaluating sites

As stated earlier, the Internet is a rich source of information for students. It is also, unfortunately, the unregulated host to sites that have been created by their authors as arenas for their ill-informed and biased opinions.

You should never let the ease of using the Internet replace using a library and using textbooks. Before an academic textbook reaches the library it has to go through a series of quality filters, including critical peer scrutiny, and may have to go through a number of amendments until the publishers are satisfied with it. Not so with the Internet. Anyone can send out into the wide blue yonder uncorrected and opinionated junk. However, the Internet can and does provide a useful starting point for ideas and the pursuit of ideas.

Reliable Internet sites can certainly be used and cited in assignments. But how can you evaluate them? Munger and Campbell (2002) and Rumsey (2004) suggest the following questions should be asked of sites to help evaluate their credibility:

Table 10.SOiii Evaluation questions

Author/purpose	Content	Design
• Who is taking 'ownership' of the information presented? • Why has this site been established – is it clear from the introduction? • Who is the sponsor of the site – who pays for it? • Who is the intended readership for the site? • Are there any biases or possible hidden agendas in the site? • Is it clear who is the originator or author for the item you want to cite? • Is there a link to any named author's email address? • Does the author have any academic or professional affiliation?	• Were you linked to this site from a reliable source? • How comprehensive is the site in its coverage? • Is the site regularly updated? When **was** the site last updated? • How are sources referenced and documented? • Are the links provided working? (*A site that is not being updated, including the hyperlinks, should not be trusted.*) • On what basis are links selected? What rationale for the links is given?	• Does it **look** professional? • Is the site easy to navigate and use? • Does the resource follow good principles of design, proper grammar, spelling and style? If it does not, beware! • Does the site include advertising? If so, might this influence the range and objectivity of the material?

Quoting from the Internet

Quoting an author directly should always be done for a particular purpose, for example, to convey a sense of the 'voice' of a particular author or organization.

Example of an extract from a student essay (following Harvard):

> However, Howard Gardner regards the term 'domain' in a completely different way: 'The domain in a society can be thought of as the kinds of roles listed in the Yellow Pages of a phone book – anything from Accounting to Zoology ' (Gardner 2005).

The reference for this quotation, which was taken from the 'Frequently asked questions' (FAQ) section of the author's website, would be referenced, as follows (example shown in the Harvard style):

> GARDNER, H. (2005). *Domains*. Howard GARDNER Homepages. FAQ, p.2, Available at www.howardgardner.com [Accessed 22 April 05].

Secondary sources on the Internet

You will also encounter many Internet sources that summarize or quote indirectly the words of others. You treat these Internet sources as secondary sources. For example, on the 'Friends of the Earth' (FOE) Internet site, FOE quote the Executive Director of

Corpwatch, Joshua Karliner, as saying that: '*51 of the 100 world's largest economies are corporations*'.

If you were unable to locate the **primary source** (i.e. Joshua Karliner) to check the accuracy of this quotation, you could cite the Friends of the Earth site, although this would not be as desirable as checking out the primary source for yourself. The citation and reference, following Harvard, would be as follows:

Citation:
(Friends of the Earth 2005, quoting Joseph Karliner); or (Joseph Karliner, as quoted by Friends of the Earth 2005)
Reference (Harvard):
FRIENDS OF THE EARTH (2005). *Corporates: corporate power*. Available at http://www.foe.co.uk/campaigns/corporates/issues/corporate_power/ [Accessed 13 Dec. 2005].

Examples of online references follow.

S1 Book online

Table 10.S1 Book online (complete book)

Harvard	APA
HARDY, T. (1887). *The Woodlanders*. [Online]. (Ed.) M. MONCUR. The Literature Page. Available at http://www.literaturepage.com/read/the-woodlanders.html [Accessed 25 July 2006].	Hardy, T. (1887). *The Woodlanders*. [Online] (Ed.) M. Moncur. The Literature Page. Retrieved July 25, 2006 from http://www.literaturepage.com/read/the-woodlanders.html
MLA	**Numerical**
Hardy, Thomas (1887). <u>The Woodlanders</u>. [Online book]. (Ed.) Michael Moncur. <u>The Literature Page</u>. 25 July 2006. <http://www.literaturepage.com/read/the-woodlanders.html>	HARDY, T (1887). *The Woodlanders*. [Online book]. (Ed.) M. MONCUR. The Literature Page. Available at http://www.literaturepage.com/read/the-woodlanders.html [Accessed 25 July 2006].

S2 Part of the same book online

Give details of the chapter name or number and the page numbers concerned, and paste in or copy out the URL address to take the reader to the first page of the source item.

Table 10.S2 Part of the same book online

Harvard	APA
HARDY, T. (1887). *The Woodlanders*. [Online]. (Ed.) M. MONCUR. The Literature Page. Ch. 18, pp.139–41 Available at http://www.literaturepage.com/read/the-woodlanders–139.html [Accessed 25 July 2006].	Hardy, T. (1887). *The Woodlanders*. [Online] Ch. 18, pp.139–41 (Ed.) M. Moncur. The Literature Page. Retrieved July 25, 2006 from http://www.literaturepage.com/read/the-woodlanders–139.html

(*Cont.*)

MLA	Numerical
Hardy, Thomas (1887). Ch. 18, 139–41 The Woodlanders. [Online book]. Ed. Michael Moncur. The Literature Page. 25 July 2006. <http://www.literaturepage.com/read/the-woodlanders–139.html>	HARDY, T. (1887). *The Woodlanders*. [Online]. (Ed.) M. MONCUR. The Literature Page. Ch. 18, pp.139–41. Available at http://www.literature page.com/read/the-woodlanders–139.html [Accessed 25 July 2006].

S3 Online reference book/encyclopedia

If an author or site compiler is named, start with this. If not, start with the title of the reference entry. Include any date recorded against the entry, title of entry, name of online reference work and other relevant identifying features. However, be cautious when using online reference sites. Check the credentials of the editor, compiler or writer, or try and ascertain what backing the site has from professional associations, universities and other reputable organizations. Ask your tutors if they have a view on the site. It is also a good idea to check the entry against other online and printed reference works to verify the level of consistency and agreement there is among them.

The first example that follows is taken from a free online source, so the URL address is given, while the second shows a restricted password-only subscription source. There is no point in citing the URL address for this, so you can just state the title of the item, name of the subscription or database source and the date the information was retrieved.

Table 10.S3i Publicly accessible site; author's name shown

Harvard	APA
HALSALL, P. (2004). Byzantine studies on the Internet. *Online reference book for medieval studies*. Available at http://www.fordham.edu/halsall/byzantium/ [Accessed 30 July 2006].	Halsall, P. (2004, July 30).Byzantine studies on the Internet. *Online reference book for medieval studies*.Retrievedfromhttp://www.fordham.edu/halsall/byzantium/
MLA	**Numerical**
Halsall, Paul. "Byzantine Studies on the Internet". Online Reference Book for Medieval Studies. July 30 2006, <http://www.fordham.edu/halsall/byzantium/>	HALSALL, P. Byzantine studies on the Internet. *Online reference book for medieval studies*. Available at http://www.fordham.edu/halsall/byzantium/ [Accessed 30 July 2006].

Table 10.S3ii Subscription site; no author's name shown

Harvard	APA
Conflict (definition). In *Encyclopædia Britannica Online*. [Accessed July 29, 2006].	Conflict (definition). In *Encyclopædia Britannica Online*. Retrieved July 29, 2006.
MLA	**Numerical**
"Conflict." Encyclopædia Britannica Online. 29 July 2006.	Conflict (definition). In *Encyclopædia Britannica Online*. [Accessed July 29, 2006].

S4 Academic journal article (originally printed, but found online)

An academic journal article has usually been subject to peer-review scrutiny. The majority of these articles retrieved from the Internet are likely to be reproduced unabridged from their original printed forms, so the journal details are referenced as if it was a printed source. You can then simply add 'Electronic version' or 'Online' to the reference; see fictitious example i that follows. However, if you have any reason to believe changes, amendments or commentaries have been made from the original print version, you should include the URL address and the date you accessed the information; see example ii that follows.

Table 10.S4i Original academic journal article

Harvard	APA
BROWN, R. (2006). Plagiarism on the net. [Online] *Journal of Referencing Studies.* Summer, pp.266–272.	Brown, R. (2006, Summer). Plagiarism on the net. [Electronic Version]. *Journal of Referencing Studies*, 266–272.
MLA	**Numerical**
Brown, Robert. Plagiarism on the Net. [Online]. Journal of Referencing Studies, Summer, 2006, 266–272.	BROWN, R. Plagiarism on the net. [Online] *Journal of Referencing Studies.* 2006, Summer, pp.266–272.

Table 10.S4ii Amended academic journal article

Harvard	APA
BROWN, R. (2006). Plagiarism on the net. [Online] *Journal of Referencing Studies.* Summer, pp.266–272. Available at http://www.JRS.org [Accessed 23 Oct. 2006]	Brown, R. (2006, Summer). Plagiarism on the net. [Electronic Version]. *Journal of Referencing Studies*, 266–272. Retrieved October 23, from http://www.JRS.org
MLA	**Numerical**
Brown, Robert. Plagiarism on the Net. [Online]. Journal for Referencing Studies, Summer, 2006, 266–272. 13 Oct.2006 <http://www.JRS.org>	BROWN, R. Plagiarism on the net. [Online] *Journal for Referencing Studies.* 2006, Summer, pp.266–272. Available at http://www.JRS.org [Accessed 23 Oct. 2006].

Example iii, which follows, illustrates referencing in action for an academic journal accessed via a freely accessible online database. However, to avoid overlong references, you can include search terms to guide the reader to the source (MLA uses the term 'path' to signal search terms).

Table 10.S4iii Academic journal article from a freely accessible online database

Harvard	APA
HALPERIN, T. et al. (2006). Detection of relapsing fever in human blood samples from Israel using PCR targeting the glycerophosphodiester phosphodiesterase. *Acta Tropica* Vol. 98, Iss. 2, May 2006, pp 189–195.	Halperin, T., Orr, N., Cohen, R., Hasin, T., Davidovitch, N. Klement, et al. (2006, May). Detection of relapsing fever in human blood samples from Israel using PCR targeting the glycerophosphodiester phosphodiesterase.

(Cont.)

[Accessed via *PubMed* online database; Search terms: as title]. 26 July 2006.

[Electronic version]. *Acta Tropica* 98: 2, 189–195. [Retrieved 26 July, 2006 from *PubMed* Online database: Search terms: as title].

MLA

Halperin, Tamar et al. "Detection of Relapsing Fever in Human Blood Samples from Israel Using PCR Targeting the Glycerophosphodiester Phosphodiesterase". <u>Acta Tropica</u> 98.2, (May 2006):189–195. Online database <u>PubMed</u>. 26 July 2006. Path: as title.

Numerical

HALPERIN, T. et al. Detection of relapsing fever in human blood samples from Israel using PCR targeting the glycerophosphodiester phosphodiesterase. *Acta Tropica* Vol. 98, Iss. 2, May 2006, pp.189–195. [Accessed via *PubMed* online database; Search terms: as title]. 26 July 2006.

Example iv illustrates referencing a source from a restricted access database. As stated previously, there is no point in citing an electronic address if access is not freely available. This example shows a reference when a password protected database was used to gather and collate data on three separate companies. You need to give details of the publishers of the database to enable others to locate the sources.

Table 10.S4iv Academic journal article from a restricted access database

Harvard

FAME: FINANCIAL ANALYSIS MADE EASY (2006). Compilation from company annual reports 2005: PC World, Currys, and UniEuro, FAME database, Bureau Van Dijk Electronic Publishers. [Accessed 22 April 2006].

APA

FAME: Financial Analysis Made Easy (2005). Compilation from company annual reports 2005: PC World, Currys, & UniEuro. Retrieved April 22, 2006 from FAME database, Bureau Van Dijk Electronic Publishers.

MLA

FAME: Financial Analysis Made Easy. Compilation from: Co. annual reports 2005: PC World, Currys, and UniEuro, 22 April 2006. FAME database, Bureau Van Dijk.

Numerical

FAME: FINANCIAL ANALYSIS MADE EASY. Compilation from company annual reports 2005: PC World, Currys, and UniEuro. FAME database, Bureau Van Dijk Electronic Publishers. [Accessed 22 April 2006].

S5 Academic journal (online only)

Table 10.S5 Academic journal (online only)

Harvard

KAUFMAN, D. et al. (1999). New compounds from old plastics: recycling PET plastics via depolymerization. An activity for the undergraduate organic lab. *Journal of Chemical Education*. November 1999, vol. 76, no. 11, pp.1525–6. Available at http://jchemed.chem.wisc.edu/Contributors/Authors/Journal/laboratory/example02/ abs1525.html [Accessed 20 July 2006].

APA

Kaufman, D., Wright, G., Kroemer, R. and Engel, J. (1999, November). New compounds from old plastics: Recycling PET plastics via depolymerization. An activity for the undergraduate organic Lab. *Journal of Chemical Education*. 76, 11, 1525–6. Retrieved July 20, 2006 from http://jchemed.chem.wisc.edu/Contributors/Authors/Journal/laboratory/example02/abs1525.html

(Cont.)

MLA
Kaufman, Don et al. "New Compounds from Old Plastics: Recycling PET Plastics via Depolymerization. An Activity for the Undergraduate Organic Lab". Journal of Chemical Education 76. 11 (Nov. 1999):1525–6. 20 July 2006: <http://jchemed.chem.wisc.edu/ Contributors/Authors/Journal/laboratory/ example02/abs1525.html>

Numerical
KAUFMAN, D. et al. New compounds from old plastics: recycling PET plastics via depolymerization. An activity for the undergraduate organic lab. *Journal of Chemical Education.* November 1999 Vol. 76, No. 11, pp.1525–6. Available at http:// jchemed.chem.wisc.edu/Contributors/Authors/ Journal/laboratory/example02/abs1525.html [Accessed 20 July 2006].

As you can see from the last example, electronic references can be quite lengthy! But, it is important to provide full details of the source supplied to help the reader quickly find the exact source you looked at, so do not stint on necessary detail. However, as stated earlier, if the URL is excessively long, you can provide search terms to cut down on the length of the reference (see example S10).

S6 Article in magazine

Table 10.S6 Article in a magazine (originally printed, but found online)

Harvard
ENSERINK, M. (2006). Influenza: what came before 1918? Archaeovirologist offers a first glimpse. [Online]. *Science*, 23 June 2006, p.1725.

APA
Enserink, M. (2006, June 23). Influenza: What came before 1918? Archaeovirologist offers a first glimpse. [Electronic Version]. *Science*, p.1725.

MLA
Enserink, Martin. "Influenza: What Came Before 1918? Archaeovirologist Offers a First Glimpse". [Online]. Science (23 June 2006]: 1725.

Numerical
ENSERINK, M. Influenza: What came before 1918? Archaeovirologist offers a first glimpse. [Online]. *Science*, 23 June 2006, p.1725.

S7 Article in online magazine

Table 10.S7 Article in an online magazine (not available in print form)

Harvard
Microsoft Windows XP (2006) 25 Best hidden programs. Issue 58, May. Available at http:// www.windowsxpmagazine.co.uk/ [Accessed 19 July 2006].

APA
Microsoft Windows XP. (2006, May). 25 best hidden programs. Issue 58. Retrieved June 19, 2006 from http:// www.windowsxpmagazine.co.uk/

MLA
Microsoft Windows XP. "25 Best Hidden Programs". 58, May 2006. 19 July 2006 <http:// www.windowsxpmagazine.co.uk/>

Numerical
Microsoft Windows XP. 25 Best hidden programs. Issue 58, May 2006. Available at http://www.windowsxpmagazine.co.uk/ [Accessed 19 July 2006].

S8 Newspaper article

If the name of the journalist or writer is shown, start with this. If not, start with the name of the online newspaper site. Give the title and date of the item or article, and the URL address to take the reader to where the article can be found.

In example i, the first date shown in the MLA reference is when the article was originally published, and the second date, which immediately precedes the URL address, is when the student visited the source.

In example ii, for the MLA entry, the date of publication, and when the student visited the site, are the same.

Table 10.S8i Newspaper article

Harvard
LISTER, S. (2006). Basic hygiene is failing in a third of NHS hospitals. *TimesOnline*. 22 Mar. 2006. Available at TimesOnlinehttp:// www.timesonline.co.uk/article/0,,8122– 2097936,00.html [Accessed 24 July 2006]

APA
Lister, S. (2006, March 22). Basic hygiene is failing in a third of NHS hospitals. *TimesOnline*. Retrieved July 24, 2006 from http:// www.timesonline.co.uk/article/0,,8122– 2097936,00.html

MLA
Lister, Sam. "Basic Hygiene is Failing in a Third of NHS Hospitals". TimesOnline. 22 Mar. 2006. 24 July 2006. <http://www.timesonline.co.uk/ article/0,,8122–2097936,00.html>

Numerical
LISTER, S. Basic hygiene is failing in a third of NHS hospitals. *TimesOnline*. 22 Mar. 2006. Available at http://www.timesonline.co.uk/ article/0,,8122–2097936,00.html [Accessed 24 July 2006]

Table 10.S8ii Newspaper article

Harvard
TIMESONLINE (2006). On the flight path of dying Ibis. 24 July 2006. Available at http:// www.timesonline.co.uk/article/0,,3– 2282913,00.html [Accessed 24 July 2006].

APA
TimesOnline (2006, July 24). On the flight path of dying ibis. Retrieved July 24, 2006 from http:/ /www.timesonline.co.uk/article/0,,3– 2282913,00.html

MLA
TimesOnline. "On the Flight Path of Dying Ibis". 24 July 2006. <http://www.timesonline.co.uk/ article/0,,3–2282913,00.html>

Numerical
TIMESONLINE. on the flight path of dying Ibis. 24 July 2006. Available at http:// www.timesonline.co.uk/article/0,,3– 2282913,00.html [Accessed 24 July 2006].

S9 Online reports or guidelines

You need to include the name(s) of the authors, and the full title, including any subtitles, in italics or underlined, plus the full URL address information (see example i).

If no author is named, start with the name of the organization sponsoring the report or guidelines (see example ii).

Table 10.S9i Online report

Harvard
INTRONA, L. et al. (2003). *Cultural attitudes towards plagiarism.* Available at http://www.jiscpas.ac.uk/apppage.cgi?USERPAGE=7508 [Accessed 13/12/2005].

APA
Introna, L., Hayes, N., Blair, L., & Wood, E. (2003). *Cultural attitudes towards plagiarism.* Retrieved December 13, 2005 from http://www.jiscpas.ac.uk/apppage.cgi?USERPAGE=7508

MLA
Introna, Lucas, et al. Cultural Attitudes Towards Plagiarism. 13 Dec. 2005 <http://www.jiscpas.ac.uk/apppage.cgi?USERPAGE=7508>

Numerical
INTRONA, L. et al. (2003). *Cultural attitudes towards plagiarism.* Available at http://www.jiscpas.ac.uk/apppage.cgi?USERPAGE=7508 [Accessed 13/12/2005].

Table 10.S9ii Online guidelines (no author's name)

Harvard
THE AMERICAN PHYTOPATHOLOGICAL SOCIETY (2006). *B&C tests: guidelines for preparing reports.* Available at http://www.apsnet.org/online/BCTests/guidelines/ [Accessed 27 July 2006].

APA
The American Phytopathological Society (2006). *B&C tests: Guidelines for preparing reports.* Retrieved July 27, 2006 from http://www.apsnet.org/online/BCTests

MLA
The American Phytopathological Society. B&C Tests: Guidelines for Preparing Reports. 27 July 2006. <http://www.apsnet.org/online/BCTests/guidelines/>

Numerical
THE AMERICAN PHYTOPATHOLOGICAL SOCIETY. *B&C tests: guidelines for preparing reports.* Available at http://www.apsnet.org/online/BCTests/guidelines/ [Accessed 27 July 2006].

S10 Online dissertation (extract from a university website)

If the work was available from a dissertation database (or commercial organization), give details of the database after the title of thesis, and any relevant search path or file name information.

Table 10.S10i Online dissertation

Harvard
DAY, S.J. (2002). *Studies of controlled substances and the enhancement of fingerprints : analysis of drugs of abuse in latent and cyanoacrylate-fumed fingerprints using raman spectroscopy.* Unpublished doctoral thesis. University of Bradford. Abstract. Available at http://ipac.brad.ac.uk/#focus Search: Chemistry; Day; 2002. [Accessed 4 Aug. 2006].

APA
Day, S.J. (2002). *Studies of controlled substances and the enhancement of fingerprints: Analysis of drugs of abuse in latent and cyanoacrylate-fumed fingerprints using raman spectroscopy.* Unpublished doctoral thesis. Bradford: University of Bradford. Abstract retrieved August 4 2006 from http://ipac.brad.ac.uk/#focus Search: Chemistry; Day; 2002.

(Cont.)

MLA	Numerical
Day, Sara, J. "Studies of Controlled Substances and the Enhancement of fingerprints : Analysis of Drugs of Abuse in Latent and Cyanoacrylate-fumed Fingerprints Using Raman Spectroscopy". Unpub. diss. Univ. Bradford. A043 Day. Abstract. 4 Aug. 2006 <http://ipac.brad.ac.uk/#focus> Path: Chemistry; Day; 2002.	DAY, S.J. *Studies of controlled substances and the enhancement of fingerprints : analysis of drugs of abuse in latent and cyanoacrylate-fumed fingerprints using raman spectroscopy.* Unpublished doctoral thesis, 2002. University of Bradford. Abstract. Available at http://ipac.brad.ac.uk/#focus Search: Chemistry; Day; 2002. [Accessed 4 Aug. 2006].

For referencing the full thesis, follow the format in the example above, but omit 'Abstract' and give chapter or section number or title and page numbers, if referring to a specific part of the thesis.

Table 10.S10ii Example of an abstract of a dissertation available online via a database

Harvard	APA
HARRIS, C.D. (2006). Organizational change and intellectual production: the case study of Hohokam archaeology. Unpublished doctoral thesis. University of Arizona. Via *ProQuest Digital Dissertations*. Abstract available at http://wwwlib.umi.com/dissertations/fullcit/3206908 [Accessed 4 Aug. 2006].	Harris, C.D. (2006). Organizational change and intellectual production: The case study of Hohokam archaeology. Unpublished doctoral thesis. University of Arizona. Abstract retrieved August 4, 2006 from *ProQuest Digital Dissertations* at http://wwwlib.umi.com/dissertations/fullcit/3206908

MLA	Numerical
Harris, Cory, D. (2006). Organizational Change and Intellectual Production: The Case Study of Hohokam Archaeology. Unpub. diss. Univ. Arizona. <u>ProQuest Digital Dissertations</u>. Abstract. 4 Aug. 2006 <http://wwwlib.umi.com/dissertations/fullcit/3206908>	HARRIS, C.D. Organizational change and intellectual production:the case study of Hohokam archaeology. Unpublished doctoral thesis. 2006. University of Arizona. Via *ProQuest Digital Dissertations*. Abstract available at http://wwwlib.umi.com/dissertations/fullcit/3206908 [Accessed 4 Aug. 2006].

S11 Conference paper or manuscript

Reference should include name of presenter, title of paper, status of paper (unpublished; working paper), name and place of conference, date delivered, URL details, date you accessed the site and any relevant page numbers.

Table 10.S11 Manuscript

Harvard	APA
ROSS, M. (2005). *Is democracy good for the poor?* Unpublished manuscript. Annual meeting American Political Science Association, Washington. 1 Sept. 2005. Available online at http://convention2.allacademic.com/one/apsa/apsa05/ index.php?click_key=1 [Accessed 2 Aug. 2006].	Ross, M. (2005, September 1). *Is democracy good for the poor?* Unpublished manuscript presented at Annual meeting American Political Science Association, Washington. Retrieved August 2, 2006 from http://convention2.allacademic.com/one/apsa/apsa05/index.php?click_key=1
MLA	**Numerical**
Ross, Michael. "Is Democracy Good for the Poor?". Unpublished manuscript. Annual meeting American Political Science Association. Washington, DC. 1 Sept. 2005. 2 Aug. 2006. <http://convention2.allacademic.com/one/apsa/apsa05/index.php?click_key=1>	ROSS, M. *Is democracy good for the poor?* Unpublished manuscript. Annual meeting American Political Science Association, Washington. 1 Sept. 2005. Available online at http://convention2.allacademic.com/one/apsa/apsa05/index.php?click_key=1 [Accessed 2 Aug. 2006].

S12 Government or other statistics online

If no author name is shown, start with the name of the publishing agency or organization. Include the year the data was originally published, title of the statistics, plus full URL address. It may also be necessary to state the country of origin, as the same name of the government agency may be used in different countries, e.g. the title 'National Bureau of Statistics' is used by more than one country.

In example i that follows, the source for just one set of UK statistics is shown.

Table 10.S12i Government Statistics

Harvard	APA
OFFICE FOR NATIONAL STATISTICS (UK). (2005). *Employment: rate rises to 74.9 per cent in 3 months to Sept 05.* Available at http://www.statistics.gov.uk/CCI/nugget.asp?ID=12 [Accessed 14 Dec. 2005].	Office for National Statistics (UK). (2005). *Employment: Rate rises to 74.9 per cent in 3 months to Sept 05.* Retrieved December 14. 2005 from http://www.statistics.gov.uk/CCI/nugget.asp?ID=12
MLA	**Numerical**
Office for National Statistics (UK). Employment: Rate Rises to 74.9 per cent in 3 Months to Sept 05. 14 Dec. 2005 <http://www.statistics.gov.uk/CCI/nugget.asp?ID=12>	OFFICE FOR NATIONAL STATISTICS (UK). *Employment: rate rises to 74.9 per cent in 3 months to Sept 05.* Available at http://www.statistics.gov.uk/CCI/nugget.asp?ID=12 [Accessed 14 Dec. 2005].

However, referencing is not always this easy! Students often gather statistics relating to different topics from one major source, e.g. national offices or bureaus of statistics, but may then be unsure how to cite and reference the different parts of the site. In this situation, the important point and principle of referencing to remember is to make it easy for your reader to locate the same source, which may mean you have to list the various URL addresses in your references.

However, if you are using Harvard, APA or MLA referencing styles your citations can separate out the relevant parts of a single source by the use of prefix letters.

For example, if you wanted to refer to three different parts of the National Bureau of Statistics (China):

a. Regulations on the Composition of Gross Wages
b. Regulations on the National Economic Census
c. Statistical Bulletin on the Input of Science and Technology, 2002

Your citations in the text of your assignment (in the Harvard style) would be shown respectively as:

- (NBOS (China) 2006**a**)
- (NBOS (China) 2006**b**)
- (NBOS (China) 2006**c**).

Do not forget, you can use abbreviations in your citations, i.e. NBOS, as this can reduce your word count. However, in the full reference details you need to start with the abbreviation and then explain it to the reader (see examples that follow).

With the APA style, you would give the full title of the organization the first time it is mentioned in the assignment, but it can be abbreviated thereafter. The full reference entry would show the full title of the organization.

The full reference details should be as follows:

Table 10.S12ii Full reference details

NBOS (China): NATIONAL BUREAU OF STATISTICS OF CHINA (2006**a**). *Regulations on the composition of gross wages*. Available at http://www.stats.gov.cn/english/lawsandregulations/statisticalregulations/t20020801_2413.htm [Accessed 23 July 2006].

NBOS (China): NATIONAL BUREAU OF STATISTICS OF CHINA (2006**b**). *Regulations on the national economic census*. Available at http://www.stats.gov.cn/english/lawsandregulations/statisticalregulations/t20050110_402222113.htm [Accessed 23 July 2006].

NBOS (China): NATIONAL BUREAU OF STATISTICS OF CHINA (2006**c**). *Statistical bulletin on the input of science and technology*, 2002. Available at http://www.stats.gov.cn/english/newrelease/statisticalreports/t20031111_119097.htm [Accessed 23 July 2006].

S13 Public records online

Detail should include name of record or source, title of specific document or list, reference number, if applicable, locality information (if applicable) and other identifying features of source, plus name of any database or URL address, and the date the information was accessed or retrieved. If referring to a specific named person, start with this (see example iii).

Table 10.S13i Census records online

Harvard
UK CENSUS 1881: *Residents of Bolton Union workhouse, Fishpool, Farnworth, Lancashire.* Available from Census Online at http://users.ox.ac.uk/~peter/workhouse/Bolton/Bolton1881.html [Accessed 8 Aug. 2006].

APA
UK Census 1881: *Residents of Bolton Union workhouse, Fishpool, Farnworth, Lancashire.* Retrieved August 8, 2006 from Census Online at http://users.ox.ac.uk/~peter/workhouse/Bolton/Bolton1881.html

MLA
UK Census 1881: Residents of Bolton Union Workhouse, Fishpool, Farnworth, Lancashire. 8 Aug. 2006 Census Online <http://users.ox.ac.uk/~peter/workhouse/Bolton/Bolton1881.html>

Numerical
UK CENSUS 1881: *Residents of Bolton Union workhouse, Fishpool, Farnworth, Lancashire.* Available from Census Online http://users.ox.ac.uk/~peter/workhouse/Bolton/Bolton1881.html [Accessed 8 Aug. 2006].

Table 10.S13ii National archives online

Harvard
THE NATIONAL ARCHIVES (2006). *Records of the Admiralty, Naval Forces, Royal Marines, Coastguard, and related bodies.* Ref. ADM 188/360. Available http://www.nationalarchives.gov.uk/documentsonline/details-result.asp?queryType=1&resultcount=1&Edoc_Id=6929949 [Accessed 10 Aug. 2006].

APA
The National Archives (2006). *Records of the Admiralty, Naval Forces, Royal Marines, Coastguard, and related bodies.* Ref. ADM 188/360. Retrieved August 10, 2006 from http://www.nationalarchives.gov.uk/documentsonline/details-result.asp?queryType=1&resultcount=1&Edoc_Id=6929949

MLA
The National Archives. Records of the Admiralty, Naval Forces, Royal Marines, Coastguard, and related bodies. Ref. ADM 188/360. 10 Aug. 2006 <http://www.nationalarchives.gov.uk/documentsonline/details-result.asp?queryType=1& resultcount=1&Edoc_Id=6929949>

Numerical
THE NATIONAL ARCHIVES. *Records of the Admiralty, Naval Forces, Royal Marines, Coastguard, and related bodies.* Ref. ADM 188/360. Available http://www.nationalarchives.gov.uk/documentsonline/details-result.asp?queryType=1&resultcount=1&Edoc_Id=6929949 [Accessed 10 Aug. 2006].

Table 10.S13iii Military record online

Harvard
BIRKS, F. (2nd Lieut. VC). (2006). *Military record.* Australian Military Units. Australian War Memorial. Available at http://www.awm.gov.au/units/people8228.asp [Accessed 11 Aug. 2006].

APA
Birks, F. (2nd Lieut. VC). (2006). *Military record.* Australian Military Units. Australian War Memorial. Retrieved August 11, 2006 from http://www.awm.gov.au/units/people8228.asp

MLA
Birks, Frederick (2nd Lieut. VC). Military Record. Australian Military Units. Australian War Memorial. 11 Aug. 2006. <http://www.awm.gov.au/units/people8228.asp>

Numerical
BIRKS, F. (2nd Lieut. VC). *Military record.* Australian Military Units. Australian War Memorial. Available at http://www.awm.gov.au/units/people8228.asp [Accessed 11 Aug. 2006].

S14 Emails

Significant email messages can be referenced, but be cautious. Wherever possible, you should obtain permission from the sender to use personal email correspondence and particularly if the correspondence will appear in the public domain. You should also save a copy of the correspondence to enable a tutor to read it.

If the message is included as a reference, do not give the email address of the sender, as this would be a breach of confidentiality and might lead to unwarranted correspondence being sent to the sender.

The following format is recommended:

- Name of sender
- Year communication received
- Medium (email)
- Title or subject of message
- Name of recipient – this may be your name
- Date communication received.

Table 10.S14 Email

Harvard	APA
BROWN, J. (2005) Email to C. HARRIS re. marketing survey, 12 Dec. 2005.	Brown, J. (2005, December 12) Email to C. Harris re. marketing survey.
MLA	**Numerical**
Brown, John. Email to Chris Harris re. marketing survey, 12 Dec. 2005.	BROWN, J. Email to C. HARRIS re. marketing survey, 12 Dec. 2005.

S15 Discussion lists

Although emails on discussion lists are entered by their senders into a limited public domain, you should, wherever possible, notify the contributors and preferably seek their permission to use their correspondence, particularly if you are hoping to publish your work.

Cite the author's name, if known, or the author's login name, nickname or nomenclature, followed by the subject of the discussion. Then state the name and address of the discussion list, or the protocol and address of the newsgroup. You should also include the date the message was posted and the date it was read by you.

Table 10.S15 Discussion list

Harvard	APA
SMITH, J. (2005). Re. skills audit. Posted 25 Nov. 2005. LDHEN discussion list. LDHEN@Jiscmail.ac.uk [Accessed 4 Oct. 2006].	Smith, J. (2005, November 25). Re. skills audit. Message posted to LDHEN discussion list. Retrieved October 4, 2006 from LDHEN@Jiscmail.ac.uk.

(Cont.)

MLA	Numerical
Smith, John. "Re. Skills Audit". Online posting. 25 Nov. 2005. LDHEN Discussion List. <LDHEN@Jiscmail.ac.uk>.	SMITH, J. Re. skills audit. Posted 25 Nov. 2005. LDHEN discussion list. LDHEN@Jiscmail.ac.uk [Accessed 4 Oct. 2006].

S16 Blogs (weblogs)

Start with the name of the owner of the weblog, and then give date of posting of item, if shown. You also need to include the title, in italics or underlined, site address and the date you looked at it.

Table 10.S16 Blog

Harvard	APA
BYFORD, P. (2006). Networking. *Phil Byford's website*. 26 July 2006. Available at http://www.byford.com/ [Accessed 27 July 2006]	Byford, P. (2006, July 26). Networking. *Phil Byford's website*. Retrieved July 27, 2006 from http://www.byford.com/
MLA	**Numerical**
Byford, Phil. "Networking". Phil Byford's website. 26 July 2006. 27 July 2006 <http://www.byford.com/>	BYFORD, P. Networking. *Phil Byford's website*. 26 July 2006. Available at http://www.byford.com/ [Accessed 27 July 2006]

S17 Text messages and faxes

The transient nature of **text messages** (see example i) are a problem and, unless saved, the lack of a permanent record of the message makes it difficult to record them in the list of references, as the reader will not be able to look at the original source. One way around this situation would be for you to save the text, copy the message into print form and then ask a neutral and objective third party, preferably the tutor marking the assignment, to witness and confirm the accuracy of the copied or summarized message. The transcribed message could then be included as an appendix item and be fully referenced. The name of the sender should come first, description of medium, name of receiver and date received.

Faxes (see example ii) produce a paper record, which can be kept and included as an appendix item, if required.

Table 10.S17i Text message

Harvard	APA
DESAI, S. (2006). Text message to J. Jones, 12 Dec. 2006.	Desai, S. (2006, December 12). Text message to J. Jones.
MLA	**Numerical**
Desai, Shoeb. Text message to Janet Jones, 12 Dec. 2006.	DESAI, S. Text message to J. Jones, 12 Dec. 2006.

Table 10.S17ii Fax

Harvard	APA
JONES, J. (2006). Fax message to S. DESAI, 13 Dec. 2006.	Jones, J. (2006, December 13) Fax message to S. Desai.
MLA	**Numerical**
Jones, Janet. Fax message to Shoeb Desai, 13 Dec. 2006.	JONES, J. Fax message to S. DESAI, 13 Dec. 2006.

S18 Referencing podcasts/downloads

Archived sound broadcasts can be referenced, as these can be publicly accessed. Start with the name of the lead commentator or presenter (if shown). If this information is not shown, start with the name of sponsoring organization, e.g. BBC. Give details of date of original broadcast or production, title of work, online address and the date you downloaded the information. If there is a transcript, print this off to make available, if required by the tutor.

Table 10.S18 Podcast/download

Harvard	APA
FINK, S. (2006). Aids in Papua New Guinea. 29 May 2006. *BBC world news: health/HIV Aids.* Available at http://www.theworld.org/health/aids.shtml [Accessed 1 Aug. 2006].	Fink, S. (2006, May 29). AIDS in Papua New Guinea. *BBC world news: Health/HIV aids.* Retrieved August 1, 2006, from http://www.theworld.org/health/aids.shtml
MLA	**Numerical**
Fink, Sheri. "AIDS in Papua New Guinea". BBC World News: Health/HIV Aids. 29 May 2006. 1 August 2006. <http://www.theworld.org/health/aids.shtml>	FINK, S. Aids in Papua New Guinea. 29 May 2006. *BBC world news : health/HIV Aids.* Available at http://www.theworld.org/health/aids.shtml [Accessed 1 Aug. 2006].

S19 Visual material online (maps, photographs, drawings, three-dimensional art, etc.)

If an author/artist/photographer or other named originator is shown, start with this. If no author name is shown, start with the name of organization hosting or organizing the site. You should include the title of work, in italics or underlined, and state the medium, if not obvious, and enclose this description in squared brackets, e.g. [photograph]. You should also include other relevant source/publication/collection information, the URL, and the date you visited the site. British Standard examples show full names of originators for visual sources for Harvard and Numerical styles of referencing.

Table 10.S19i Map

Harvard
MULTIMAP.COM (2006). *Map of Poland*.
Available at http://www.multimap.com/map/
browse.cgi?lat=51.6301&lon=17.068&scale=
2000000&icon=x [Accessed 2 Aug. 2006].

APA
MultiMap.Com (2006). *Map of Poland*.
Retrieved August 2, 2006 from http://
www.multimap.com/map/browse.cgi?lat=
51.6301&
lon=17.068&scale=2000000&icon=x

MLA
MultiMap.Com. Map of Poland. 2 Aug. 2006
  <http://www.multimap.com/map/browse.cgi?lat=
  51.6301&lon=17.068&
  scale=2000000&icon=x>

Numerical
MULTIMAP.COM. *Map of Poland*. Available
http://www.multimap.com/map/browse.cgi?lat=
51.6301&lon=17.068&scale=2000000&
icon=x [Accessed 2 Aug. 2006].

Table 10.S19ii Photograph

Harvard
CAMERON, Julia. (1864). *Suspense*.
[Photograph]. National Museum Film and
Photography. Available at http://www.
nmpft.org.uk/insight/collectiononline_
group.asp?exid=44 [Accessed 12 Aug. 2006].

APA
Cameron, J. (1864). *Suspense*. [Photograph].
  National Museum Film & Photography. Retrieved
  August 12, 2006 from http://www.nmpft.org.uk/
  insight/collectiononline_group.asp?exid=44

MLA
Cameron, Julia. Suspense. Photograph. 1864.
  Nat. Mus. Film and Photogr. 12 Aug. 2006,
  <http://www.nmpft.org.uk/insight/
  collectiononline_group.asp?exid=44>

Numerical
CAMERON, Julia. *Suspense*. 1864.
[Photograph]. National Museum Film and
Photography. Available at http://www.
nmpft.org.uk/insight/collectiononline_
group.asp?exid=44 [Accessed 12 Aug. 2006].

Table 10.S19iii Painting

Harvard
KLEE, Paul. (1937). *Legend of the Nile*.
[Painting]. Kunstmuseum Bern. Available at
WebMuseum http://www.sai.msu.su/wm/paint/
auth/klee/ [Accessed 16 Aug. 2006].

APA
Klee, P. (1937). *Legend of the Nile*. [Painting].
  Kunstmuseum Bern. Retrieved August 16, 2006
  from WebMuseum http://www.sai.msu.su/wm/
  paint/auth/klee/

MLA
Klee, Paul. "Legend of the Nile". Painting.
  1937. Kunstmuseum Bern. 16 Aug. 2006
  WebMuseum <http://www.sai.msu.su/wm/paint/
  auth/klee/>

Numerical
KLEE, Paul. *Legend of the Nile*. [Painting].
1937. Kunstmuseum Bern. Available at
WebMuseum http://www.sai.msu.su/wm/paint/
auth/klee [Accessed 16. Aug. 2006].

Table 10.S19iv Cartoon

Harvard	APA
BELL, Steve. (2006). The Government energy review. [Cartoon]. *The Guardian* 12 July 2006. Available at http://www.guardian.co.uk/cartoons/stevebell/0,,1818593,00.html [Accessed 30 July 2006].	Bell, S. (2006, July 12). The government energy review. [Cartoon]. *The Guardian* Retrieved July 30, 2006 from http://www.guardian.co.uk/cartoons/stevebell/0,,1818593,00.html
MLA	**Numerical**
Bell, Steve. "The Government Energy Review". Cartoon. The Guardian 12 July 2006. 30 July 2006. <http://www.guardian.co.uk/cartoons/stevebell/0,,1818593,00.html>	BELL, Steve. The Government energy review. [Cartoon]. *The Guardian* 12 July 2006. Available at http://www.guardian.co.uk/cartoons/stevebell/0,,1818593,00.html [Accessed 30 July 2006].

Three-dimensional art work (e.g. sculpture)

If the URL is a very long and complicated one, you can use the home or search page address, but include a relevant search term or terms to guide others to the online source.

Table 10.S19v Glass sculpture

Harvard	APA
SWINBURNE, Elizabeth. (1991). *Life cycles* [Glass sculpture]. London: V & A Museum, ref. C.8–1994. Available at http://images.vam.ac.uk/ixbin/hixclient.exe?_IXSESSION_=&submit-button=search&search-form=main/index.html [Search terms: glass, Swinburne, Life Cycles]. [Accessed 1 Aug. 2006].	Swinburne, E. (1991). *Life cycles* [Glass sculpture]. London: V & A Museum, ref. C.8–1994. Retrieved August 1, 2006 from http://images.vam.ac.uk/ixbin/hixclient.exe?_IXSESSION_=&submit-button=search&search-form=main/index.html [Search terms: glass, Swinburne, Life Cycles].
MLA	**Numerical**
Swinburne, Elizabeth. Life Cycles [Glass sculpture]. London: V & A Mus. Ref. C.8–1994. 1991. 1 Aug. 2006 <http://images.vam.ac.uk/ixbin/hixclient.exe?_IXSESSION_=&submit-button=search&search-form=main/index.html> Path: glass; Swinburne; Life Cycles	SWINBURNE, Elizabeth. *Life cycles* [Glass sculpture]. London: V & A Museum, ref. C.8–1994. Available at http://images.vam.ac.uk/ixbin/hixclient.exe?_IXSESSION_=&submit-button=search&search-form=main/index.html [Search terms: glass, Swinburne, Life Cycles]. [Accessed 1 Aug. 2006].

S20 Portable databases (DVD/CD-ROM)

Detail to include:

- Author/editor
- Year
- Title of work, in italics or underlined
- Title and type of database, e.g. DVD

- Volume, edition, and item number
- Other identifying features
- Place of publication and name of publisher
- Page numbers, if applicable.

If no author is shown, start with the title of item. However, you do not need to include the terms 'Accessed' or 'Retrieved', with the date, as you would with an online source. The main thing is to state the database to help others locate the source.

Table 10.S20i DVD, no named author

Harvard	APA
Sports injuries (2006). 2nd edn. [DVD]. Wigan: Open Software Library.	*Sports injuries* (2006). 2nd edn. [DVD]. Wigan: Open Software Library.
MLA	**Numerical**
Sports Injuries. 2nd edn. DVD. Wigan: Open Software Library, 2006.	*Sports injuries* (2006). 2nd edn. [DVD]. Wigan: Open Software Library.

Table 10.S20ii CD-ROM, name(s) of author(s) shown

Harvard	APA
MERRITT, F.S., M.K. LOFTIN, and J.T. RICKETTS (1995). *Merritt's standard handbook of civil engineering.* 4th edn. [CD-ROM]. New York: McGraw Hill.	Merritt, F.S., Loftin, M.K. & Ricketts, J.T. (1995). *Merritt's standard handbook of civil engineering.* 4th edn. [CD-ROM]. New York: McGraw Hill.
MLA	**Numerical**
Merritt, Frederick. S., M. Kent Loftin, and Jonathan T. Ricketts. Merritt's Standard Handbook of Civil Engineering. 4th edn. CD-ROM. NY: McGraw Hill, 1995.	MERRITT, F.S., M.K. LOFTIN, and J.T. RICKETTS. *Merritt's standard handbook of civil engineering.* 4th edn. [CD-ROM]. New York: McGraw Hill, 1995.

For the Harvard and Numerical references, et al. could have been used, if preferred; e.g. MERRITT, F.S. et al.

Appendix 1

Answers to the quiz on understanding when to reference

1   When you include tables, photographs, statistics and diagrams in your assignment. These may be items directly copied or a source of data collation which you have used   ✓

2   When describing or discussing a theory, model or practice associated with a particular writer   ✓

3   When you summarize information drawn from a variety of sources about what has happened over a period and the summary is unlikely to be a cause of dispute or controversy   ☐

4   To give weight or credibility to an argument that you believe is important   ✓

5   When giving emphasis to a particular idea that has found a measure of agreement and support among commentators   ✓

6   When pulling together a range of key ideas that you introduced and referenced earlier in the assignment   ☐

7   When stating or summarizing obvious facts, and when there is unlikely to be any significant disagreement with your statements or summaries   ☐

8   When including quotations   ✓

9   When you copy and paste items from the Internet and where no author's name is shown   ✓

10   When paraphrasing or summarizing (in your own words) another person's work that you feel is particularly significant, or likely to be a subject of debate   ✓

Appendix 2

Plagiarism quiz answers

The answer to all questions, apart from 6, 8 and 12 is 'Yes'.

6   No
    However, be cautious when doing this and always try to establish the name
    of the original author. If an author's name is shown, this must be cited. If the
    idea is an **original** one (as opposed to 'interesting'), it would be wise to
    reference the website if no author's name is shown

8   No
    It is not plagiarism if you present a summary of what has happened in the
    past, providing you draw from a range of sources and there is no significant
    dispute between commentators on the events you describe. However, if you
    just use one source, or you quote directly, or paraphrase, from any particular
    source, the author(s) should be cited and referenced

12 No
    Plagiarism is to **knowingly** take and use another person's work and claim it
    directly or indirectly as your own. This is an example of carelessness and you
    could be criticized for it, but it is not plagiarism. However, you should always
    check out ideas as thoroughly as you can before claiming any originality for
    them. You could, for example, discuss your ideas with your tutor, as the tutor
    is likely to know if others have published ideas similar or identical to your
    own

Appendix 3

Exercise: Is it plagiarism?

Example 4.1

This is a clear example of worst-case plagiarism. The extract from the article has been copied directly into the essay without any attempt to acknowledge the source.

Example 4.2

This is plagiarism. Although the original authors are cited, the article has been copied, with only very minor changes, directly into the essay. Copying on this scale, even if the source is acknowledged, will be regarded by most UK universities as plagiarism.

Example 4.3

This is plagiarism. Although an attempt has been made to summarize in part the original article, the authors are not acknowledged. The extract contains important background information that cannot be regarded as 'common knowledge', particularly the last sentence, so the authors and original source should have been cited.

Example 4.4

This is plagiarism. Although the authors have been cited, and some of their words directly quoted, the student simply copies a large part of the original, and the implication is that the sections outside the quotations are the student's own words – which they are not.

Example 4.5

This is not plagiarism. The original source is acknowledged and the student has made a reasonable effort to summarize the extract in his or her own words.

Example 4.6

This is not plagiarism. The original source is acknowledged and the student has made a very good effort to summarize the extract in his or her own words.

Example 4.7

This is plagiarism. Although this is a very good summary of the original extract, it is plagiarism, as the original authors are not cited. The original work containing the ideas of authors must be acknowledged. It is only if knowledge becomes publicly well known (or 'common knowledge') that summaries of generally undisputed facts can be presented without referencing the sources. Sentences two and three can be regarded as common knowledge, as the information in these could be derived from a general reference book. However, the following paraphrased sentences reflect the specialist work of the authors, who should have been cited at the end of this section:

> Since 1979, China has loosened opened and stimulated its economy by foreign direct investment (FDI), international technology transfer (ITT), and from the influence of multinational enterprises (MNEs). However, these developments have also focused attention on the issue of intellectual property rights (IPR) and until recently in China there has been no effective system of intellectual property protection (IPP).

If in doubt, always cite the source.

Appendix 4

How can theories of managing change be applied in life planning? Give examples to illustrate your answer

'Change is not made without inconvenience, even from worse to better' (Samuel Johnson). Johnson's observation summarises a paradox that many people feel: the tension between remaining in a familiar state, or making a change; a change that is likely to cause some 'inconvenience', or more likely, uncertainty. Therein lies the paradox: it is tempting for many people to stay with a situation that has the comfort of familiarity, rather than risk moving into territory for them as yet uncharted. But this assumes a choice over the matter. People are often propelled unwillingly and unexpectedly into situations not of their choosing.

> **The author of the quotation is cited. If the quotation is by a well-known person, and is just included to add colour and general interest to your writing, it does not need to be given a full reference entry.**
>
> **But if in doubt, always supply a full reference entry for this type of quotation.**

This essay will present and discuss some models for managing change and is aimed at people in three broad categories: first, those who exercise discretionary choice over a given life situation; second, those who are faced with choices they would prefer not to make, but nevertheless have ultimate control of the process; and third, those who have change thrust arbitrarily on them by fate in all its many forms. The examples given will be related to how practitioners charged with the responsibility of managing or supporting others facing change might support the 'change-seekers' or 'change-victims' concerned. In a business context these practitioners are likely to be members of a Human Resources team, but could also include external trainers, management or life planning consultants.

Change is not received or perceived in a homogeneous way. Gerard Egan, for example, draws a distinction between 'discretionary and non-discretionary change' (Egan 1994).* In the former, the individual has a choice about change to make and makes it willingly. The outcome may be 'inconvenient' or challenging, but the change, nevertheless, is desired and embraced. In the case of 'non-discretionary change', people are faced with situations that are deeply uncomfortable, but they stay in trouble because it is easier to do so than make the emotional effort to change. Egan traces the roots of inertia in emotional passivity, learned helplessness, disorganisation or 'vicious circle' self-defeating behaviour. The 'non-discretionary' nature of change is because non-change is likely to result in the person concerned becoming ill or making others suffer. The third form of change is by Harold Kushner in his book of the same name: '*When Bad Things Happen to Good People*'† (Kushner 1981). These 'bad things' manifest themselves in crisis, misfortunes or traumas in all their malignant shades. These things happen because they happen – but some models of change can at least help in the understanding of process, and support for, those involved.

> *The particular theorist is mentioned and the source is cited.

> †The name of the author is confirmed and year of publication.

For those actively wanting and seeking change, Maslow's theory of Hierarchy of Needs (Maslow 1968)* offers an explanation as to why individuals seek transition and change in their lives. As basic and intermediate needs (food, shelter, affection) are met, aspirations rise, and people reach out to meet more intrinsic needs, for example, the chance to gain more status at work or opportunity to develop a new interest. In this situation, the 'Managing Change Approach'† (Coleman 1991) offers a model for plotting the stages involved. Coleman envisages six steps, including the first trigger step of '*transition*': a sense of wanting change and being able to identify and articulate the reasons and feelings for this. This is an important first step, as it allows the decision-maker a sense of control over the process and gain 'ownership' of the idea. The decision-maker proceeds then to steps two and three: *information gathering*, and *considering the options* available. This leads to a *choice* (step four), *action* (step five) and later a process of *reassessment and evaluation* (step six).

> *Theory mentioned here, so the source is cited.

> †A particular model is mentioned, so the source is cited.

For this model to succeed there are, arguably, a number of assumptions to make about the discretionary decision-makers. Veronica McGivney suggests a number of favourable determinants in adult lives that can motivate them to return to formal learning (McGivney 1993), and these can be adapted to connect with the Coleman model. The first determinant of success for the Coleman model is that the person concerned has a belief that he or she could cope with the transition and final change desired. The second is that the person concerned knows, or can find out, where to seek the information necessary to make an informed decision. The third and fourth, crucially, are that the person concerned has enough optimism about the future to contemplate change – and feels that he or she **has** some control over their life. These latter points are critical pre-requisites for those plotting a life course through the Coleman model of managing change.

> A particular commentator is mentioned, so the source is cited.

The Coleman model connects too, with one advanced in recent years by Bill Law: a 'Career Learning Theory', although Law has been at pains to point out that the theory is relevant to all life choices, not just vocationally biased ones (Law 1996). Law proposes a four stage model for managing change: *sensing, sifting, focusing* and *understanding*. The first three of these connect with Coleman's middle and latter stages, although Law advances his third stage (*focusing*) by asserting that this is achieved by a decision maker engaging with three specific questions: *is the choice idea salient*; is *it valued* (in terms of acceptable to self and others); and *is it credible* (perceived as a sensible or wise decision by self or others)? Law's fourth stage: '*understanding*' is explained in terms of an individual's ability to justify overall a particular course of action chosen. This connects with Coleman's first stage, but Law pursues the issue further by arguing '*understanding*' also relates to an ability to identify and explain the relationship of past events to future action, which forms the basis for sustainable action. The process of understanding is also about being able to anticipate or visualise the probabilities or consequences of actions.

> The source of the theory is cited.

Coleman's model appears to assume, while Law's is more explicit in this respect, that making choices involves a certain level of risk-taking. Law explicitly points out that action always entails risk, but that risk can be assessed so that probabilities are estimated:

Autonomous action must involve some such visualisation (whether rational or not) of . . . 'this is what will probably happen if I do this . . .' It requires the imagination of possible selves in possible futures (Law p.65).

> As a quotation is used, the author name is confirmed and the page number is shown (notice how the quote is indented).

Perhaps the Coleman and Law models are at their most salient in relation to confident, intelligent people who are faced with relatively straightforward economic-related decisions: career, work, accommodation, and money. But perhaps they are less applicable when considering change in the realms of human emotion? The role of practitioners however, in these discretionary choice situations can be one of 'oiling the wheels' of change for the decision-maker; these would include supplying information, listening, encouraging and generally offering support and guidance. The process of change is likely to happen without the practitioner's support, but with it change can happen often faster and more effectively.

> The student presents at this point a personal reflection on the topic. These reflective sections in an assignment can go unreferenced, providing no new evidence is presented.

However, a common scenario is one where a person is faced with stark choice, particularly of the emotionally charged variety; the choice is often change or suffer. At one level there is 'choice', but as Egan (1994) has argued it is of the 'non-discretionary' kind. Egan has noted that people in this situation can vacillate and remain static, rather than face change.

> The date of the source is confirmed.

This emotional stasis has been related by some commentators (for example, Bandura 1991)* to both lack of confidence – that a particular choice path will lead to certain desirable outcomes, and pessimism about outcomes that might follow from the change. In this scenario, the 'Stages of Change' model proposed by Prochaska and DiClemente (1984)† offers a way of understanding the process of change – or a relapse back into the 'old habits'. Prochaska and DiClemente related their model specifically to smoking, but it can be equally applicable to any pattern of behaviour rooted in addiction, habit or compulsion. In this model, the process of change begins with '*contemplation*', and the notion that change is for the better. However, there can be an inner voice that warns: change is 'risky', so 'why change?' This can produce oscillation between wanting and not wanting change.

*Only one commentator is cited. As the essay refers to 'some commentators', it would have been better for the student to have included one or two others for extra emphasis.

†Cites year of publication.

However, whatever the accelerant might prove to be, the person concerned can 'commit' and be ready for change, which propels them forward, and leads to the 'maintenance' stage of maintaining change. The new situation in time becomes the norm, but there is the possibility of *relapse*, and going back to the stating point of the circle.

The practitioner has a particularly key role to play in helping in the process of reflection at these different stages in the decision-maker's life. Egan suggests six ways of helping people in this situation strengthen self-efficacy to stay on track with a chosen decision. The first is to help people develop any necessary skills to succeed in the belief that self-efficacy is based on ability. The second is to offer feedback on any deficiencies in performance. This helps decision-makers avoid situations of self-delusion, where they rationalise any lapse or diversion from their original goals. The third is to help the decision-maker see how a change of behaviour or direction produces results, which connects with the fourth: about promoting others as role models of success. Steps five and six are related to reducing the anxiety faced by people overly fearful of failure: by encouragement and being generally supportive, and reminding the decision-maker of their original motivations (Egan 1994).

Year of publication is confirmed.

The third group (the change victims) requires of practitioners the greatest level of understanding about the anguish of change that people can experience. People are often unwilling victims of change, including redundancy, sudden bereavement, financial disaster.

Many of the models of change that are applicable to this situation are similar in tracing a pattern of shock, guilt, bewilderment (or anger), a search for meaning, then gradual acceptance of the change (see Sinfield 1985; also Coleman and Chiva 1991, in relation to redundancy; and Kubler-Ross, 1970, in relation to death and dying).

Cites a number of sources to make connections between ideas.

Some of the earliest studies that noted this pattern date back to the 1930s with studies of unemployment, particularly the experience of older workers (Eisenberg and

Lazarsfield 1938, as cited in Sinfield 1985, p.191). These noted then the impact of shock on the newly unemployed, followed by an active hunt for work, during which the individual is still optimistic. But when all job-seeking efforts fail, the person becomes anxious and suffers depression, which can lead to fatalism and adaptation to a narrower state.

> **Gives details of the studies – note use of secondary source.**

More recent studies have confirmed this pattern still applies today, particularly for the older worker (see Harrison 1976, for example). Two commentators, Kubler-Ross (1970) and Coleman and Chiva (1991), both note that anger is often a feature of the response to sudden changes, as well as guilt, self-doubt and depression. The anger is of the 'why me' variety, and when there is often no rational answer to this question depression can follow, arising from a realisation of the powerlessness of individuals in the path of unstoppable forces.

> **Gives example of such a study; also cites the commentators.**

There is however, a gradual acceptance of and adaptation to the situation. Alvin Toffler suggests too, that an ability to cope (and recover) from traumatic change depends on the relative security of other aspects of our lives. He argues that we can cope with enormous amounts of change, pressure, complexity and confusion, provided at least one area of our life remains relatively stable (Toffler 1970). He suggests that there are five main 'Stability Zones':

> **Cites a particular commentator.**

1. **Ideas**: for example, deeply felt religious beliefs, or strong commitment to a philosophy, political ideology or cause;
2. **Places**: places that individuals can relate to, on either a large scale (a country) or smaller scale, such as home, street or even office;
3. **Things**: favourite, familiar, comforting possessions, and especially things related to childhood or emotional events;
4. **People**: particularly valued and enduring relationships with others, especially friends;
5. **Organization**: institutes, clubs or societies offering an important source of stability and focus for self-identity.

The role of the practitioner with responsibility for managing or supporting change in all three situations outlined is to firstly ascertain whether the person concerned is a discretionary or non-discretionary change seeker, or thirdly a change-victim, as each require different types of help or support, in ways outlined earlier. The practitioner's support for the change-victim can be particularly valuable. This support can take the form of encouraging the individual to talk through the change experiences and to release feelings of anger. An understanding of these stages can help the practitioner locate a stage the change-victim appears to be in and assist that person to begin to explore relevant new life options and possibilities.

> The conclusion pulls ideas together. As these ideas were referenced earlier in the assignment, there is no need to reference them again in the conclusion.

> You would list your references at the start of a new page; see next page for the list of references for this essay.

References (Example Essay)

BANDURA, A. (1991). Human agency: the rhetoric and the reality. *American Psychologist*, 46, pp.157–161.

COLEMAN, A. and A. CHIVA (1991). *Coping with change-focus on retirement*. London: Health Education Authority.

EGAN, G. (1994). *The Skilled Helper: a problem-management approach to helping*. Belmont: Brooks/ Cole Publishing Company.

HARRISON, R. (1976). The demoralizing experience of prolonged unemployment. *Department of Employment Gazette*, 84, April, pp.330–349.

KUBLER-ROSS, E. (1970). *On death and dying*. London: Tavistock Publications.

KUSHNER, H.S. (1981). *When bad things happen to good people*. London: Pan Books.

LAW, B. (1996). A career-learning theory, In A. WATTS et al., *Rethinking careers education and guidance: theory, policy and practice*. London: Routledge.

MCGIVNEY, V. (1993). *Adult learners, education and training*. London: Routledge/Open University.

MASLOW, A (1968). *Toward a psychology of being*. New York: Van Nostrand.

PROCHASKA, J. and C. Di CLEMENTE (1984). Stages and processes of self-change of smoking: towards an integrated model of change. *Journal of Consulting and Clinical Psychology*, vol. 51 (3) pp.390–435.

SINFIELD, A. (1985). Being out of work. In C.R. LITTLER (Ed.), *The experience of work*. Aldershot: Gower/Open University.

TOFFLER, A. (1970). *Future shock*. NY: Random House.

Recommended reading

ANGÉLIL-CARTER, S. (2000). *Stolen language? Plagiarism in writing.* Harlow: Pearson education.

APA: AMERICAN PSYCHOLOGICAL ASSOCIATION (2005). *Concise rules of APA style.* Washington, DC: American Psychological Association.

FRENCH, D. (1996). *How to cite legal authorities.* London: Blackstone.

GIBALDI, J. (2003). *The MLA handbook for writers.* New York: Modern Language Association of America.

GRAFTON, A. (1997). *The footnote: a curious history.* London: Faber and Faber.

LEVIN, P. (2004). *Write great essays!* Maidenhead: Open University Press.

LI, X. and N.B. CRANE. (1996). *Electronic styles: a handbook for citing electronic information.* Medford (N.J.): Information Today.

MAIMON, E.P. et al. (2007). *A writer's resource: A handbook for writing and research.* New York: McGraw Hill.

MHRA: MODERN HUMANITIES RESEARCH ASSOCIATION (2002). *A handbook for authors, editors, and writers of thesis.* London: as author.

MUNGER, D. and S. CAMPBELL. (2002). *Researching Online.* 5th edition. New York: Pearson Education.

OXFORD STANDARD FOR CITATION OF LEGAL AUTHORITIES (2005). http://denning.-law.ox.ac.uk/published/oscola.shtml). [Accessed 10/01/2006].

PEARS, R. and G. SHIELDS (2005). *Cite them right: the essential guide to referencing and plagiarism.* Newcastle upon Tyne: Pear Tree Books.

WALKER, J.R. and T. TAYLOR (1998). *The Columbia guide to online style.* New York: Columbia University Press.

References

AGGARWAL, R. et al. (2002). A study of academic dishonesty among students at two pharmacy schools. *The Pharmaceutical Journal*. Vol. 269, 12 October.

ANGÉLIL-CARTER, S. (2000). *Stolen language? Plagiarism in writing*. Harlow: Pearson education.

APA: AMERICAN PSYCHOLOGICAL ASSOCIATION (2005). *Concise rules of APA style*. Washington, DC: American Psychological Association.

ASHTON, D. and FIELD, D. (1976). *Young workers*. London: Hutchinson and Co.

BARRETT, R. and J. MALCOLM (2006). Embedding plagiarism in the assessment process. *International Journal for Educational Integrity* [online], vol. 2, no. 1. Available at http://www.ojs.unisa.edu.au/journals/index.php/IJEI [Accessed 28 Aug. 2006].

BOWERS, W.J. (1964). *Student dishonesty and its control in a college*. New York: Bureau of Applied Social Research, Columbia University.

BRITISH COUNCIL (2006). *IELTS band and descriptions*. Available at http://www.britishcouncil.org/taiwan-exams-ielts-ielts-bank-and-descriptions.htm [Accessed 28 Aug. 2006].

BRITISH STANDARD INSTITUTION (BS). (1983). *Recommendations for citation of unpublished documents*. BS 6371:1983. London: BS.

BRITISH STANDARD INSTITUTION (BS). (1989). *Recommendation for references to published materials*. BS 1629:1989. London: BS.

BRITISH STANDARD INSTITUTION (BS). (1990). *Recommendations for citing and referencing published material*. BS 5605:1990. London: BS.

BRITISH STANDARD INSTITUTION (BS). (1997). *Information and documentation – bibliographic references – part 2: Electronic documents or parts thereof*. BS ISO 690–2:1997. London: BS.

BRITISH STANDARD INSTITUTION (BS). (2000). *Copy preparation and proof correction – part 1: Design and layout of documents*. BS5261–1:2000. London: BS.

BULLEY, M. (2006). Clunky writing is proof positive of lazy thinking. *Times Higher Education Supplement*, 2 June 2006, p.14.

BUTCHER, D. (1991). *Official publications in Britain*. 2nd ed. London: Library Association.

CABLE, J. (2001). *Harold Freeman and his nine novels*. Colchester: Bloozoo Publishing.

CARROLL, J. (2005). Institutional issues in deterring, detecting and dealing with student plagiarism. Available at www.jisc.ac.uk/uploaded_documents/plagFinal.doc [Accessed 15 Mar. 2006].

CBI: CONFEDERATION OF BRITISH INDUSTRY (2006). *Employment trends survey 2006*. London: as author.

CHERNIN, E. (1988). The 'Harvard system': a mystery dispelled. *British Medical Journal*, vol. 297, pp. 1062–1063.

CSU: CHARLES STURT UNIVERSITY (2004). *Referencing style guides survey*. CSU 8/9/2004. Available at www.caul.edu.au/surveys/style-guides2004.doc [Accessed 8 May 2006].

CULWIN, F. et al. (2002). *Source code plagiarism in UK HE computing schools: issues attitudes and tools*. London: South Bank University, SCISM Technical Report 2000–2001.

DALY, J.A. and L. STAFFORD (1984). Correlates and consequences of social-communicative anxiety. In J.C. MCCROSKEY and J.A. DALY (Eds.) *Avoiding communication: shyness, reticence, and communication apprehension*. London: Sage Publications.

DENNIS, L.A. (2005). Student attitudes to plagiarism and collusion within computer science.

University of Nottingham. Available at http://eprints.nottingham.ac.uk/archive/00000319/. [Accessed 15 Mar. 2006].

DORDOY, A. (2002). *Cheating and plagiarism: staff and student perceptions at Northumbria*. Working Paper presented Northumbrian Conference: 'Educating for the Future', Newcastle 22 Oct. 2003.

EISENSTEIN, E.L. (1983). *The printing revolution in Early Modern Europe*. New York: Cambridge University Press.

GIBALDI, J. (2003). *The MLA handbook for writers*. New York: Modern Language Association of America.

GRAFTON, A. (1997). *The footnote: a curious history*. London: Faber and Faber.

GUSTAVII, B. (2003). *How to write and illustrate a scientific paper*. Cambridge: Cambridge University Press.

HA, PHAN LE (2006). Plagiarism and overseas students: stereotypes again? *ELT Journal*, vol. 60, no. 1, pp.76–78.

HAMPDEN-TURNER, C. and F. TROMPENAARS (2000). *Building cross-cultural competence*. New York: John Wiley and Sons.

HANDY, C. (1995). *Beyond certainty. The changing worlds of organisations*. London: Hutchinson.

HANSEN, J. (2005). *Is there still time to avoid 'dangerous anthropogenic interference' with global climate? A tribute to Charles David Keeling*. Presentation given 6 Dec. 2005 at the American Geophysical Union, San Francisco.

HART, M. and T. FRIESNER (2004). Plagiarism and poor academic practice – a threat to the extension of e-learning in higher education? Academic Conferences Limited. Available at www.ejel.org [Accessed 13 Mar. 2006].

HOPKINS, J.D. (2005). *Common knowledge in academic writing*. Guidance to students, University of Tampere, FAST Area Studies Program, Department of Translation Studies, Finland. Available at http://www.uta.fi/FAST/PK6/REF/commknow.html [Accessed 26 Oct. 2006].

HOWARD, R.M. (1995). Plagiarisms, authorships, and the academic death penalty. *College English*. No. 57, pp.788–806.

HOWARD, R.M. (1999). The new abolitionism comes to plagiarism. In L. BURANEN and R. ROY (Eds.). *Perspectives on plagiarism and intellectual property in a postmodern world* (pp.87–95). Albany: State University of New York Press.

ICMJE: INTERNATIONAL COMMITTEE OF MEDICAL JOURNAL EDITORS (2006).*Uniform requirements for manuscripts submitted to biomedical journals: sample references*. Available at http://www.icmje.org/ [Accessed 14 Oct. 2006].

IEEE: INSTITUTE OF ELECTRICAL AND ELECTRONICS ENGINEERS (2006). *Transactions, journals, and letters: information for author*. Available online from http://www.ieee.org/web/publications/authors/transjnl/index.html [Accessed 20 Aug. 2006].

INTRONA, L. et al. (2003). *Cultural attitudes towards plagiarism*. Report. Lancaster: Lancaster University (Dept of Organisation, Work and Technology).

JONES, K.O. et al. (2005). *Student plagiarism and cheating in an IT age*. Paper presented at International Conference on Computer Systems and Technologies – CompSysTech 2005, 16–17th June 2005.

KELLY, G. (1955). *The psychology of personal constructs*. Two vols. New York: Norton.

LAKE, J. (2004). EAP writing: the Chinese challenge; new ideas on plagiarism. *Humanising Language Teaching*, year 6, iss.1, January. Available at http://www.hltmag.co.uk/jan04/mart4.htm [Accessed 27 Aug. 2006].

LENSMIRE, T.J. and D.E. BEALS (1994). Appropriating others' words: traces of literature and peer culture in a third-grader's writing. *Language in Society*. Vol. 23, pp.411–425.

LEVIN, P. (2003). Beat the witch-hunt! Peter Levin's guide to avoiding and rebutting accusations of plagiarism, for conscientious students. Student-Friendly Guides dot com available at http://www.student-friendly-guides.com/plagiarism/index.htm [Accessed 14 Feb. 2006].

LEVIN, P. (2004). *Write great essays*. Maidenhead: Open University Press.

LI, X. and N.B. CRANE. (1996). *Electronic styles: a handbook for citing electronic information.* Medford (N.J.): Information Today.

McCROSKEY, J.C. and V.P. RICHMOND (1987). Willingness to communicate. In J.C. MCCROSKEY and J.A. DALY (Eds.). *Personality and interpersonal communication.* (pp.129–156). London: Sage Publications.

McCROSKEY, J. C. et al. (1977). Studies of the relationship between communication apprehension and self-esteem. *Human Communication Research.* Vol. 3, no. 3, pp.269–277.

MAIMON, E.P., J.H. PERITZ and K.B.YANCEY (2007). *A writer's resource: a handbook for writing and research.* New York: McGraw Hill.

MAIZELS, J. (1970). *Adolescent needs and the transition from school to work.* London: Athlone Press.

MHRA: MODERN HUMANITIES RESEARCH ASSOCIATION (2002). *A handbook for authors, editors, and writers of thesis.* London: as author.

MUNGER, D. and S. CAMPBELL (2002). *Researching Online.* 5th edition. New York: Pearson Education.

OXFORD STANDARD FOR CITATION OF LEGAL AUTHORITIES (2005). Available at http://denning.law.ox.ac.uk/published/oscola.shtml [Accessed 10 Jan. 2006].

PEARS, R. and G. SHIELDS (2005). *Cite them right: the essential guide to referencing and plagiarism.* Newcastle upon Tyne: Pear Tree Books.

PENNYCOOK, A. (1996). Borrowing others' words: text, ownership, memory and plagiarism. *TESOL Quarterly.* Vol. 30, no. 2, Summer 1996, pp. 210–223.

PENROSE, A.M. and C. GEISLER (1994). Reading and writing without authority. *College Composition and Communication.* Vol. 45, no. 3, pp. 505–520.

RICHMOND, V.P. (1984). Implication of quietness: Some facts and speculations. In J.C. McCROSKEY and J.A. DALY (Eds.). *Avoiding communication: shyness, reticence, and communication apprehension.* (pp. 145–155). London: Sage Publications.

ROBERTS, K. (1968). The entry into employment: an approach toward a general theory. *Sociological Review.* No. 16, pp.165–184.

ROBERTS, K. (2001). *Class in modern Britain.* New York: Palgrave.

RUMSEY, S. (2004). *How to find information: a guide for researchers.* Maidenhead: Open University Press.

SAUNDERS, M. et al. (2003). *Research methods for business students.* Harlow: Prentice Hall.

SCOTT, C.R. and S.C. ROCKWELL (1997). The effect of communication, writing, and technology apprehension on likelihood to use new communication technologies. *Communication education.* Vol.46, pp.44–62.

SHAPLAND, M. (1999). *Evaluation of reference management software on NT (comparing Papyrus with ProCite, Reference Manager, Endnote, Citation, GetARef, Biblioscape, Library Master, Bibliographica, Scribe, Refs).* University of Bristol. Updated Apr. 2001. Available at http://eis.bris.ac.uk/~ccmjs/rmeval99.htm [Accessed 17 Nov. 2006].

SHERMAN, J. (1992). Your own thoughts in your own words. *ELT Journal.* Vol. 46, no. 2, pp.190–198.

THES: TIMES HIGHER EDUCATION SUPPLEMENT (2006). Polls find elite top cheats list. 17 Mar. 2006, p.9.

THOMPSON, C. (2005). Authority is everything: A study of the politics of textual ownership and knowledge in the formation of student writer identities. *International Journal for Educational Integrity*, vol. 1, no. 1 (12 pages). Available at http://www.ojs.unisa.edu.au/journals/index.php/IJEI [Accessed 29 Aug. 2006].

UNIVERSITY OF QUEENSLAND (2006). *Policy no. 3.40.12 Academic integrity and plagiarism.* Available at http://www.uq.edu.au/hupp/index.html?page=25128 [Accessed 25 Aug. 2006].

WALKER, J.R. and T. TAYLOR (1998). *The Columbia guide to online style.* New York: Columbia University Press.

WILDE, S et al. (2006). *Nuffield review of 14–19 education and training: research report: Nuffield review higher education focus group preliminary report.* London: Nuffield Foundation.

WINCHCOMBE, A. (1978). Thomas hardy: A wayfarer. Dorchester: Dorset County Library and the Thomas Hardy Society.

YANG, D. (2005). Culture matters to multinationals' intellectual property businesses. *Journal of World Business*. Vol. 40, pp.281–301.

YANG, D. and P. CLARKE (2004). Review of the current intellectual property system in China. *International Journal Technology Transfer and Commercialisation*. Vol. 3, no. 1, pp.12–37.

Index

GRAMMAR
A FRIENDLY APPROACH

Christine Sinclair

- Do you feel that your writing lets you down?
- Do you have problems turning your thoughts into writing?
- Do you randomly scatter commas throughout your written work and hope for the best?

You are not alone – and this book is just what you need!

This is a grammar book with a difference. It brings grammar to life by giving examples of grammatical problems in the contexts where they arise by including a soap opera. As the characters' grammar improves, so will yours.

It blends a story about three students – Barbara, Kim and Abel – with advice on specific areas of grammar. The characters' story builds throughout the book, but each chapter can be read separately if readers want to focus on specific grammatical issues.

The book examines and clearly explains aspects of grammar, language use and punctuation such as:

- Academic language
- Standard English
- Correct use of tenses
- Active and passive voices
- Sentence construction and punctuation
- When and where to place an apostrophe
- Using grammar checkers

There are exercises to encourage the reader to relate the issues to their own practice and experiences, as well as an extensive glossary which defines the terms that are used throughout the book.

Grammar: A Friendly Approach is based around issues at university but students from schools and colleges will also love this irreverent look at the rules of grammar: Their teachers and tutors will also see rapid and noticeable improvements in students' written work.

Contents
Introduction – Bad language – Mangling and dangling participles – Getting tense with verbs – Active and passive voices – What is the subject? – The complete sentence – Relationships and relatives – How to be offensive with punctuation – Possessive apostrophes and missing letters – Checking the checker – Finale – Glossary – Appendices – Bibliography – Index.

March 2007   144pp
978–0–335–22008–3 (Paperback)   978–0–335–22009–0 (Hardback)

UNDERSTANDING UNIVERSITY

Christine Sinclair

- Does university seem like another planet?
- Does everyone else seem to speak another language?
- What can you do to make the grade?

If these are the kind of questions you are asking, then this is the book you need. After the excitement of being accepted, the reality of life at university or college can be daunting, but help is at hand.

This practical book guides new students through the terminology used at university and shows you:

- What a student needs to know
- How to be accepted by students and lecturers
- How to get the best out of your institution and yourself
- How to communicate using appropriate language in higher education institutions
- How to learn the conventions of your specific subject area
- How to be confident and competent in your new world

All new students find the move to university slightly bewildering, but with this book you can be one step ahead. The author has spent time talking to students across a broad range of different universities and uses her first-hand experience as a basis for the book.

Understanding University provides a lifeline for new students in further and higher education offering everything from practical advice on studying, to explanations of frequently used terms. If you don't know the difference between a seminar and a tutorial or want to know what 'matriculation' means, then this is where to start.

Need a little assistance? Just open this book. And remember – you are not alone.

2006   176pp
ISBN-13: 978–0–335–21797–7   ISBN-10: 0–335–21797–4 Paperback
ISBN-13: 978–0–335–21798–4   ISBN-10: 0–335–21798–2 Hardback